To Bub,
From Mom & Dad
March 1985

The Second
Texas Infantry

"The Battle of Corinth", a Kunz and Allison Print.

The Second Texas Infantry

From Shiloh
To Vicksburg

Joseph E. Chance

EAKIN PRESS
Austin, Texas

FIRST EDITION

"Though years have stretched their weary length between, and on your grave the mossy grass is green . . .
I hear you calling me."

From an old Irish Ballad

An engraving showing the defenses of Vicksburg, Mississippi, taken from the *Tri-Weekly Telegraph* of Houston, Texas, April, 1863. Note position 7, east of Vicksburg, the site where the Second Texas Infantry skirmished with Federal gunboats in January, 1863.

— *Barker Texas History Center, UT*

TABLE OF CONTENTS

Brigadier General John Creed Moore, P.A.C.S.

— *Colonel E.C. Moore (ret)*

FOREWORD

Dr. Joe Chance with this well written and documented history of the Second Infantry Regiment has filled a long gap in Texas-Confederate history. Texas historians and publishers would be wise to emulate those of Virginia where a project has recently been undertaken to write and publish histories of all Virginia regiments that fought in the War between the States. Joe Chance and Ed Eakin have led the way!

The Second Texans Infantry was commanded by outstanding soldiers and Texans, Colonels John C. Moore, William P. Rogers, Ashbel Smith and Major George W.L.Fly. Other officers of note, assigned to Regimental Headquarters were, Majors Xavier Blanchard Debray, Hal G. Runnels, Nobel L. McGinnis and William C. Timmins. Both Debray and Moore were later promoted to general rank, although the former was never confirmed by the Confederate Congress.

The Second Texas was raised for the most part in the Galveston-Houston area, and served on both sides of the Mississippi River during its career. The Regiment was originally assigned to duty in Texas, but in the spring of 1862 was transferred to northern Mississippi as part of the Army of the West. Later it served in the Army of the Mississippi and the Department of Mississippi and East Louisiana. The Regiment was captured at Vicksburg and then was reorganized after being exchanged. It served in the Trans-Mississippi Department in 1864 and 1865.

The Regiment saw much action during the War and participated in more than twenty-five engagements during its Civil War service. Major engagements included the battles of Iuka (September 19, 1862), Corinth (October 3–4, 1862), Chickasaw Bluff (December 29, 1862), Champion's Hill (May 16, 1863), Big Black River Bridge (May 17, 1863), Vicksburg (May 18–July 4, 1863), Mansfield (April 8, 1864), and Pleasant Hill (April 9, 1864).

No greater heroism was shown during the Civil War of the Sixties than the charge led by Colonel William P. Rogers of the Second Texas Infantry at the Battle of Corinth. On this fateful day for Confederate arms, the Texas Colonel, commanding a Brigade of Texas, Mississippi and Alabama troops charged Battery Robinett three times in direct assaults. Decimated by both the frontal and enfilade fire, the brigade reached (and momentarily held) the Battery, but after severe hand-to-hand fighting against overwhelming numbers, was forced to fall back. This left Colonel Rogers and many of the officers and men of the gallant Second Texas on the field of battle.

During late 1864 and 1865, the Second Texas Infantry operated primarily along the upper Texas Coast with headquarters at Galveston. It was during this time that a yellow fever epidemic broke out in the Regiment taking the lives of many of the men. The Second Texas Infantry was included among the Confederate units of the Trans-Mississippi, surrendered formally at Galveston on June 2, 1865, by E. Kirby Smith. However, the Regiment had disbanded shortly before June 2 rather than surrender.

Eakin Press of Austin, Texas, and Dr. Joe Chance of Pan American University, Edinburg, Texas, have combined their talents to add an illustrious chapter to Confederate and Texas History.

Harold B. Simpson
Hillsboro, Texas

PREFACE

Although highly praised by its contemporaries for deeds of valor and daring, few records exist today on the Second Texas Infantry and its participation in the Tennessee-Mississippi Campaign. Dr. Ashbel Smith, in the last years of his life, made efforts to collect information for a regimental history. At the time of his death, however, the project had not been completed, and no other member of the regiment took the task to completion. What little information that is known today on the regiment resides in many scattered sources. It is the purpose of this book to pull together these fragments and create the type of regimental history, perhaps, that Ashbel Smith had in mind.

I have attempted to describe the history of the Second Texas, whenever possible, with eyewitness accounts written by the men of the regiment, and to describe their day-to-day life in the camps. One may criticize these accounts as sometimes being less than factual, but my purpose is to convey the impressions and feelings of the Confederate soldier as he daily confronted death from bullets and sickness. Exaggeration is often a valid medium of expression for such sensations. Through these accounts the men express their pride in the regiment and a devotion to the South and its institutions which may appear peculiar to us as we read them some 120 years later.

The primary source of information for this book came from the factual account of the Second Texas Infantry written by Charles I. Evans, a Private of Company G, that appeared in *A Comprehensive History of Texas 1685 to 1897,* edited by Dudley G. Wooten, and printed in 1898. To supplement the account of Evans, the less factual but extremely perceptive and humorous account written by Ralph Smith, a private from Company K, was found to be useful. Smith's privately published book, printed in San Marcos, Texas, in 1911, is entitled *Reminiscences of the Civil War and Other Sketches*. This rare book was reprinted in 1962 by W.M. Morrison of Waco, Texas, with even the reprints being considered rare. Writing in his seventies, Smith's memory had begun to fail him on dates and names, but he could still remember lines of verses and songs, and many of the humorous anecdotes and practical jokes that occurred while the regiment was in Mississippi. It is, thanks to Smith the self-titled "Sometimes Private," that we affectionately learn about Dr. Ashbel Smith's extremely high temper, and how Smith earned the irreverent name, "Jingle Box," from the men of the regiment.

A valuable source of personal letters and information about the regiment came from *The Tri-Weekly Telegraph* published in Houston, Texas throughout the war. Battle reports and casualty lists from the officers of the regiment, news about the condition of the men, and private letters were published regularly in that paper. These reports and letters offer a valuable view of the life of a Texas soldier away from home in Mississippi in 1862–1863.

Additional sources of information on the regiment came from the Ashbel Smith papers and the William P. Rogers papers located in the Eugene C. Barker Texas History Center at The University of Texas at Austin, The Ashbel Smith papers contain regimental orders, battle reports, and several letters of reminiscences written by the men of the regiment in later years after the end of the war. The William P. Rogers papers consist of letters written by Rogers in Mississippi to his wife in Texas about the progress of the war and conditions in the camps.

A good source of information about the regiment during the time of the defense of Vicksburg is found in the personal diary of Major Maurice Simons, kept from April 16, 1863, until October 5, 1863. A copy of this diary can be found in the Texas State Library and Archives, Austin, Texas.

Use was made of microfilm copies of the regimental muster rolls supplied by The National Archives, Washington, D.C.

Extensive use was made of the 128 volume series, *War of the Rebellion: Official Records of the Union and Confederate Armies.*

Using these battle reports, especially the exquisitely detailed reports of Brigadier General John C. Moore, movements of the regiment throughout the first day of the Battle of Shiloh and the two days of the Battle Cornith can be traced. These reports further allow the student of these battles to accurately determine which regiments of the Federal Army the Second Texas encountered in each battle.

Several personal accounts of battles written by John C. Moore, memorials and remembrances written to the memory of William P. Rogers, and an account of how George Washington Lafayette Fly brought his family across the Mississippi River under the nose of Yankee gunboats, all appearing in the *Confederate Veteran,* were used as a part of the story of the Second Texas.

The descendants of several of these brave Texas Confederates kindly furnished unpublished manuscripts, private letters, and pictures for the use of which the author is grateful.

An artist's concept of a Federal attack on the Vicksburg defenses, from an engraving appearing in *Harper's Weekly*, March 7, 1863. From the topography of the fort and its surroundings, this scene suggests how the Federal attack of March 22, 1863, on the Second Texas Lunette, might have appeared.

— Chicago Historical Society, Clark Street at North Avenue, Chicago, Illinois 60614

The marker erected to Colonel Rogers in Confederate Park at Corinth, Mississippi, paid for by the people of Texas by private subscription.

— From private collection of the Author

ACKNOWLEDGMENTS

Without the help and cooperation of many people this book would not have been possible. To those people I wish to express my deepest gratitude.

Much of the research done for this work was the result of correspondence with libraries and the inter-library loan program. Thanks are due to the following institutions: The National Archives, Washington, D.C.; The Eugene C. Barker Texas History Center, The University of Texas at Austin; Texas State Library and Archives, Austin, Texas; The Pan American University Learning Resource Center, Edinburg, Texas; The Rosenberg Library, Galveston, Texas; The San Jacinto Museum of History Association, La Porte, Texas; and The Sam Houston Memorial Library, Huntsville, Texas. In particular, I wish to express thanks to Michael J. Dabrishus and Carol M. Finney of the Texas State Library; George Gauss, Susan Hancock, Nicole McKelvy, and Gerald Whittaker of Pan American University; and Jane Kenamore of the Rosenberg Library.

Many individuals associated with Texas county historical survey committees generously donated their time and efforts in behalf of this book. I wish to acknowledge the help and support given by Mrs. Catherine Alford of Burleson County, Mrs. Genevieve Vollentine of Gonzales County, Mr. Maurice Shelby of Jackson County, Mrs. Jan Conn of Lee County, and Mr. Kendon Clark of Chambers County.

The descendants of members of the regiment kindly furnished letters, pictures, and manuscripts that greatly aided in the preparation of this book. The author is indebted to Mr. Thomas Archer Simons III, Houston, Texas; Dr. W. Lamar Fly, Cuero, Texas; Judge Robert M. Hill, Dallas, Texas; and Colonel E.C. Moore, Dallas, Texas.

Other individuals who helped to answer to endless questions that I posed them are Mrs. Jane Evans, San Marcos, Texas; Mr. Cox Robert Crider, Mexia, Texas; Mr. Brownson Malsch, Edna, Texas; Ms. Elizabeth Silverthorne, Temple

County Junior College; Colonel Harold Simpson, Hill Junior College; Dr. Charles D. Spurlin, Victoria College; Mr. Kirk Lyons, Galveston County Historical Museum; and Mr. Albert Blaha, Houston, Texas.

A very special debt of gratitude is owed to my friend and colleague, Mr. Jon P. Harrison of Pan American University, whose scholarship on the Confederacy he freely shared with me and whose advice and counsel I came to depend upon heavily.

Many people in the great state of Mississippi shared their knowledge of history with the author and were ever eager to help. In particular, I wish to thank Mrs. Mary Travis from Quitman, Mississippi, and Mrs. L.B. Buckley from Enterprise, Mississippi, who furnished information on the history of the Texas Hospital and helped me locate its abandoned cemetery.

My wife, Carolyn Louise, spent many hours proofing the rough drafts and making suggestions that improved the style of the manuscript.

Mr. Mike Whelan, McAllen, Texas, was kind enough to introduce me to the Confederate manual of arms and demonstrate the firing of a Civil War vintage Enfield rifle and Colt revolver.

Finally, I cannot close without mentioning the tireless efforts of Mrs. Edith Hatfield of Pan American University in transcribing the hopeless jumble that I gave her into the manuscript you see before you.

1

Organization of the Second Texas Infantry

We went direct to Houston and joined the Second Texas Infantry, commanded by Colonel John C. Moore, a West Point Graduate and a brave and gallant officer but not a Christian, for he was red-headed, red-bearded, red-faced, and extremely high tempered. It was only a short time until I had strong suspicions that I had joined a regiment of devils.

Ralph Smith, Company K.

The Second Texas Infantry, as did most Confederate regiments, consisted of ten companies of riflemen, a company of musicians, regimental officers, a quartermaster, an adjutant, a surgeon, and a chaplain. The commanding officer held the rank of colonel, with a staff consisting of a lieutenant colonel and a major. Each of the ten companies was commanded by a captain. At full company strength, Confederate Army regulations specified that

". . . a company should consist of one captain, three lieutenants, four sergeants, four corporals, two musicians, and not less than sixty-four nor more than one hundred privates, to serve during the war if not sooner discharged . . ." [1]

The ten companies that made up the Second Texas Infantry were originally organized as militia immediately after public ratification of the Ordinance of Secession on February 23, 1861. The newly formed Confederate State Government of Texas called upon each county to organize a militia for its defense, and to appropriate money for the purchase of military supplies. The county commissioners responded by informally selecting someone within the county having military experience and leadership qualities to organize the militia. On a prescribed day, men wishing to volunteer for military service met at a site within the county and enlisted for service in the company. In the tradition of the volunteer militia, company officers were elected by popular vote of the men, and a local designation was selected for the company. Military instructions began immediately, and Colonel W.J. Hardee's book, *Rifle and Light Infantry Tactics,* was universally adopted by the militia as a text on the deployment and training of troops.

The ranks of these companies were filled mostly by proud young volunteers imbued with a spirit of adventure and eager to serve. When the government at Richmond, Virginia, passed a Conscription Act in late 1862 to fill the numerous gaps within the ranks caused by war, these same original volunteers bitterly resented having to serve alongside conscripts. In the words of Ralph Smith,[2] as he described a comrade in arms,

> . . . Bill had been one of the first to respond to his State's call to arms and expressed his firm belief that every male from sixteen to one hundred able to shoulder a gun, should be in the field under his country's banner. He swore that the only cause for our failure to crush the United States and end the war in a year was a mortifying fact that there were thousands of able-bodied men in the South who not only refused to volunteer but were skulking in the brush to escape being conscripted. He could not abide a conscript, his idea being that a man who had to be forced into the army would not fight and was good for nothing but to dig trenches after he got there.

Information on the specific details and organizations of the ten militia companies that were incorporated into the Second Texas Infantry is far from complete. County courthouses have burned, and the few written recollections and eye witness accounts of the veterans have been diluted by apportionment among heirs. Many of the sources are in the form of personal letters, out-of-print books and undated newspaper clippings from long-defunct papers.

The data that this author could find follows.

Company A, originally known as the San Jacinto Guards,[3] was organized as a militia company by Captain Hal G. Runnels at Lynchburg in Harris County. Captain Runnels, a native of Mississippi, was listed in the 1860 Federal Census as a contractor with three children.

The other elected officers were: first lieutenant, Dan Gallaher; second lieutenant, John Roach; and junior second lieutenant, Joe Smith. Shortly after induction into the Second Texas Infantry, Captain Runnels was promoted to major, and an election was held among the men of the company to fill the captain's vacancy. The outcome of the election was unexpected; Sergeant William Christian from Company B was elevated to the rank of captain by an unanimous vote.

Company B was recruited as militia by Captain William C. Timmons from the city of Houston in Harris County and was known as the Confederate Guards.[4] Other officers were: first lieutenant, James W. Mangrum; second lieutenant, James D. McCleary; and junior second lieutenant, Andrew S. Mair. Another distinguished member of this company was Sergeant Major A.T. Paul, the highest ranking non-commissioned officer in the regiment.

Company C, the Bayland Guards, came from the Cedar Bayou area of Harris County and West Chambers County.[5] Dr. Ashbel Smith, a man well-known to Texans, organized the company on April 27, 1861. Dr. Smith was born in Hartford, Connecticut, on August 13, 1805.[6] He graduated from Yale Phi Beta Kappa in 1824, and returned there to complete a medical degree in 1828. He studied medicine in Paris and became acquainted there with the Marquis de Lafayette, Samuel F.B. Morse, and James Fenimore Cooper. In 1837 Smith came to Texas and was appointed by Sam Houston as

Surgeon General of the Texas Army. He further served the Republic of Texas as chargé d'affaires to England and France in 1842 and 1843, and Secretary of State to the Republic in 1844. Dr. Smith served in the Mexican War in 1846 and was elected to a term in the Texas Legislature in 1855. He could have chosen to serve the Confederate Government in many higher positions, but instead, at the age of 56, organized his neighbors into a militia company and was elected its captain. Among the men he recruited were Sam Houston, Jr., eldest son of the general who opposed his young son's enlistment, and Albert Jones 2nd, son of Anson Jones, the last President of the Republic of Texas.

Dr. Smith drilled the Bayland Guards on his plantation, "Evergreen," in eastern Harris County. The recruits from Baytown, Cedar Bayou, and Barbers Hill quickly gained the martial skills necessary to become known as one of the best schooled companies in the State. Their fine appearance was noted by a reporter of the *Galveston Weekly News*, September 3, 1861, who wrote,

> Coming up the Strand last evening, we stopped a while to witness the Bayland Guards, recently arrived from up the Bay and enlisted for Coast Defense, go through their maneuvers. Their commander is an old Texian, whom to name is sufficient to show that in mature age as in early manhood, he is ready to respond to the call of his country.
>
> Dr. Ashbel Smith can be congratulated on the fine appearance of his men and their excellent drill. They have evidently received much instruction from competent hands. In the ranks marched two youthful sons of two ex-Presidents of the Republic of Texas — Gen. Sam Houston and Dr. Anson Jones — and near them and in the ranks also, we noticed that estimable citizen and old soldier, Colonel Mills of Cedar Bayou, who served in the U.S. Army through the Florida War, and is entitled by his services in the field and military knowledge, to hold an important command. He chose the position of a private, however, in order to set a good example to the young men.

The Bayland Guards made a memorable entrance into Houston, in December, 1861, as they were moved to Camp Bee to complete training.[7] Captain Smith, being a man of diminutive stature, naturally chose to carry a quite large sword which he wore while marching at the head of his troops. This immediately caught the eyes of the citizens of Houston as an eccentricity; however, the company band was even more appealing. Music, in the form of a well-played fiddle, was all that accompanied the marching detail. Captain Smith could not procure a fife or drum for his company, so he detailed Corporal Jim Hagerman to supply the company music with a fiddle. The men marched into Houston to the strains of the foot-stomping fiddle tune, "The dog he ate in the corner and wiped his mouth with a straw." Captain Smith, when questioned about this breach of military protocol, replied, "My men are so rambunctious and eager for war that I have to use stringed instruments to soothe them." [8]

General Sam Houston himself claimed to be a private in Company C and visited the drills often. "To the inquiry if he (General Houston) was not too feeble for the service, he would reply, 'I can at least stand on the right of the line and be counted.' " [9] General Houston boosted the morale of the men with his biting sense of humor. This anecdote told about the General was taken from the *Southern Intelligencer,* an Austin, Texas, newspaper, on October 25, 1866.

> It was while Captain of the Bayland Guards that General Houston, at Ashbel's request, officiated as drillmaster.
> "Bayland Guards!" said the General, "Eyes right!" This evolution being performed, the General said: "Do you see Louis T. Wigfall?"
> Being answered by them — "No!"
> The General gave his second command: "Eyes left!" which being obeyed, he inquired: "Do you see Williamson S. Oldham?"
> This was answered, "No!"
> Then the General gave his third and last command: "Eyes Front!" and asked — "Do you see either of them in front?" Whereupon being answered in the negative, the old hero said: "No! Nor you never will!" [10]

The other officers in this company were: first lieutenant, J.P.

Harrell; second lieutenant, M.A. Lea; and junior second lieutenant, P.M. Woodall.

Company D was organized by Captain Edward F. Williams in Harris County and was probably known as the Confederate Grays.[11] Its other officers were: first lieutenant, Ed Daly; second lieutenant, Andrew Gammel; and junior second lieutenant, James E. Foster.

Company E was organized by Dr. Belvedere Brooks who was elected the first captain. The recruits came from around Wheelock Prairie in Robertson County and western Brazos County. Dr. Brooks, a native of Tennessee, settled in Texas at Wheelock in Robertson County in 1850. He was a physician, merchant, and large landowner. Dr. Brooks's son later became an executive of Western Union Telegraph Company in New York after the war.[12]

Dr. Brooks schooled the company in infantry tactics at Block House Springs west of the Brazos River in Robertson County. By fall of 1861, the men were marched overland to Millican, a railroad terminal in Robertson County, and were embarked by rail for Houston to join the regiment. A rousing farewell party was given before boarding and "few tears were shed, for the people believed it was a great adventure for the men, and in a short time they would return as heroes." [13]

The junior officers of the company were: first lieutenant, J.H. Feeney; second lieutenant, George Green; and junior second lieutenant, J.L. Arnett. John H. Feeney, a Wheelock resident, was a delegate from Robertson County to the Secession Convention.

Company F was recruited from the city of Galveston by Captain John Muller, and its ranks were filled almost entirely by German immigrants. Captain Muller was an early advocate of secession, belonging to the "Committee of Safety" organized after the election of Abraham Lincoln to popularize the idea of secession among the citizens of Galveston County. Captain Muller was elected as delegate to the Secession Convention from Galveston County.[14]

Other officials elected to serve in the company were: first lieutenant, Jackson McMahan; second lieutenant, Gustave Prellwitz; junior second lieutenant, Ferdinand Halley.

Company G, known locally as the Burleson Guards,[15] was raised by Captain John W. Hood from men living in the area around Caldwell in Burleson County. The volunteer force was certified by the Chief Justice of Burleson County on March 1, 1861. Recruits were expected to furnish their own arms and equipment, but the county commissioner's court voted to allow each soldier $4.00 to be used for necessary equipment. However, this allowance was later denied, as there were no funds in the county treasury.[16] The officers elected by the company were: first lieutenant, C.C. McGinnis; second lieutenant, E.J. Chance; and junior second lieutenant, Joseph C. Rowland. E.J. Chance served as a representative from Burleson and Robertson Counties to the Seventh Texas Legislature, and later in the Confederate Tenth Texas Legislature. Two veterans of the Texas Revolution also served in this company.

Company H was raised in the western part of Burleson County, which later became a part of Lee County. This company, known as the Lexington Grays,[17] was recruited from the area around Lexington by Captain Nobel L. McGinnis. The junior officers of the company were: first lieutenant, Thomas S. Douglass; second lieutenant, Jerome I. McGinnis; and junior second lieutenant, George Harris. Lieutenant Douglass rose to the rank of captain in the company during the war and was active in later years in the formation of the annual Confederate Reunion, held at Wimberley Lake, near Lexington. This annual camp for the veterans was named in his honor.[18]

Company I, known as the Gonzales Invincibles, was recruited from citizens living in Gonzales County by Captain George Washington Lafayette Fly. The company was certified by the County Clerk on July 9, 1861. However, the thirty-one privates recruited were apparently insufficient to form an infantry company. The Gonzales Invincibles were combined with the thirty-eight privates of the "Wilson Rifles," another militia company from Gonzales County, to form the militia company thereafter known as the "Wilson Rifles." By September 27, 1861, G.W.L. Fly was signing quartermasters' requisition forms as "Capt. Wilson Rifles."

Captain Fly was born in Yalobosha County, Mississippi, on June 2, 1835. He attended the University of Mississippi in 1851, the year of its first graduating class, and completed his education at Madison College in Sharon, Mississippi. In 1855, he settled in Gonzales County at Big Hill Prairie. Prior to the war, he was a planter and a slaveholder. His political views were ably expressed in a letter from G.W.L. Fly to the Reverend Walter J. Johnson,[19] written December 5, 1899.

I was raised and educated in the old school of politics and have always been a strict construction States Rights Democrat, always taking an active part in politics as a private citizen. When the crisis came in 1861, I thought the South had endured until endurance ceased to be a virtue; the time had come for a determined stand for what I then believed and still believe to be the right. To a friend who was an ardent secessionist and who said, "There will be no war; if there is it will not last four months; I will agree to drink every drop of blood that will be shed," I replied, "If you looked at the matter as I do, I fear you would not vote for secession. I will vote that way believing that we will have the bloodiest war ever fought. If it ends under ten years it will be with the subjugation of the South." This was my opinion then, and I still believe that had we acted on the defensive altogether and preserved our men and thus had continued the war, we would have succeeded in establishing the independence of the Confederacy. I am not one of those who think that our defeat was evidence of the unrighteousness of our cause. I cannot subcribe to the fearful doctrine that might makes right. The fearful departure from every principle upon which our Government was founded as evidenced by the present condition of things is evidence that should convince every reasonable person that the principles against which the Confederacy fought are subversive of every principle of constitutional liberty.

Captain Fly was a noted orator in antebellum southeastern Texas and a staunch supporter of States Rights as evidenced by his previous statements. In the crucial election of 1860, political clubs formed in many of the towns of Texas to debate the merits of each of the presidential candidates. The clubs of Columbus, Texas, invited Captain Fly to speak in favor of the Breckinridge-Lane slate, an invitation that he accepted. The captain, however, wore his welcome thin with a three hour address that had the good people of Columbus quite restless. Finally the crowd began to chant, "Robson," the name of Captain Fly's rebuttal speaker, in an effort to move the debate to a climax. Robson arose and, standing on a bench in the audience, effectively silenced the oratory of G.W.L. Fly by saying, "Ladies and gentlemen, Mr. Fly has spoken more than three hours, the night is warm and you are worn out. If you will meet me here tomorrow evening, I promise to clip that Fly's wings so short he will never be able to buzz in this community again." [20]

Other elected officers of the Gonzales Invincibles were:

first lieutenant, W.D. Goff; second lieutenant, Reuben de Borde; and junior second lieutenant, George Weakley.

Company K, known as the Texana Guards, was organized in old Texana in Jackson County by Captain Clark L. Owen, a Texas patriot.[21] Captain Owen was born in Shelby County, Kentucky, in 1808. He came to Texas in March, 1836, and enrolled as a private in Captain T.H.D. Rogers's company on July 18, 1836. He was discharged in November of the same year with the rank of lieutenant. He later joined the army with the rank of captain in 1837 and participated in the Plum Creek Fight against the Comanches in 1840. In 1842, he participated in the Mier Expedition. President Houston appointed him as commander of the troops in southwestern Texas at the rank of colonel in 1843, after he declined the cabinet post as Secretary of the Treasury. He represented Jackson, Matagorda, and Victoria Counties in the Senate of the Sixth and part of the Seventh Congress. Owen made his home in old Texana and engaged in farming and ranching on Carancahua Creek in Jackson County.[22]

Captain Owen was "a strong Union Man"[23] but joined the Confederate Army, as so many others did, to protect Texas from a Northern invasion. So, at the age of 53, the old Texas soldier organized another military unit to defend his state.

A veteran of the Mexican War, Maurice Kavanaugh Simons enlisted in this company and was elected second lieutenant. Simons was born in Halifax, Nova Scotia, on March 4, 1824, and came to Texas in 1834.

The service record and war experiences of Maurice Simons in the Mexican War were assembled in an undated and unpublished manuscript written by Dr. J.E. Conner,[24] now retired from the Department of History at Texas A and I University, Kingsville, Texas. Dr. Conner, having access to the papers and diaries of the Simons family, recorded many of the personal experiences of M.K. Simons with the American Army in Mexico.

The following narration of Simons's service in the Mexican War is taken from this account.

Maurice Simons was attached to the Commissary Department of General Taylor's Army and helped to supply it with beef while it was located at Corpus Christi. When the invasion of Mexico became imminent, he joined, on April 16, 1846, the Texas Ranger Company of Samuel H. Walker and served as a scout for the army. Simons narrowly missed being killed by the Mexicans on a scouting expedition near the Rio Grande River just prior to the Battle of Resaca de la Palma.

One of the scouts, a man named Taylor, in Walker's Company killed an old Mexican in an unprovoked act that enraged the rancheros of the area. That night two hundred Mexicans crossed the river and attacked the Ranger's camp, killing five of the eight men on duty. In later years, Maurice Simons's wife, in a letter to her daughter, related the incident from Maurice Simons's point of view:

> Once they (Maurice Simons and George Washington Trahern) and six men who went with them to drive the beeves were camping out when they heard Mexican Soldiers. They ran undressed and barefooted, scattered in every direction. Maurice hid under some cactus and saw one of his men killed. A Mexican officer cut him open with a sword. The prickly pear was so dense that while he was there two of the Mexican soldiers stopped near enough to him to light their cigars and he could hear what they said. They were saying that they would rather have those 2 black headed devils (he and Wash) than all the others. He staid there until dark then made his way to headquarters . . .

A similar version of this incident is described by George Washington Trahern[25] who gives an exciting narrative of his wartime adventures with Maurice Simons. Simons served in the Battle of Resaca de la Palma as guide to the left wing of Taylor's Army and later participated in the capture of Monterrey. However, Simons's greatest service to the American Army came on the night of February 22, 1847. General Taylor's Army of 6,000 men, camped near Saltillo, was surrounded by the 20,000-man Mexican Army of General Santa Anna. Isolated from part of his artillery which was in Rinconado several miles away, Taylor realized that his army would need the extra fire power this ordnance could provide. Summoned to General Taylor's tent, Simons and Trahern were asked by Taylor to volunteer for a dangerous mission. When they agreed to accept the assignment, General Taylor ordered them to ride immediately to Rinconado with orders to bring up the artillery. Both rangers slipped through the 3,000 men of General Miñon's Cavalry Division assigned to guard the Monterrey road and delivered the message. The artillery, along with infantry reinforcements, arrived by the early morning of February 24, too late to engage the defeated Mexicans. Maurice Simons refused a $500 reward from General Taylor for his service, believing that what he had done was only the duty required of a soldier.

Simons's career with the United States Army was brought to an end by a serious wound he received while on assignment near Papagallos, between Monterrey and Cerralvo. In an undated letter written by Simons's wife to a niece, she tells about the incident:[26]

> On the day of April 27, 1847, he and Wash were riding together when Mexican Guerillas fired on them. Maurice's horse ran into a thicket and fell dead, and he fell from him. This was 10 o'clock in the morning and no relief came until sundown. Wash had escaped and came with soldiers to look for him. When the surgeon saw how badly he was hurt, he said there was no chance to save his life but to take off his leg. Maurice said he would rather die, and the Dr. gave it up for he said he didn't think he could live anyway, but after Wash begged him to have it taken off he consented. The surgeon said he had no surgical instruments and Maurice told him to saw if off with a butcher saw which he did. He cut flesh with a butcher knife and the bone with a meat saw.
>
> When the operation was done he fainted, and they all thought he was dead, and they went and sat around the camp fire. After a while Wash went to look at him, thinking he was dead. He took his hand and pressed it as if to say "Good-bye," and your uncle returned the pressure gently. Wash called the Dr. and he bound up the wound and gave him restoratives. After he revived he said, "Dr. is there any chance for me to live?" "About one chance in a hundred," said the Dr.

He was taken to a house and made comfortable and the next morning the Dr. went to see him and he had broken out with Small Pox. He said, "Well, that takes away the other chance, does it?" The Dr. said, "Yes," and hurried and got the soldiers away from there, for fear the Small Pox would break out in the Army, and left him to his fate. Mexican women nursed him but it was 18 months before he was able to come home.

Young Simons had his right leg amputated close to the hip joint due to the wound caused by a musket ball fired from ambush. Yet even on a crutch, Maurice Simons willingly volunteered to hobble off to war with Texana Guards.

When the Texana Guards arrived at Galveston to be mustered into military service for the Confederacy, the officer in charge informed Lieutenant Simons that it was impossible for a one-legged man to serve in the infantry. The men of the Texana Guards became incensed and refused to take the oath of service without Maurice Simons as a member of the Company. With such a large body of troops at stake, the officer relented in his decision and Lieutenant Simons of the Texas Militia became Lieutenant Simons of the Provisional Confederate States Army.

The other junior officers of Company K were first lieutenant, A.B. Dodd, and junior second lieutenant, Joseph M.B. Haynie. Ralph Smith, "the sometimes private," served in this company, as well as Dr. James Woolfork, a surgeon who was cited for treating wounded soldiers at the battle of Shiloh.

These ten independent militia companies, each organized for defensive purposes, rapidly became consolidated into a regiment. Orders sent to Ashbel Smith on July 31, 1861, from the Adjutant General of Texas stated, "Captains H.G. Runnels, W.C. Timmins, E.F. Williams, and Ashbel Smith's Companies of Infantry will prepare themselves to be mustered into the service of the Confederate States, to form a part of a body of ten companies destined to the defense of the Coast of Texas." [27]

The task of locating the remaining companies and schooling them as a regiment was assigned to Captain John Creed

Moore, a regular in the Confederate Army. To go along with this new assignment, Moore was promoted to the rank of colonel in the Provisional Confederate Army. Colonel Moore was born in Hawkins County, Tennessee, February 28, 1824. He attended Emory and Henry College and graduated from the United States Military Academy at West Point in 1849, seventeenth in a class of forty-three. He fought in the Seminole War and served tours of duty in Santa Fe and Baton Rouge. He resigned his military commission in 1855 and was teaching at Shelby College, Kentucky, in 1861. Moore's previous assignment as a Confederate captain of artillery was to erect coastal defenses for Galveston.[28]

The regiment was brought to full strength by September, 1861, and Richmond was so notified. The Confederate War Department enlisted Moore's regiment as the First Texas Infantry Regiment, which it proudly accepted. However, by the political influence of Senator Wigfall, now in Richmond, this designation was changed. Several independent companies of Texas volunteers had rushed to Virginia, against orders, to join the Army of Northern Virginia. Senator Wigfall had claimed the right for this collection of troops to be designated as the First Texas. Richmond acquiesced to his demands, and Moore's regimental designation was changed to Second Texas Infantry Regiment. The First Texas became a part of Hood's Brigade soon after Senator Wigfall, then Brigadier General Wigfall, relinquished command on February 20, 1862, to serve in the Confederate Senate from Texas.[29]

While Richmond could waver in a political decision, it did not fail the regiment in filling the slot of lieutenant colonel by naming William P. Rogers to the post. Rogers was born in Georgia on December 27, 1817, and was raised on a plantation in Aberdeen, Mississippi. He studied medicine to please his father and graduated from a medical college before the age of 21. His father set him up in medical practice in Lowndes County, Mississippi, but at the age of 21, he abandoned his practice to study law. To support himself while a student, he edited a Whig newspaper in Aberdeen. The newspaper failed, but his law studies were a success, and he became a practicing attorney. Rogers served in the Mexican War as captain of Company K (The Tombigbee Guards) of the famous First Mississippi Regiment. This regiment, known as the Mississippi Rifles, was commanded by Colonel Jefferson Davis and Lieutenant Colonel A.K. McClung, the noted duelist. Rogers quickly gained a reputation for bravery and leadership in Mexico that was later to become his hallmark. He was first cited for bravery in the capture of Monterrey. With General Zachary Taylor watching, McClung and Rogers, in that order, were the first and second Americans to enter the Mexican fort Tenería while under heavy enemy fire. In the battle of Buena Vista, the Mississippi Rifles formed one wing of the famous "V" that helped the Mexican Cavalry charge of General Miñon and saved an outnumbered American Army. After the war President Taylor appointed Rogers United States Consul at Vera Cruz, Mexico, where he remained four years. He settled in Texas in 1851 and practiced law in the old town of Washington-on-the-Brazos. He rapidly achieved fame as a defense attorney and in 1859 resettled in Houston, Texas. Rogers was a cousin of General Sam Houston's wife and a lifetime political supporter and personal friend to the General. He supported the Know-Nothing party during its existence and campaigned the state for General Houston during the gubernatorial race of 1859. Rogers felt that secession was not the answer to the problems of the South, but he also felt a deep loyalty to the Southern people, and accordingly cast his lot with the Confederacy. He was elected to the Secession Convention as a delegate from Harris County and voted for the Secession Ordinance. Jefferson Davis offered him the command of the First Texas Infantry, then a regiment in Virginia, but at his wife's urgings, he accepted the junior command of the Second Texas Infantry.[30]

The other regimental staff position of major was filled by Captain Hal G. Runnels of Company A; William Christian being elected to the vacated position as captain of Company A.

The new regiment was billeted in Galveston in warehouses and cotton compresses. The officers set to work immediately with drill for the men six hours a day except Sunday.

Hardly had the drill begun before Lieutenant Colonel Rogers had an opportunity to renew acquaintance with the unexpected appearance of a comrade in arms from the Mexican War, Lieutenant Maurice Simons. Mrs. Elizabeth Simons, in a letter, relates this fateful reunion as told to her by her husband:[31]

> When he joined the Confederate Army at Galveston he was riding horseback and the Lieutenant Colonel of the Regiment rode up by him on his good side, and began talking, and asked him if he had any brother in the Mexican War. He said he did, and Rogers said, "I was with a company of soldiers sent to rescue a man by the name of Simons who had been shot by Guerrillas," and went on and told about the Dr. taking his leg off, and how well he stood it, etc., and asked if that man was his brother. He said, "I am that man." Rogers said, "No that man died."
>
> When Maurice convinced Rogers, he rode around on the other side, and saw he had lost a leg. He said, "By . . . its the same man."

Rogers had described the incident of Simons's wounding, tersely, in his own diary[32] with his April 28, 1847, entry stating, "Today our Butcher rode ahead of the train with 2 or 3 others and was shot in the thigh — his leg was taken off he killed one of the Mexicans that shot him."

Under the eyes of Moore and Rogers, the regiment slowly began to coalesce as a fighting unit. Colonel Moore earned the reputation of a disciplinarian, acting in a strict manner toward the men. But all the veterans of the Mexican War well understood the necessity for discipline and drill, having seen green volunteers panic and run in battle, endangering the lives of all the men on a battlefield. However, beneath this stern West Point exterior existed a man who sincerely cared for the welfare of his troops. He immediately set out to find uniforms for his men when none were to be had. Finally, in desperation Moore clothed his rag-tag regiment in Federal uniforms captured from Yankee troops in Texas at the time of the secession. These same captured troops also furnished rifles and muskets to fill out the armament needs of the regiment.[33]

The stoic routine of drill is described by Maurice Simons in a letter to his wife, Elizabeth, from Galveston on November 3, 1861.[34]

> . . . For the last few days we have been kept pretty busy. We have dress parade in the Regiment every morning and evening, which with our company drills keeps us pretty constantly engaged. On Sunday we have dress parade, but do not drill in company.
>
> On tomorrow we will have general inspection of all the troops. There will be some 4 or 5 thousand. General Herberd [Paul Hebert] will revue them.

With such a regimen of drill, the regiment became known as the finest-schooled military unit in the state, and would later become known as the finest regiment in the Army of the West while in Mississippi.

Simons's letter continues,

> . . . You said in your last that I must say something about Green. Well Green is not much attached to this kind of life, I assure you. He says that he would rather be at home with Miss Bettie and the baby. He always says this when anyone asks him how he likes living in the army. His foot has gotten nearly well. He is the same old Green. He is quite attentive to me and enjoys seeing the troops drill very much.

Green was a Negro slave who accompanied Lieutenant Simons throughout his service in the Confederate Army. This practice was fairly common with the soldiers of the Confederacy. Not only officers, but some enlisted men too had slaves to serve them. Simons was greatly attached to Green, and the entries in his Vicksburg Diary showed a concern for him as one friend to another, exceeding the bounds of a master-slave relationship.

Describing the privations of army life, Simons stated in his letter,

Last night Captain Owen and I were invited by a friend of the Capt. to supper which invitation we excepted, and I tell you we supped to the full extent. We had a splendid supper. It was the first time that either of us has sat down to a table since we left home. Our table is the floor, and we all form a circle about the dishes. You see the great advantage of this kind of table is that we can increase the size to suit any number of persons. We will get so in the habit of sitting down in [on] the floor to take our meals that I would not be surprised that when we return home you will have to indulge us in the habbit.

The regiment was moved to Camp Bee in Houston in December, 1861. However, even with all the necessary preparations for war, there was still time for social events. From *The Galveston Weekly News*, January 14, 1862, comes the following item:

The military ball given by Moore's regiment to the ladies of Houston, came off on Wednesday night, in Perkin's Hall, and was well-attended. We regret our inability to be present, but learn from those who were there, that it was a brilliant affair, and gave very general satisfaction. The evening was rather unfavorable, on account of the weather, but this did not prevent the ladies from venturing out, as we understand the large hall, which is said to be the finest in the State, was crowded to excess. "And all went merry as a marriage bell."

A war hysteria gripped many of the citizens of Texas, and the regiment was caught up in its throes. As Ralph Smith, the young private from Texana, so ably put it:[35]

I wish I were able to describe the glorious anticipation of the first few days of our military lives, when we each felt individually able to charge and annihilate a whole company of blue coats. What brilliant speeches we made and the dinners the good people spread for us, and oh the bewitching female eyes that pierced the breasts of our grey uniforms, stopping temporarily the heart beats of many a fellow that the enemies bullets were destined soon to do forever.

On the 10th of October we were ordered to Houston where we were mobilized into the Second Texas Infantry commanded by Colonel John C. Moore, our company designated Company

K. Here again all was excitement and all felt that it was only a matter of few months until we would return home covered with glory and renown. The possibility of such a thing as defeat never for a moment entered the mind of a member of our inexperienced corps. Day after day we were dined, wined, and flattered. Night after night we floated on a sea of glory. The ladies petted and lionized us; preachers prayed with and for us, declaring that the lord was on our side, so we need have no fears. Alas how soon we were to realize the truth of epigram that the lord was on the side with the biggest guns.

The routine of sham battles and socials continued until March, 1862, when Colonel Moore received orders to report to General Van Dorn in Arkansas. Before departure, the ladies of Houston, in a gala send-off, presented the regiment with a silk battle flag. No record now exists as to what insignias or designs were borne on the flag, and one can only suppose that it must have appeared as pictured in the Kurz and Allison print "the Battle of Corinth." [36] This flag is essentially the State flag of Texas, perhaps mistakenly pictured as being flown upside down (red on top, white on bottom) with the Lone Star encircled with two olive branches, and the words "SECOND" above and "TEXAS" below the star. Union General Stephen A. Hurlbut, in his official report on the battle of Shiloh, reported being attacked by a Texan Regiment bearing "Lone Star" flags.[37] Due to Hurlbut's location on the Shiloh battlefield, the unit must have been the Second Texas Regiment. Thus, the battle flag must have been emblazoned with a large star and gives credence to the depiction in the Kurz and Allison print.

All the festivities, patriotic speeches, and blaring band music set the spirits of the regiment soaring, and the men felt that a great adventure had begun. Only the veterans of war knew better. Of all the speeches and ceremonies conducted that day, the men would remember in later years most clearly the prophetic words uttered in a speech given by General Sam Houston to the departing men of the Second Texas. General Houston told the men that the resources of the north were almost exhaustless and of the ease with which the Confederacy could be split by capture of the Mississippi River. He suggested a policy of concentration west of the Mississippi and a prolongation of the war until the South received diplomatic recognition from the great European powers. Finally, the grizzled old warrior told the men that he was not ashamed to have his name associated with the regiment; he felt that the regiment would reflect credit on the state. In an emotional ending to the speech he told the soldiers to be strong and valiant, that he had committed his own beloved son to the fate of the regiment, and that his eyes and prayers would follow.[38]

The next day, March 18, 1862, the men departed from Houston by railroad, serenading the many wives and sweethearts at the depot with "The Girl I Left Behind Me." Within a month the families and friends of the regiment would be trying to find the small settlement of Pittsburg Landing, Tennessee, on their maps, where the regiment was to be tested in battle for the first time. This battle site is more commonly named by Southerners for the small church located nearby — Shiloh.

2

The Battle
of Shiloh

... I thought the Yankees are better fighters than they are.
I can assure you that every time our regiment got after them
they run. They could not stand the cold steel. At one time,
our boys run three thousand of them.

A letter to home from a soldier in Company H.

At this point, a brief description of some of the strategic and
logistic considerations leading up to the battle of Shiloh is important.

Corinth, a city in northeastern Mississippi, held the key
to the railway supply of the Confederate States east of the
Mississippi River. The Mobile and Ohio Railroad, which ran
from the Gulf of Mexico, intersected the Memphis and
Charleston Railroad, an east-west railroad artery, at Corinth.
The Federal Army, flush from easy successes in the capture of
Forts Henry and Donelson, initiated a plan on March 4, 1862,
that would terminate in the capture of Corinth. On this date
the Army of the Tennessee, under its commander, General
Ulysses S. Grant, departed from Cairo, Illinois, by steam-
boats for Pittsburg Landing, Tennessee, on the Tennessee
River. The landing was a steamboat supply station about
twenty-five miles northeast of Corinth. Grant, when rein-

forced by General Don Carlos Buell and the Army of the Ohio, planned to attack Corinth. General Buell was to march overland from Columbia, Tennessee, with his army for the rendezvous at Pittsburg Landing.

A small Methodist church, known as Shiloh, was three miles west of the landing on a topography of undulating ground cut with brush-filled ravines and small hills covered with oak and pine trees. A few small fields and meadows dotted the landscape, but, for the most part, the surface features of the land were disconnected and would not permit the coordinated movements of large bodies of troops. Pittsburg Landing was an excellent defensive site bounded by Lick Creek on the south and Owl Creek on the north which could be useful to prevent flanking movements and could be reinforced in the rear by the Tennessee River under the control of the Federal Navy riverboats.

The Army of the Tennessee was staffed with many volunteer regiments manned by green troops and led by commanders having no battle experience. General Grant had no previous command experience over an army of this size but was chosen for command chiefly because of his victories at Forts Henry and Donelson. He quickly demonstrated his lack of respect for Southern arms by not improving his defensive position. No entrenchments or earthworks were constructed during the three weeks that his army lay idle at the Landing. No abatises were fashioned from the numerous trees, nor clearings chopped in the brush for lines of fire. No cavalry scouting missions were organized for reconnaissance of the countryside, so Grant remained uninformed as to Rebel troop movements. Pickets and sentries were placed haphazardly around the perimeter of the camp to protect it, with each division responsible for its own security. In short, General Grant was not planning to fight a battle at Pittsburg Landing.

Meanwhile in Corinth, the Confederates (under General Albert Sidney Johnston who had arrived there on March 22) were feverishly attempting to assemble the Army of the Mississippi to defend the city, General Johnston consolidated his forces with those troops led by Generals Beauregard, Bragg, Polk, Ruggles, and Hardee. A plan of action evolved that would utilize the element of surprise. The Confederate command agreed on a plan to attack the Army of Tennessee at Pittsburg Landing before it could be reinforced by General Buell and the Army of the Ohio. The Army of the Mississippi, with sufficient time to execute this battle plan, slowly frittered away its advantage. Ten days were required to organize the Army and to develop marching orders and a plan of attack. Additional days were spent waiting for the arrival of General Van Dorn's troops from Arkansas. On April 2, General Johnston's scouting reports noted the close proximity of General Buell's forces to Pittsburg Landing, and the Confederate general realized that an attack must be mounted immediately for success.

The next day the Confederate Army, still lacking Van Dorn's reinforcements, was set in motion toward Pittsburg Landing in a badly planned order of march. The roads from Corinth to Pittsburg Landing had become mired by unusually heavy spring rains, and the march slowed to a crawl, interrupted by bogged-down ammunition wagons and confused corp commanders. The plan to attack the Federals on Saturday, April 5, had to be delayed until Sunday, April 6. The battle plan, as originally envisioned by General Johnston, would consist of a heavy thrust at the Federal left on Lick Creek, driving them in past the Landing, which would then be captured by the Confederates. The Federal Army, separated from its point of supply and reinforcements, and trapped against the Tennessee River, could then be destroyed.[1] The attack would be mounted by three parallel rows of corps, commanded by Generals Hardee, Bragg, and Polk, respectively, in order of attack. While the Confederate Army had been slow in arriving at its destination, it had done so in relative secrecy, and the Federals remained unaware that a large hostile army was poised to attack. Thus, the stage was set. Grant, with 40,000 troops of the Army of the Tennessee, was unwittingly about to be attacked by Johnston and 44,000 men of the Army of the Mississippi.

The Second Texas Regiment, having departed from Houston on March 18, 1862, by train, proceeded to Beaumont, Texas. From this site, travel was by steamboat up the Neches River to Weiss's Bluff, followed by a march overland, east from there through the thickets and swamps to Alexandria, Louisiana. From Alexandria, travel continued by steamboat on the Red River to its junction with the Mississippi River and thence up that river to Helena, Arkansas. At Helena, orders were received to report to Corinth, Mississippi. Again by steamboat, they traveled on the Mississippi from Helena to Memphis, Tennessee, and completed the journey with a march overland to Corinth, arriving there on April 1, 1862.[2]

Before departure from Houston, Colonel Moore had sent an agent to New Orleans to requisition gray uniforms for his blue-clad soldiers, fearing that on the battlefield they might be mistaken for Yankees. The new uniforms waiting in Corinth to greet the regiment on their arrival there were unconventional, to say the least. Bundles of white wool uniforms had been sent with no designation as to size. The uniforms were issued, and a comical scene ensued.

> Soon the company grounds were full of men strutting up and down, some with trousers dragging under their heels, while those of others scarcely reached the tops of their socks; some with jackets so tight they resembled stuff toads, while others had ample room to carry three day's rations in their bosoms. The exhibition closed with a swapping scene that reminded one of a horse-trading day in a Georgia county town.[3]

With such distinctive uniforms they would soon attract the attention of the Federals of Shiloh. One Federal prisoner referred to the regiment as ". . . them hell-cats that went into battle dressed in their grave clothes."[4]

The regiment spent but one day at Corinth, resting from the march and cooking the remaining meager rations provided for them. Each regiment had been issued four days of

rations for the battle, but the Second Texas, due to its late arrival at Corinth, received the remaining supplies on hand at
the commissary and could issue only two- and a-half days rations to the men.

On April 3, the regiment joined the army and took up the
march toward Pittsburg Landing on a road choked with men
marching four abreast, ankle deep in mud. Many of the officers and men of the regiment had worn out their shoes in
transit to Corinth and were barefooted, but no replacements
were available. The first day of the march was spent mostly
waiting as the roads were choked with men from other regiments, and at nightfall the Texans had moved barely two
miles from their earlier camp. By Saturday morning, April 5,
the regiment's rations were exhausted. Rain continued to fall
as the soldiers of the Army of the Mississippi slogged into their
assigned locations in the battle formation. The men of the Second Texas bedded down in a muddy cornfield without tents
or a blanket for cover. They had cast off their knapsacks and
bedrolls two days earlier at the sound of rapid firing from a
minor skirmish, sure that the battle was imminent. The road
had been littered for miles with knapsacks and every kind of
clothing cast off by the Texas, Mississippi, and Tennessee regiments.[5]

From this cornfield, the Second Texas was within three
to four hundred yards of the Federal camps and was ordered
to speak in whispers so as not to alert the unsuspecting Federal pickets. They overheard the Federal evening roll call and
occasional conversations. An anxious night was spent by
many of the men, and some felt that premonition of death that
often occurs as a prelude to battle. Captain Belvedere Brooks
and Lieutenant J.H. Feeny of Robertson County had both
written wills before leaving Corinth and, as fate would have it,
were spending their last few hours on earth.[6]

Sunday, April 6, dawned as a beautiful day. The regiment had been assigned to the Third Brigade commanded by
Brigadier General J.K. Jackson of the Second Division commanded by Brigadier General J.M. Withers of the Second

Corps and all commanded by Major General Braxton Bragg. The Second Division had been ordered to serve as a reserve unit for the attack by General Bragg.

The spirits of the regiment were boosted as General Albert Sidney Johnston rode up, accompanied by Lieutenant Colonel Rogers. The regiment had left Rogers in Houston, Texas, seriously ill when it departed for Corinth. Rogers, having partially regained his health, had rushed to join the regiment, finally overtaking it that morning. The men of the regiment began to cheer, but were silenced by the officers, lest alarm be spread to the Federal camps.[7]

The Rebel assault was unleashed on the unsuspecting Federal camps at daybreak, but the attack on the Federal left slowed by 8:30 A.M. and the reserves were prepared to enter the battle. The Second Division was sent to fill a gap on the Confederate right flank bordering on Lick Creek. Jackson's Brigade was centered between the Brigade of General Gladden on the left and the irrepressible Mississippians of Chalmers's Brigade which formed the extreme right of the Confederate line of attack. Federal skirmishers opened fire on the Second Texas immediately, mortally wounding Captain Brooks of Robertson County, and heavy fighting began. After a quick advance the regiment approached a heavily guarded camp. This camp, a collection of log cabins surrounded by tents, was the Headquarters for Stuart's Brigade of General W.T. Sherman's Division, consisting of the 55th Illinois, the 54th Ohio, and 71st Ohio.[8] Stiff resistance was met from the Federals at this point, and the attack ground to a halt. General Johnston, who was in personal command of the right flank, ordered an immediate bayonet charge.

> 'Where is that Texas Regiment?' asked General Johnston, and on our gallant Colonel answering, 'Here they are,' were ordered by the General to charge the enemy and drive them 'out of the camp.' After opening our fire and repulsing the enemy's charge three times, Col. Moore gave the command, 'Charge Bayonets' and with a yell, in we went; the Federals ran in great disorder, although we learned afterwards from prisoners that they numbered 3000, whilst our regiment had less than 730.[9]

Another Texas soldier wrote of the charge,

About 10 o'clock, on Sunday, our regiment was ordered to charge on the encampment of the 55th Illinois Brigade. There was a number of old log houses in the centre, and after advancing a short distance, we found these buildings to be filled with Federals, who fired through the cracks at us. Our men fell back a short distance and formed again, and charged with a terrible yell. The Yankees dropped guns, cartridge boxes, and even threw off their coats, to get beyond our reach. We captured ten of them, however.[10]

A soldier from Captain McGinnis's Company H was later to write home to Burleson County, "I have one thing to say — I thought the Yankees are better fighters than they are. I can assure you that every time our regiment got after them they run. They could not stand the cold steel. At one time, our boys run three thousand of them." [11] The 7th and 9th Mississippi Regiments of Chalmers's Brigade also participated in the charge.[12] The unguarded Federal camp was a sight to behold for the Texas troops. Sam Houston, Jr. reported in amazement what he found,

. . . and a moment later we advanced to find ourselves in the most complete canvas city imaginable. The streets, great and small, upon which the tents faced, were arranged with the precision of those in a well regulated city, and everything seemed as permanent as if the residents had located with an intention of remaining forever. . . . Throughout the camp, preparations for a meal were in progress, and having eaten little or nothing for three days, I severely scalded my hand in fishing from a camp kettle, a piece of beef, weighing some three pounds. . . . Pots of coffee were boiling and loaves of bread waited to be served. These things were promptly issued and though the rations reached other mouths than those for which they were intended, they could certainly have found none more appreciative.[13]

Captain Fly of Company I from Gonzales County was to relate in later years in an unpublished manuscript how he grabbed a skillet of fried meat from a campfire and ate it on the run while chasing the fleeing Federals.[14]

Sam Houston, Jr. continued,

The pangs of hunger allayed, our fellows showed a disposition to
take in the camp, but were forbidden to enter any tents except
those immediately along our line — not from any moral stand-
point, of course; the restriction was merely to keep us together,
as we were now in the extreme front and the enemy might at any
moment attempt to regain their lost ground.

Those of us who did secure plunder certainly displayed
queer taste in its selection. One notorious sloven from Company
H became the proud possessor of a magnificent dressing case,
and another party, who had secured a silver mounted revolver,
immediately traded it to a comrade for a hand mirror.

. . . One pillager must have happened on the pay-master's
quarters, for he came out with a tin cash box which when prized
open with a bayonet, proved to be completely filled with fresh,
smooth dollars, varying in denomination from one to one
hundred dollars. I will not attempt to estimate their aggregate
amount, but it was certainly sufficient to place several men in
decidedly comfortable circumstances. As it was, we knew nothing of the value of Uncle Sam's I.O.U.s and regarded them as so
much worthless paper. The soldier, who captured all this
wealth, gave the box a contemptuous kick and the crisp notes
fluttered around as unheeded as so many autumn leaves.[15]

John Hirschfield, a soldier from Company B, mailed
home to Houston a certificate for $500 worth of stock in the
Mound City Manufacturing and Real Estate Company. The
most popular item for the Texans though, appeared to be sta-
tionery and envelopes emblazoned with Federal devices.
"They embrace all sorts of illustrations of flags, liberty trees,
sinking worlds, scriptural quotations, crowing cocks, etc., etc.
A stranger, to see them might think our boys were tinctured
with unionism. Some of the boys, fearing the postmasters
might be misled by appearance, take the precaution to write
on the outside of the envelopes how they happen to go under
such colors." [16] While the men of the regiment were selecting
battle momentos from the tents, officers were searching to
find medical supplies desperately needed by the Second
Texas. Major Hal G. Runnels wrote,

I presume some of our army surgeons have supplied themselves
from the Yankee camp, as I examined several surgeon's tents,

and found that someone had been ahead of me at each place and left nothing but the common medicines. I could find no quinine, chloroform, morphine, or anything valuable. And from the confusion in which I found everything, I think the Yankees had taken nothing, but our men had taken all the valuable drugs.[17]

It is now about 12 A.M., and the confusion reigns supreme in both Army of the Mississippi and the Army of the Tennessee. The front extends more than three miles from Owl Creek to Lick Creek, and Confederate Corp Commanders have lost communication with their troops. The three Confederate Corps, which were to attack in waves, have become hopelessly entangled, and due to the rough terrain, many small isolated battles are being fought between opposing regiments and a few brigades; but no coordinated frontal attacks at the corp level are being executed. General Johnston remains with the Confederate right flank to push for the capture of Pittsburg Landing, so crucial to Confederate success.

On the Federal side, the ferocious Confederate bayonet attacks of the morning have broken the will to fight of many of the green troops, who have bolted from the battle lines and run for their lives. These inexperienced Union Troops remain huddled below Pittsburg Landing in numbers estimated by Union General Don Carlos Buell to range as high as fifteen thousand men. General Grant is busily riding from one flank of his line to the other, giving commands to his division commanders and trying to boost the morale of his remaining men. The Federal battle perimeter is steadily shrinking, and Grant must soon face the possibility of being driven into the Tennessee River. However, General Benjamin Prentiss has reorganized his broken division, and with Generals Hurlbut and Stuart, falls back and reforms a second defensive position on the left. The center of this position is a sunken road flanked on either side by open fields. At this location the hardest fighting of the day will take place. By nightfall, Confederates will have named this location "Hornets' Nest" in honor of the fierce struggle by General Prentiss. It is in this area that the Second Texas Infantry will meet more determined opponents.

Suddenly a rumbling sound announces the arrival of a Union artillery battery, having lost its way and crossed the battle lines in the midst of the Second Texas. The Texans capture the field piece intact, with horses, drivers and full ammunition chest, without firing a shot.[18]

At the sound of rapid firing from the right flank, Colonel Moore detached the companies of Smith, McGinnis, and Christian to aid Chalmers's Mississippians. They advance at a double quick and aid in rolling back a line of Union soldiers resisting the Confederate advance. "As we passed over the ground in front," Colonel Moore wrote, "the number of dead and wounded showed that our balls had done fearful execution in the ranks of the enemy." [19]

The line of attack is re-formed and ordered to sweep westward by a slow wheel. The regiment moves about a half mile to the west in the direction of the sound of heavy rifle and cannon fire. Moore's regiment is about to attack General Hurlbut's defensive line that covers the left flank of the "Hornets' Nest." They are entering the regimental camps of the 41st Illinois and 3rd Iowa. At this location heavy fire is turned upon the Texans. The regiment's battle line is in an awkward position; the right flank is in a deep ravine, and the left flank is positioned on a high hill. The left flank takes heavy fire, and Colonel Moore orders the regiment into a prone position. The fire is so intense that several of the prone soldiers are wounded. The left flank of the Second Texas battle line recoils and retreats fifty yards to regroup. Colonel Moore regroups the regiment and charges the camp in the face of intense rifle and cannon fire. The Federals are routed from their camp, and General Hurlbut's left flank crumbles. At the northwest edge of this camp a Federal colonel on horseback tries to deceive the Texans. "Boys, for God's sake stop firing, you are killing your friends," he shouts at the regiment, then wheels his horse to ride for safety. When he fails in the command to halt, he and his horse both become casualties of the battle.[20] Another officer attempts to flee and drives off at a hasty gallop in a buggy but is shot dead for his efforts. This charge is not without its casualties, however. Captain Ashbel Smith is felled with a severe wound of the arm and taken to the rear,[21] but unknown to the regiment, the most important casualty of the battle, and perhaps the war, has been sustained on a hilltop that overlooks the captured camps. General Albert Sidney Johnston, watching his Texas regiment advance, is struck in the leg by a stray minié ball, severing the artery. General Johnston refuses to have the wound treated and soon topples off his thoroughbred bay, Fire-eater, and dies. It is now 2:30 P.M.

General Hurlbut sends word to General Prentiss that he cannot maintain his position any longer. He retreats, and advancing Confederates prepare to complete the encirclement of General Prentiss and the "Hornets' Nest." General Prentiss has maintained this position throughout most of the afternoon, withstanding eleven heavy Confederate frontal assaults. Confederate General Ruggles, in desperation, forms an artillery line of sixty-two cannons that fire into the "Hornets' Nest," but still General Prentiss fails to yield ground. This heroic defense has bought the time needed to save the Army of the Tennessee.

With the capture of the regimental camps, Colonel Moore and the Second Texas have completed the encirclement of the "Hornets' Nest." However, the regiment is unaware of its success. A large force of Federals suddenly appear to the front of the Texans, and Colonel Moore assumes that a counterattack is being mounted that will attempt to turn his left flank. Colonel Moore orders the regiment to re-form, when suddenly a white flag appears. A Federal officer on horseback approaches Colonel Moore and informs him that 1,000 Federal troops wish to surrender to the Texas regiment. Under a flag of truce, Colonel Moore sends Captain J.W. Hood of Company G, Burleson County, to accept the surrender. Captain Hood returns with a double arm-load of swords that the union officers have presented him; but before the surrender can be completed, a Confederate cavalry regiment marches the Federal troops to the rear, and Colonel Moore never learns the name of the unit surrendering to the Second Texas.[22]

Colonel Moore is now ordered to advance in a northerly direction, meeting only token resistance from the few stragglers left in the deserted camps of General Hurlbut's division, another large tent city. As the regiment approaches Dill's Branch, a deep, brush-filled ravine forming the southern boundary of Pittsburg Landing, a large shell explodes in the ranks, killing two Jackson County soldiers from Captain Owen's Company K. The Federal Navy, anchored offshore from Dill's Branch in the Tennessee River, has commenced firing upon the advancing Confederates. The Federal gunboats, *Tyler* and *Lexington,* commanded by Captains Gwin and Shirk, have been ordered to shell the advancing Confederate Brigades of Generals Jackson and Chalmers, now within a short distance of their objective, the Landing. The gunboats, with a firepower of four 20-pound Parrott guns, begin lobbing the large shells ineffectually into the Confederate lines. A last line defense consisting of siege cannons and field artillery, facing south from the Landing, also commences firing upon the Confederates. This row of cannons, hastily formed by General Grant, is the Federals' last hope to stop the onrushing Rebels. To escape this concentration of firepower, the Second Texas is ordered to take cover in the bottom of a steep ravine, and the shells pass overhead striking the opposite bank.

It is now almost the twilight of an early spring day, and the weary confederates attempt to re-form for an attack of Pittsburg Landing. Chalmers's Brigade has exhausted its ammunition supply, and Jackson's brigade has only a few cartridges left. Word is sent to the rear that, with reinforcements and ammunition, Pittsburg Landing can be taken. As there is not time to supply either commodity before darkness, a bayonet attack is ordered. Chalmers and Jackson's Brigades advance from Dill's Branch, and coming face to face with the row of heavy artillery, realize the futility of such an attack against an organized defense. The attack is called off just at the onset of darkness, and Pittsburg Landing is saved. Colonel

Moore would write in later years that the Second Texas had been delayed two or three hours in the ravine awaiting orders to attack the Landing.[23] But the death of General Johnston at 2:30 P.M. had paralyzed the Confederate attack, and it was at least an hour later before General Beauregard began to function in his new position of command.

Colonel Moore is ordered back to the regimental camps of the 41st Illinois and 3rd Iowa, taken by storm that afternoon, and where the men of the Second Texas are bivouacked for the night. Vainly, Moore searches the darkened woods to rejoin Jackson's Brigade, but it cannot be located. The Second Texas will not rejoin the Brigade until several days after the battle.[24] Meanwhile the Texans dine this evening on rations supplied by the Federal Government. "Oh how empty we found ourselves," remembered Ralph Smith, "when we had time to think of it. Having inflated our anatomies with crackers, sausage, pigs feet, macaroni, sugar, coffee, etc., we began to select such blankets, overcoats and other clothing as we felt the need of."[25]

Colonel Moore sends Lieutenant Daniel Gallaher of Company A to look for ammunition, but he strays too close to Federal lines in the darkness and is captured.[26] The men fill their canteens from a pond in the area of the camp but report the water as unfit to drink, being strongly tinctured with blood.[27]

Private Sam Houston, Jr. removes the Bible from his knapsack to read by campfire and discovers a bullet hole in the back cover.[28] The path of the bullet penetrates the New Testament and finally halts at Psalm 70, one of the greatest prayers for deliverance in the Bible: "Make haste, O God, to deliver me: make haste to help me, O Lord." "Let them be ashamed and confounded that seek after my soul: let them be turned backward, and put to confusion, that desire my heart . . ."

As the exhausted soldiers bed down, a cold deluge of spring rain begins to fall, and they will spend another night exposed to the raw elements of nature. To add to this discomfort, the gunboats *Lexington* and *Tyler* continue to bombard confederate positions throughout the night at ten-minute intervals. The 8-inch shells burst in the air with brilliant flashes that shower the confederates with falling limbs and branches, disturbing their rest. However, the most disheartening sounds of the night come from the cheering of federal soldiers that signals the arrival of General Buell and the battle-tested soldiers of the Army of the Ohio. These reinforcements arrive at Pittsburg Landing by steamboat to reinforce the left flank of the Union line. The right flank is reinforced by the belated arrival overland of General Lew Wallace with 5,000 troops. The weary Confederates must rise tomorrow to fight a fresh army of battle-tested veterans.

Before dawn on Monday, April 7, General Buell organizes the Army of the Ohio into battle formations, and the Second Texas finds itself behind Federal lines. Moving south along the Tennessee River, the Texans reorganize on Lick Creek, where they entered the battle on Sunday. Colonel Moore, for his valor on Sunday, receives a battlefield promotion to brigadier general and relinquishes command of the Second Texas to Lieutenant Colonel W.P. Rogers who is promoted to colonel. General Moore's Brigade consists of the Second Texas and the Nineteenth and Twenty-first Alabama Regiments.

In the first few minutes of the second day of battle at Shiloh many Texans become casualties, and the Second Texas becomes the center of a controversy that will rage throughout the war. General William Hardee is given command of the right flank of the Confederate Army and orders General Moore's Brigade into a line of battle. From General Moore's official report,[29] the opening battle on Monday is described:

> . . . Having formed the brigade in a line of battle, as ordered (the Twenty-first Alabama on the right, the Second Texas in the center, and the Nineteenth Alabama on the left), a general officer and staff rode up and inquired for General Withers, who had just left our position. He ordered me to throw forward skirmishers, cover our front, feel the position of the enemy, and then fall back. On asking from whom I received the order, I was answered, "General Hardee." The order was immediately given for deploying the skirmishers, but before it could be executed it was countermanded, and the brigade, except a part of the Nineteenth Alabama, which acted as a support, advanced under the personal direction of Gen-

eral Hardee and staff, who generally gave orders directly and not through myself as Commander of the brigade.

... If, as commander of the brigade, I had taken upon myself the responsibility of advancing upon the enemy without first feeling his position with skirmishers, then I might justly be held responsible for the results; but such was not the case.

Before the advance was ordered we were told that the brigade was to act as a support to General Breckinridge, who was engaging the enemy in front, and while advancing we were warned again and again by one or more staff officers not to fire on our friends in front. The greater part of the Second Texas passed over an open field and the enemy allowed them to approach near their lines before firing. Even after the enemy opened fire, the officers of the Second Texas report the order was still given not to fire on our friends, and in one instance, after a private returned the fire of the enemy, a staff officer rode up and drew his pistol, threatening to blow off the man's head if he fired again.

Major Runnels reports that while the order not to fire was being reported to the regiment he saw that the force in front were not friends, and ordered the men to charge them; but just at that time a most galling cross-fire was poured into the regiment and the cry, "fall back," being heard in a voice unfamiliar to him, he countermanded the order; but it was too late to be effective. The men fell back in great confusion . . .

I doubt not that our failure to drive back the enemy at this time and place may be attributed wholly to the mistake regarding the character of the force in front, the multiplicity of commands, and the consequent confusion of the men not knowing whom to obey.

The grim reaper strikes. "When they were ordered to charge a battery Monday morning, they were ordered to charge upon an open field, and while charging were ordered to halt, and received a murderous fire from the enemy lying in ambush. Our loss in ten minutes was greater than the whole of Sunday," reports Captain William Christian.[30] Great losses indeed they were for the regiment.

Texas patriot Captain Clark Owen is felled by a Belgian musket ball, entering the stomach and exiting near the backbone, and is carried from the field mortally wounded.[31] Lieu-

tenant J.H. Feeney from Robertson County is struck down
while rallying his men. Sergeant Major A.T. Paul from Harris
County, eulogized as "one of the bravest of the brave," is
killed.[32] Ralph Smith estimates that 150 men were lost by the
regiment in the ambush, and shortly later he, himself, is shot
in the left leg and taken prisoner.[33] Private Sam Houston, Jr.,
receives a serious wound in the upper part of the thigh and is
struck on the knee by a spent ball in this field, and, in reports
sent to General Houston in Texas, is listed as dead. Colonel
Rogers, in a letter to his wife, writes, "Young Sam Houston is
no doubt dead. I had diligent search made for his body but
could not find it, he was I suppose buried by the enemy as was
also our poor friend Paul. The blow to his mother will be
great. How sad it was that my advice was not taken by the
General." [34]

This ambush, as reported by General Moore and Cap-
tain Christian, has not been perceived as such by General
Hardee and his staff who accuse the regiment of cowardice. In
General Hardee's report he states:

> . . . Many of our best regiments, signalized in the battle of Sun-
> day by their steady valor, reeled under the sanguinary struggle
> on the succeeding day. In one instance, that of the Second Texas
> Regiment, commanded by Colonel Moore, the men seemed ap-
> palled, fled from the field without apparent cause, and were so
> dismayed that my efforts to rally them were unavailing.

In a subsequent letter on the subject, he further states:

> . . . On the morning of April 7, at the battle of Shiloh, being in
> command of the right of our line, I ordered Colonel Moore's
> Second Texas Regiment into action, I was near the regiment
> when it was moved foreward, and could not have been more
> than 40 yards from it when it was placed in line of battle. I was
> about the same distance from it when it commenced firing; and
> apparently before half the pieces of the regiment were dis-
> charged it broke and fled disgracefully from the field. I [then]
> sent Captain Clare, then acting on my staff, to pursue and rally
> the regiment. He afterward informed me that it could not be ral-
> lied; that a portion of the regiment swore they would not return
> to the field, and when told that I would call them a "pack of

cowards," said they did not care a damn what I might call them. So far as I know the regiment did not return to the field on that day.[35]

Thus the facts in the matter appear to be as follows: the Second Texas was ordered to advance on the enemy without proper use of skirmishers to probe for enemy strength. During this advance, the proper chain of command was not maintained. General Hardee's staff gave direct orders to the troops. As an immediate consequence of this action, several different commands from unfamiliar voices were given to the troops simultaneously, while under fire, causing widespread confusion in the ranks. In addition, General Hardee's staff failed to know the correct location of General Breckinridge's troops, and failed to exercise good judgement in repeatedly ordering the troops to withhold fire in the face of an evident enemy attack. Thus the regiment quite likely saved itself from complete destruction by not returning to the battlefield under such poor leadership. It should also be noted that General Hardee specified in his report that General Moore commanded the Second Texas Infantry, while, in fact, he did not. Colonel Rogers was in command. However, the Second Texas Infantry and General Moore have both made a very powerful enemy in General Hardee, who has substantial political influence in Richmond, and this slanderous story of cowardice will continue to demoralize the regiment throughout the war.

After the ambush, the regiment falls back and reforms. The Texans take the battlefield again and attack a Federal battleline. The line breaks in retreat, and the Second Texas pursues the fleeing enemy almost half a mile.[36] However, the battle-weary Texans do not have the stamina to match General Buell's fresh troops and are slowly repulsed, as is the entire Confederate battleline. With his troops on the verge of collapse, General Beauregard breaks off action with the Federals at 3:00 P.M., and withdrawal begins uninterrupted by Federal attacks. The Corinth road, now a sea of mud, is once again choked with troops, this time in retreat. Wagons are loaded with wounded soldiers laid in like sacks of grain. The

Confederate field hospitals and surgical staff are woefully inadequate to handle the large number of wounded soldiers. Doctors Nedlett and Woolfork from Company K receive special commendation for their tireless efforts on behalf of the regimental wounded, but with no drugs or medical supplies, little can be done to alleviate the suffering.[37] Additional casualties not previously reported include the death of Captain Edward F. Williams of Company D and the severe wounds received by Captains J.W. Hood and G.W.L. Fly of Companies G and I, respectively. Total regimental casualties are reported as thirty-three and one-third percent, with known killed as ten percent. The final reported casualties for all Confederates are listed as killed 1,728, wounded 8,012, and missing 959. The Federals' report include killed 1,754, wounded 8,408, and missing 2,885.

Company commanders on both sides now begin the painful process of writing letters home to inform loved ones of the loss of a son, husband, or sweetheart. For Captain Ashbel Smith, the pain is more acute in several ways. His wounded right arm makes writing an arduous detail; but the worst pain is caused by the anguish he feels as he writes General Sam Houston about the news of his missing son. General Houston and his wife had both attempted to stop Sam Jr. from enlisting in the Army, but the seventeen-year-old lad had prevailed over his parents. If he must enlist, they felt he would be safest in the Bayland Guards under the watchful eye of an old friend, Ashbel Smith. With a heavy heart, Dr. Smith writes the following letter.[38]

"To Gen. Sam Houston

"April 16, 1862

"My dear Old Chief

"Writing is extremely painful — a wound involving the right armpit and weakness from many days fever — my arm is laid out on the table. This is my first effort except a short scrawl. No amanuensis, alone on a negro plantation.

"You have heard of the battle of the 6th and 7th — I shook hands with Sam on the morning of the 7th. I was carried to Camp 16 miles from the battlefields on the night of the 7th —

during the 8th most of our company arrived in camp, or *were accounted* for. Sam and some 7 or 8 others were in no way accounted for, which led to apprehension being entertained for their safety. — On the 9th I was sent to the hospital in Memphis — since leaving I have not heard a word from Camp. And being sent away from Memphis for safety, though 30 miles nearer Corinth I seem cut off from information till I can myself travel.

"I by no means despair of Sam's safety — indeed, I trust he may now be in Camp — 16 miles from the battlefields to camp, the roads inconceivably muddy, and our men worn down with fighting, hunger and marches by night — I feel confident that several of the missing must needs have lain down by the wayside and taken some of the repose which all required — and they have subsequently returned to Camp. — Some too may have been wounded — and perhaps have fallen into the hands of the enemy, where at least they will be decently treated.

"The battle — where all fought most gallantly — as did all the Bayland Guards — to name individuals would be invidious. But Sam with some others were conspicuous — he fought like a hero and with the coolness of a veteran. He was in the front rank, and I saw him repeatedly having loaded his gun step foreward a pace lay his gun to his shoulder throw his eye along the barrel till the sight covered the enemy and then having discharged his piece, he would drop back and reload. I occasionally cautioned him with a friendly threat to tell his mother of his so exposing himself. — Sam always replied with a pleasant smile and a cheery word.

"I trust my dear Command[er]; that Sam will be restored to yourself. [three lines obscured] . . . From our leaving Houston till Monday evening 7th when I shook hands with him Sam's conduct and bearing was all that his mother and father could desire.

"Though weak and full of pain I hope in a week or two to be again strong and on duty — Public affairs look as gloomy to us here as they can do to you at a distance.

"May God bless and you and yours.

"Truly you old friend
"Ashbel Smith"

But what happened to Sam Houston, Jr.? After the regiment is led into an ambush on April 7 by General Hardee's staff, he receives a gaping wound in the groin of his right leg and falls on the battlefield, left for dead by his retreating comrades. On a field littered with Federal and Confederate wounded, Sam lies waiting to be attended to by a Union Surgeon. The surgeon, rushing to treat both Federal and Confederate casualties, hurriedly examines the location and severity of Sam's injury and pronounces the wound fatal, stating that the femoral artery has been severed.

Sam, a youth of seventeen, lies on this remote battlefield feeling his strength ebb away and prepares himself as best he can to face death. A Union chaplain kneels beside Sam to offer spiritual consolation. As a dying request, Sam asks the chaplain to send his bullet-creased Bible back to his mother in Texas. In perusing the flyleaf of the Bible, the Chaplain discovers Sam's name, and that he is the son of former Senator Sam Houston of Texas. Suddenly the chaplain shouts excitedly for the surgeon to return to young Houston and examine his wounds thoroughly. The surgeon probes Sam's wound with his finger and feels the pulsing femoral artery still intact. Litter bearers are summoned and the young lad is removed to a dressing station with the chaplain trotting beside him attending his needs. In the ensuing days, the chaplain works tirelessly to save Sam's life, and when the crisis has passed, tells young Houston of a pledge made in antebellum days. The chaplain, before the war, had been sent as a member of a non-denominational committee of ministers to Washington to plead with the United States Senate not to repeal the Missouri Compromise Bill. The committee of clergymen were ignored by all the Senators they approached, except Sam Houston of Texas. He championed their cause and forced the Senate to grant them a hearing on the floor of the Senate. ". . . the members of the Committee expressed their gratitude for his help, but one particular minister, the last to leave, held him by the hand and told him if the time ever came that he could do anything for him or for anyone who meant anything to him he would be glad to render the service." [39] The chaplain was this minister.

Both sides claim a victory at Shiloh and from camp in Corinth on May 1, Colonel W.P. Rogers writes, "The gallantry of our Reg[iment] is spoken of by all. Our charges were magnificent. The last charge on Sunday evening and two on Monday were truly grand. Those I lead in person, am commanding carrying our battle flag. It has six holes through it one in the staff— my horse slightly wounded in the shoulder. I received a blow from a limb cut off by a cannon ball." [40]

3

Camp life in Mississippi

The romance of soldiering has pretty nearly worn off, . . .
When we first arrived in Corinth, we were told that the
Texians were readily recognized by being the *dirtiest* troops in
the command, . . .

Letter from "Confederate" to the
Tri-Weekly Telegraph.

The weary survivors and those wounded that can be
moved begin to arrive in camp at Corinth on Monday night
and Tuesday morning, April 9, 1862. The severely wounded
are left on the battlefield to be tended by the Federals. The
twenty-five mile march from Pittsburg Landing to Corinth is
made through heavy rain and hail storms. Muddy roads are
churned ever deeper by the transit of wagons and artillery
caissons, and ankle-deep mud becomes knee-deep. The Regiment finds on its return to Corinth that no arrangements have
been made to organize a hospital for Texas troops, and there
are no medicines and drugs to be issued. Major Runnels
writes on April 13,

Eight days ago the great battle of Shiloh was fought, in which
Texans lost many brave and noble Spirits. Some of our

wounded have, as yet, not even had their wounds dressed. They are scattered all over the army, in various hospitals. God knows what attention they have received. Many are in camp not only wounded, but sick, without medicine or medical attendance, in tents and on the wet ground, no place for a sick or wounded man.[1]

It is small wonder that the regiment will experience such a high mortality rate among wounded, and the mixing of sick and well troops will cause communicable diseases to sweep like wildfire through the camps. Major Runnels further states that the State of Texas has appropriated money for a regimental hospital for the Second, Ninth, and Terry's Regiments, but no action has been taken to purchase supplies. Finally, Runnels suggests that agents be sent to Mexico to purchase medicine for use in the Mississippi hospitals. The kind people of Mississippi respond to this sorry plight as best they can and, as Captain William Christian writes, ". . . her people are hospitable; our sick are scattered at every farm house." [2] Sickness instead of Yankee bullets now begin to take its toll of the Texans. Captain Christian, in a correspondence to Houston, Texas states, "Two of my best men have died since the battle of Shiloh of disease, John White and John Muir, both of Harris Co.[County]. They braved the battle of Shiloh like heroes, returned to camp and were cut down by sickness."[3] Death from sickness becomes a commonplace event in the camps; Colonel William P. Rogers explains in a letter to his brother's widow, ". . . disease is so fatal in my Reg. . . . One and sometimes two of my Reg. die in camp every week. I have been writing this while listening to the solemn funeral dirge of one of my best officers, Sergeant Major Gadtler. Poor fellow he has answered his last roll call on earth."[4]

Miss Kate Cumming, a courageous young woman from Mobile, Alabama, is in Corinth during this time as a volunteer nurse. Over the strong disapproval of her family, Miss Cumming travels by train to reach Corinth on April 11, 1862, and meets the incoming wounded. In her diary[5] she writes about her shock at the crude medical facilities for the troops,

As it had been raining for days, water and mud abounded. Here and there were wagons hopelessly left to their fate, and men on horseback trying to wade through it. As far as the eye could reach, in the midst of all this slop and mud, the white tents of our brave army could be seen through the trees, making a picture suggestive of any thing but comfort.

. . . We are at the Tishomingo Hotel, which, like every other large building, has been taken for a hospital. . . . Mrs. Ogden tried to prepare me for the scenes which I should witness upon entering the wards. But alas! nothing that I had ever heard or read had given me the faintest idea of the horrors witnessed here. . . . Gray-haired men — men in the pride of manhood — beardless boys — Federals and all, mutilated in every imaginable way, lying on the floor, just as they were taken from the battle-field; so close together that it was almost impossible to walk without stepping on them. . . . The foul air from the mass of human beings at first made me giddy and sick, but I soon got over it. We have to walk, and when we give the men any thing, kneel, in blood and water; but we think nothing of it at all.

Rations supplied to the men are of the poorest quality. The mainstay is flour, made into a dough that is usually cooked over the campfires on musket ramrods and passes for biscuits. This fare is supplemented with pickled beef, described in flattering terms as, "unpalatable." S.B. Barron of the Third Texas Cavalry describes[6] the procedure used by Confederate troops in Corinth to obtain drinking water:

water we had to drink was bad, very bad, . . . we procured [water] by digging for it; the earth around Corinth being very light and porous, holding water like a sponge. When we first went there the ground was full of water, and by digging a hole two feet deep we could dip up plenty of a mean, milky-looking fluid; but as the season advanced the water sank, so we dug deeper, and continued to go down, until by the latter part of May our water holes were from eight to twelve feet deep, still affording the same miserable water. My horse would not drink a drop of the water the men had to use, and if I failed to ride him to a small running branch some two miles away he would go without drinking.

The regiment's stay in Corinth is brief, for on Wednesday night they are ordered on picket duty to Monterrey, eight miles north of Corinth on the road to Pittsburg Landing. The few men that can answer roll call fall into formation and hobble to their assigned posts. Thus begins the first in a series of picket duties the Second Texas will participate in to monitor the slow, cautious advance of the Union Army upon Corinth. Under the command of General Halleck, this army, complete with huge, siege cannons anticipated for the defenses of Corinth, will swell in size to over 100,000 men. Observers predict that when these two great armies clash again, the bloodiest battle in the history of the world will be fought. Rains continue to fall, and the men are constantly exposed to the privations of war while serving on picket duty with no tents and very little food. More and more men's names swell the sick list, many dying from the influenza and other communicable diseases that sweep the camps in Corinth. In a note to the *Tri-Weekly Telegraph* of Houston, a correspondent observes, "Could your readers see our regiment today, and compare them to what they were two months ago, they would indeed think that life is changing. Out of 850 brave, healthy men who left Houston, only some 175 or 200 will be able to go into the fight. Many on the sick list will go into the fight."[7]

On May 8, 1862, an action is taken by the Confederate Army at Corinth to dislodge an advanced guard of Federals from the small town of Farmington, Mississippi, eight miles east of Corinth.

The Second Texas, as a part of General Ruggles's Fourth Brigade, leaves Corinth on the evening of May 8 in a southerly direction and suddenly veers east to Farmington in an all night march over boggy ground. At Farmington several brigades under command of General John Pope have taken the city from Confederate pickets and are camped east of the city. The Federal encampments straddle the bridge over the marshy Seven Mile Creek, with one brigade camped on the east side and the remainder protected by the creek on the west side. The Confederate plan of attack calls for the first three brigades of General Ruggles's Division to feign a frontal assault on the single Union brigade, causing the remaining Federal forces to cross the bridge to the east side of the creek, and relieve the beleaguered brigade. The Confederate Fourth Brigade, lying in wait with its forces to the southwest, will then attack in a movement up the creek and burn the bridge, trapping the Federals on the east side of Seven Mile Creek.[8] But, unknown to the Confederates, Union General Halleck has ordered General Pope not to cross Seven Mile Creek to provoke a general engagement.[9] On daylight on May 9, the Confederate Brigade of General Patton Anderson strikes the Federal front on the east side of the creek, and a sharp engagement ensues. The Federal troops handle themselves well until the arrival of the Rebel Fourth Brigade from the southwest. The Yankees flee the field and cross the bridge to join forces on the west side of the creek and avoid entrapment. The battlefield is littered with knapsacks dropped by escaping Federals, which supply food and articles of clothing desperately needed by the men of the Second Texas. One of the Texans, finding a copy of a St. Louis, Missouri newspaper on the battlefield, reads of the fate of several regiment members. Held as prisoners of war in St. Louis are: Lieutenant Dan Gallaher of Company A, B. Buddy, W.R. Anthony, Joe Wright, James A. Rhea, and H. Bartlett, all reported as missing at Shiloh.[10] Thus ends the small battle of Farmington, with the Confederates burning the bridge and returning to Corinth. The Confederate harassment tactics at Farmington fail to slow the cautious advance of General Halleck, and by May 23th, his army faces the northwestern defenses of Corinth, with the two great armies eye to eye. Federal artillery shells begin to fall in the Confederate camps, and Colonel William Rogers reports, "The Yankees bombarded us two days before we left Corinth and killed my horse, one I bought here." [11]

General Beauregard, in a movement that surprises even his own troops, orders Corinth evacuated on the night of May 29. The 47,000 Confederates, greatly outnumbered by their besiegers, withdraw south to Baldwin, Mississippi. Under the cover of darkness Confederate forces avoid encirclement by employing the clever ruses of General Beauregard. Wooden "Quaker guns" are in emplacements, manned by padded dummies, and several trains pull into Corinth throughout the night with loud cheering and a brass band, causing the Federals to suspect the arrival of reinforcements. On the dawning of May 30, reveille bugles are blown throughout the city, and the Yankees are still unaware of the retreat until midday when the few supplies that cannot be transported are fired, and several ammunition dumps explode.

The Second Texas leaves Corinth on the night of May 29, not in retreat, but to prevent their capture by Federal cavalry of Boonville, Mississippi, and the destruction of a disabled ammunition train within the city. The march pace throughout the night alternates between quick and double-quick, but the Federals win the race. At 2:30 A.M., the 2nd Iowa and 2nd Michigan cavalry regiments capture the train, and before daylight the Second Texas can see the glare and explosions on the horizon caused by the burning train. Colonel Washington L. Elliott of 2nd Iowa Cavalry receives lavish praise from General Pope for this raid, which represents the largest single amount of supplies destroyed from the fleeing Confederates.[12]

The regiment is now bivouacked at Camp Ingraham, forty miles south of Corinth on the Mobile and Ohio Railway. The camp is named in memory of a staff member of General Van Dorn, killed in the battle of Farmington. At this camp several promotions are authorized for the regiment: Colonel Moore is promoted to the rank of brigadier general subject to approval of the Confederate Senate at Richmond, and Lieutenant Colonel William Rogers is promoted to the rank of colonel. Major Hal Runnels is passed over for promotion, and he resigns his commission in an embittered state. Due to his seniority, the rank of lieutenant colonel passes to Captain William Timmons, who waives his right in favor of Captain Ashbel Smith saying, "Captain Smith is an old man, who has long been in public life, and has served the republic and the State of Texas in various civil capacities, and I am a young man and can afford to wait."[13] With this chivalrous act, the rank of lieutenant colonel passes to Ashbel Smith, and William Timmons is promoted to major.

The army is moved to Tupelo, Mississippi, where it is reorganized and reassigned. The Second Texas remains at Tupelo with the corp commanded by General Sterling Price of Missouri. "Pap," as the men call him is one of the most loved and respected officers in the Confederate Army. The other corp, under General Braxton Bragg, will later march northward into Tennessee. On June 11, the Second Texas receives two honors from General Dabney Maury, its division commander. It receives a unit citation reading, *For conspicuous gallantry in the battle of Shiloh, the Second Texas Regiment will have Shiloh inscribed on its battle flag.*[14] The same unit citation had been given to the regiment earlier by General Beauregard when it was encamped at Corinth, becoming the first regiment in Price's Army of the West to receive such a distinction.[15] The second honor is their selection as the "sharpshooters" regiment of General Moore's brigade. This designation means that the Second Texas will lead all attacks made by the brigade, and form the rear guard for any retreats. Hereafter, the regiment will often be referred to as the Second Texas Sharpshooters, an honor which will the cost the Texans dearly in casualties.

Around June 19, Colonel Rogers receives disturbing news that certain individuals in Houston are spreading rumors that the regiment had behaved badly on the second day of the battle of Shiloh. By return mail, Colonel Rogers, writing to his wife, replies,

> . . . I received lately two letters from you — the one about the letter of Runnels and the other of June 3. Please say nothing to anyone about Runnels. If he wrote as you supposed its falsehood will be fixed. He has gratified my Reg one and all by resigning. He was not promoted and one of my capts. was and so have I been. Facts speak for themselves. He never has been at any time even for one hour in command of the Reg. — The Reg. did not run it fell back 2 or 3 hundred yards. I with others of my officers lead it again to the fight and for its conspicuous gallantry I have

been by Gen. Beauregard authorized to inscribe Shiloh on my flag.

The companies all fought well and so did all of my Capts. My old Houston Companies were conspicuous for their gallantry and indeed none of them wanting in deeds of valor. Since I have been promoted my Reg. has received the distinguishing honor of being designated as advance sharpshooters. I deal in truth when I say to you that 2nd Texas stands today ahead of all others in drill and discipline, and behind none in deeds of daring valor and gallantry. I cannot believe that Runnels wrote as you heard he did.[16]

Colonel Rogers is deeply upset by this news and corresponds with Dr. William McCraven, editor of the *Tri-Weekly Telegraph* of Houston, Texas, to reassure him and the community of Houston that the regiment behaved in a gallant manner. This letter has been lost, but we can judge much of its content by the return letter Dr. McCraven writes,

. . . We are *proud* of them all but we have a *special* interest in "2nd Texas" as well for the laurels it has won as because it is so largely made up of Harris County boys. Don't be alarmed my dear Colonel for the reputation of the "2nd Texas" in this community — or suffer a moments anxiety lest its glorious laurels should be tarnished or *could* be tarnished by any slanders that may have been circulated and apparently intended to prejudice the regt. It is true there have been rumors of reports tending in that direction. I hope they have arisen either from misconception or exaggeration. But admitting that they meant *mischief* be perfectly assured that they have not and will not *touch* the reputation of the regiment, but with just and inevitable retribution recoils on the head of the slanderers. The banner of the "2nd Texas" is in itself a refutation of any slanderous imputation inferring the courage of the regiment. I do not say that these rumors have met with no countenance from individuals. On the contrary I believe they have been countenanced by a few persons connected with discontented parties in or from the regiment. But so insignificant has been the influence that it could not even raise a ripple on the wave of public opinion. You may rest satisfied that those leaving the regiment from disappointed aspirations can never tarnish its glory no matter with what animus they may be impelled. The glory of *your regiment* is something we would not willingly let die.[17]

While the ugly rumors will never surface in print at home, they have done their job; for Colonel Rogers feels that he must now prove the bravery of the regiment, and in so doing will later lose his life. In future letters to his wife he continually reassures her of the regiment's bravery, thereby building an image that he must maintain at all costs.

While the health of the regiment improves with warmer weather, their resupply by the State of Texas with equipment and clothing continues to be a haphazard affair. To the *Telegraph* in Houston, a soldier of the regiment ironically writes,

Since our hegira from Corinth, as you probably know, we have had but little fighting to do, and the attention of the public mind has been gradually turned from the great army of the West to the still greater one in Virginia, and we have been allowed to rest quietly in camps; improving our health by the daily practice of the skirmish drill — a very pretty manoeuvre when executed upon the parade grounds of Camp Bee, with the accustomed congregation of fair spectators — but not considered so by the poor private, over a ploughed field with the mercury standing at 90 degrees in the shade, with a momently increasing prospect of having to "rally on the reserve," some 400 yards in the rear, at a "double quick."

The romance of soldiering has pretty well worn off, and it has become reduced to facts and figures; I might with propriety say *bare facts*, for clothing, in common with other earthly things, will wear out — new supplies are "unavoidably detained" and *something* (a "military necessity" I reckon, as that is responsible for most all slight commissions or omissions) keeps pay-day in the same place it has been for the last eight months, to-wit; still in the perspective, thereby preventing us from furnishing ourselves. When we first arrived at Corinth, we were told the Texians were readily recognized by being the *dirtiest* troops in command; but experience proved to us that a new system had been adopted, as our retreat illustrated. In answer to the often repeated inquiry, "What regiment is that?" one of our boys merely raised the skirts of his coat, by way of a reply, and the dilapidated condition of his nether garments seemed to solve all doubts in the querist's mind as he immediately rejoined, "Oh! yes, you are Texians." Well, we can console ourselves with the quotation that "a hole may be but the accident of a day; but a patch is the sign of premeditated poverty." [18]

A more indignant letter to the *Telegraph* is written by Captain William Christian, a former enlisted man, about the sufferings of Texas soldiers:

> Our regiments have not been paid yet, and long months have the soldiers been without a cent. The officers were paid several days ago, and when we ask why the privates are not paid, all the satisfaction we get is, "No money for the soldiers yet." Yes, the poor soldier, who finds himself far away from home and friends, who risks his life for his country, is neglected, he falls sick, is sent to the hospital with not a dime in his pocket to buy any of the luxuries that a sick man requires. Vegetables are paraded before him, No money he says, and turns over and suffers. Week after week he lingers, and then fills an unmarked grave. Readers, if you were ever in a camp then you know something of the hardships of a soldiers life. Guard duties, fatigue duties, etc., often boiling down many a proud spirit by disease. You can easily see then the injustice done the private, by paying their officers from $85 to $130 per month regular and have no work to do, while the soldiers receive but $11; and have but this pittance to supply their wants. I say you will agree with me that a wrong has been inflicted on the 2nd Texas Regiment. Every other regiment in the service have been paid regular every two months as the army regulations require.[19]

In the camps at Tupelo, Colonel Rogers resumes regimental drill, as do the other regiments of the Army. As idle men will do, speculation runs rampant through the army as to which regiment is the best drilled. Competition develops, and as Captain Fly of Company I reports,

> At Tupelo, among other commands was the Brigade commanded by Brigadier General Whitfield from Lavaca County, Texas. In this Brigade was the 3rd Louisiana, which was recognized as one of the best drilled regiments in the Confederate Army. There had long been a rivalry between these regiments as to their superiority in drill. There was to be a general review of the troops before General Bragg. Colonel Rogers and General

Whitfield agree to back their opinions as to which of these regiments was better drilled, and put up $500 each, to be paid to Rogers if the 2nd Texas won in the contest, and to General Whitfield in case the 3rd Louisiana won. The judges were to be appointed by General Bragg and the contests to come the day after the General Review. In marching in review, the 3rd Louisiana was permitted to break ranks and await the coming of the 2nd Texas. After the review was over, General Whitfield rode to Colonel Rogers's tent and, calling him out, asked if he would not agree to withdraw the wager, admitting that the 2nd Texas was superior to the 3rd Louisiana in drill. After some chaffing, the Colonel agreed to declare the contest off, provided the General would admit that the 2nd Texas was the better drilled regiment. To this the General agreed, to the delight of the 2nd Texas who, it must be admitted, had but little faith in their success, having on several occasions seen the 3rd Louisiana maneuvering.[20]

It is at about this time that Ralph Smith makes a joyous reunion with the regiment. When we left Ralph, he was in a camp for prisoners of war, (a Federal prison in Alton, Illinois) nursing the wound in his leg he received at Shiloh. The Federals exchange Ralph in about July, 1862, (trade him for a Federal prisoner), and he is taken by guarded transport down the Mississippi River and released at Vicksburg, Mississippi. Teaming up with other soldiers who have also been exchanged, they march overland to reunite with the regiment, probably now at Tupelo. No sooner has this group of pilgrims struck camp then they are summoned to General Moore's tent.

No sooner had we halted than the General appeared, grasped each of us by the hand and with tears trickling down his cheeks spoke to us of the joys he felt at seeing us back again safe and sound and congratulated us upon our perseverance in overcoming so many obstacles in our efforts to array ourselves once more under the flag of our beloved Second Texas. I shall remember that scene as long as my mind endures for it taught me to appreciate the fact that men are not always what they seem. General Moore was a graduate of West Point, a strict disciplinarian with rather a haughty air, but when we saw him mingling his tears with those of the ragged, foot-sore returned prisoners we knew that beneath his grim and cold exterior there beat a heart as tender as a child's. Such expressions of feeling together with sympathetic acts of a thousand kinds afforded a bond of trust between many of our officers and their men that nothing but death could break.[21]

Ralph's feelings about John C. Moore and the regiment have changed quite a bit since his arrival in Houston as a shy young private to enlist in the infantry. At that time he had said, "We went direct to Houston and joined the Second Texas Infantry, commanded by Colonel John C. Moore, a West Point graduate and a brave and gallant officer, but not a Christian, for he was red headed, red-bearded, red-faced, and extremely high-tempered. It was only a short time until I had strong suspicions that I had joined a regiment of devils." [22]

As the hot summer wears on, the idle men in the camps at Tupelo find mischief to get into. Observing the unloading and storage of a forty gallon barrel of peach brandy, the Texans plot to sample its contents. The barrel is secured in a building posted by a sentry day and night. However, the building is on three-foot pilings, and it doesn't take "Sargent Bill" of the regiment very long to crawl under the building in the dead of night and quietly drill from beneath the floor with an auger. Filling many vessels with "joy to the world" tonic, he drives a plug into the barrel and retreats to share his pilferage with the regiment. At dress parade the next morning, it is apparent that the leaking barrel's contents have not been wasted on the ground.[23]

Even though many previously sick soldiers are returning to active duty and exchanged prisoners are filtering into camp, the regiment is still undermanned. Over the protests of the regiment, Lieutenant Colonel Ashbel Smith is sent back to Texas to enroll a group of conscripted soldiers into the the Second Texas. The Government at Richmond, Virginia has passed a Conscription Act drafting all able-bodied men into military service. Colonel Rogers writes his protest of this action to Dr. McCraven of Houston,

I have still left about 500 effective men and Col. Smith goes to

Texas to bring conscripts to me. I will not have them if I can help it. I do not want to command men who have been passed by law into the ranks — no give me the brave men who made a free offering of their services to their country rather than take them I shall ask that my regiment be reduced to Battallion and my rank to that of a Major, not withstanding my *Cols. spurs were won at Shiloh and Farmington.* If they still force them upon me, I must take the fellows and do the best I can with them.[24]

In the same vein Colonel Rogers writes his wife, "Lt. Col. Smith goes to Texas this evening in search of conscripts for my Reg. which I hope he will not get for I do not want them, etc. I write by him. If Gen. Price forced them upon me I shall get mad." [25]

Colonel Rogers's star is on the rise, and the qualities of leadership he exhibits while in the camps at Tupelo attracts the attention of his fellow officers. He writes to his wife,

I have lately had a very high compliment paid to me by my brother officers of this division. The Cols., Lt Cols., and Majors of about 20 regiments from the States of Texas and Arkansas have addressed a letter to Richmond urging my appointment as a Major General to command the troops from their two states now on this side of the river. Learning that the president is still vindictive to me I hardly hope for the appointment, but is nevertheless a very high compliment to me and one which I valued.

. . . They view me as a drill officer, as a disciplinarian and they have seen and tested my capacity to command in battle. For these reasons the compliment is a higher one even if it is thwarted by the personal hostility of the president. They have sent for a special messenger (Lt Col Walson of Arkansas) to urge my claims at Richmond. They allowed me to know nothing of it until it was acted upon.[26]

It is now September 3, and the army has lain idle for three months. The men begin to feel the coolness of the nights that signal the onset of autumn. Suddenly, officers begin to scurry about; marching orders have been received. A soldier from the regiment writes,

We have orders that are unmistakable in their meaning,

which is a foreward [*sic* forward] movement, and by the time this reaches you, our gallant regiment (the 2nd), under the command of the much loved and brave Col. W. P. Rogers, will have met the vandal hordes of Lincoln, and make them feel what it is to resist the charge and fury of true Southerners.

The health of the regiment has improved very much. The boys are very much pleased at the thoughts of a foreward [*sic*] movement, though it takes them farther from home and into a cold climate. Speaking of cold climates — cannot our friends at home send us a few blankets, and thereby enable us to get through the winter: for we are very near destitute of such things as blankets and underclothing, in consequence of our retreat from Corinth, and have not been supplied by the military authorities.[27]

As the regiment prepares to march into battle again, many new faces appear in the ranks as company commanders. The captains of Companies A through K are now respectively: William Christian, Jas. D. McCleary, P.M. Woodall, Ed Daly, William Holder, John Muller, C.C. McGinnis, Nobel L. McGinnis, G.W.L. Fly, and W.D. Goff. Lieutenant Maurice Simons has been promoted to the post of brigade quartermaster for General Moore's Brigade at the rank of major.

The Confederate army at Tupelo, known as the Army of the West, is set in motion towards the small village of Iuka, Mississippi, thirty miles east of Corinth. Its commander, General Sterling Price, has received orders to block the advance of Union General Rosecrans's army into Tennessee to unite with General Buell's army. The Confederates move rapidly, by forced march, with the last forty-five miles covered in thirty hours, and the last five miles at the "double-quick." Preceding the army, the Confederate cavalry dashes into Iuka in time to prevent the hastily retreating Federal garrison from putting the torch to their immense storehouse. General Price is pleased with the captured goods and issues his troops bread, cheese, crackers, and canned goods to fill their knapsacks. The countryside around Iuka has suffered greatly from the ravages of the war, and is dotted with the burned-out farmhouses of Southern sympathizers. The pathetic scenes of thinly-clad, barefoot women and children gathered around the ashes that once were their homes, fill Confederate soldiers with anger.[28]

General Grant, having monitored the movements of the Army of the West closely, decides that it can be encircled at Iuka. Sending General Ord with 6,500 men to block the northern road from Iuka, and General Rosecrans with two divisions of men to block the two southern roads leading from Iuka, the trap is set. However, Rosecrans is delayed in his arrival to Iuka, so Grant orders Ord to delay his actions until he can hear the sound of cannon fire from Rosecrans's attack. Fortune smiles on the Confederates, however, because a stiff breeze from the north — at the back of General Ord — will carry the sound of the battle to the south away from his ears. Ord's forces will not attack the entire day of September 19, leaving one jaw of the trap unsprung. In another error, the Federals fail to block both southern roads as ordered, leaving the road to Fulton, Mississippi, open as an escape route. On the morning of September 19, General Price receives a communication from Ord, who is now north of Iuka, demanding his surrender. Ord states that Price and his Confederates are surrounded, but since Rosecrans has been delayed in transit and is nowhere to be seen, the communication is ignored. However, by 2:30 P.M. Rosecrans arrives on the Tuscumbia Road from the south and spearheads an attack into Iuka. General Price has earlier ordered Maury's division, which contains the Second Texas, to move north of Iuka and intercept the advancing force of General Ord. The Division of General Henry Little moves on the advancing column of Union soldiers from Rosecrans's two divisions as they move into Iuka from the south on the Tuscumbia Road. A bloody battle ensues on the narrow roadway, in which the counterattacking Confederates drive the union troops back and capture nine cannons, but not without losses. General Little is struck by a minie ball in the forehead and killed. Total Confederate casualties are placed at 700, with the Union losses at 790. Little's Division has borne a heavy assault, while Maury's Division encounters only light resistance. Early the next day the Confederates, burdened with their captured supplies, escape the trap planned for them in Iuka by retreating south on the unguarded Fulton Road. The Federals, eager to regain their lost stores, pursue the retreating Confederate rear guard closely along the heavily wooded Fulton Road in order to provoke another battle. An ambush planned by Colonel Rogers is executed by the Second Texas Sharpshooters, which turns the tide and forces the Federals to break off the engagement. For this daring action the Second Texas and Colonel Rogers are cited by both General Price and General Maury in their official reports of the battle of Iuka.

An eyewitness account of the battle is given by Colonel Rogers in his September 24th letter to his wife.

Since I last wrote you, now 14 days ago, we have had stormy times. We have been to Iuka, captured it with a great deal of army stores say $4 or 500,000 and all without a fight. We took Iuka on Sunday and as the Yankees fled we supposed we would have to go further for a fight, but on Tuesday evening at 2 P.M. the booming of cannon announced the enemy was returning. I formed the old Reg. and advanced it deployed as skirmishes in front of the 1st Brig — The enemy soon greeted us with minnie balls — we returned their fire for two hours drove them before us, until night put a stop to our work. 2nd Texas was the only Reg. in the fight and during $2^1/_2$ or 3 hours was exposed to the fire of the enemies sharpshooters and artillery. About sundown their cavalry made a dash at the Reg. which we repulsed in fine style — our loss was only 2 killed and 3 wounded. We were from a half to $^3/_4$ of a mile ahead of the Brigade all the time . . .

We slept on our arms all night and at dawn of day I sounded the advance and forward we went for a mile or more through forest, fields, and brush finding no enemy I now halted as it was clear that the enemy was gone. The two succeeding days gave no indication of an enemy in force. During all this time 2nd Texas was in line of battle $1^1/_2$ miles ahead of the Brigade sleeping on arms.

On Friday morning it was evident they were again advancing. I was now put in command of a Brigade of 3 Regiments —

to wit — my own Adams Arkansas Reg. and Stearman's Reg. of Sharpshooters. The enemy approached us from 3 roads. I was in command of the center in advance. It also happened that they only attacked our left, late in the evening — a fierce and angry battle for about 40 or 50 minutes ensued in which we lost about 100 killed and wounded among the killed was Gen. Little. We captured 9 pieces of artillery and drove the enemy back. The loss of the enemy was much greater. At dark I was ordered to fall back from my advanced position in the center to the scene of battle. We reached there in one hour and found all quiet except the groans of the wounded and dying. We slept on the battlefield and at daybreak our General ordered a retreat, for it was clear that we were surrounded by a force greatly larger than ours. Yes we were surrounded by a largely superior force and although we had whipped them in every skirmish they had demanded an unconditional surrender. Things were dark around us. Gen. Maury rode up and put 2nd Texas and Bledsoe's battery of 4 guns in the rear. We took the Fulton Road the only one not occupied by the enemy. It was clear that 2nd Texas would have to fight. They permitted us to pass 7 miles, when they drove in our Cavalry rear guard, where I again called on 2nd Texas to present a wall of fire between the enemy and our retreating army. The line of battle was formed across the road. With Bledsoe's 4 guns in the centre — the Yankees approached within 100 or 200 yds and our fire opened, in 5 minutes the Yankees were gone and 2nd Texas was again victorious. The loss of the enemy is estimated 30 or 40 ours at only 3 slightly wounded. This is a witness to the fact that our line was masked by underbrush and they did not see us until we delivered our fire. They followed us no farther and we took up camp there about 40 miles from Iuka on the evening of the 22nd.

. . . In all of these engagements the Regiment displayed the cool, obstinate and determined bravery of veterans and the Counties of Harris, Burleson, Robertson, Galveston, Gonzales, and Jackson may well be proud of them. The hardships to which they are subjected are indeed great, for many of them are without blankets, tents, or shoes. We have been in the last 10 days, exposed to rain 3 days and nights. The nights are getting quite cool and the men are suffering.

I begged in vain for blankets, tents, and shoes, I will submit to it 4 weeks longer. They must supply them or there will be trouble.

The Reg. now numbers 551 of these 128 are about sick leaving for duty 423 — of these 71 are on detached service as teamsters, mechanics etc. leaving me really only 342 fighting men.[29]

The narrow escape from Iuka was remembered by Captain G.W.L. Fly, who in later years gave this version.

Finding that General Rosecranz was approaching from Corinth with a large force, our General began to retreat in the direction of Tupelo, from which we had come. It was then that the 2nd Texas was called to the post of danger. We had been sent to the front to meet the enemy as he came in, but had not met him as he chose a different route from that we expected. Now, as our army was about to retreat, we were called in from our skirmish line and formed in the rear of our retreating army. We were duly drawn up in line of battle, on a ridge in the southern portion of the town and there held until the army could move out, we to bring up the rear. After waiting here for some time, we saw the enemy marching on the opposite side of town. Seeing this, Colonel Rogers rode in front of the regiment and said: "Men, again you are called to the post of danger, which is the post of honor. Do your duty like men." After this short speech there was not a man of the Regiment, but would have died rather than disappoint the expectations of their beloved Colonel. As the head of the enemy's column came within a half mile of us, they began placing their batteries and forming lines of battle. Just at this juncture, the entire army of Confederates having moved out, we were ordered to follow, which we did in the finest order, moving as if on parade, and anxious for the enemy to come near enough for us to have a strike at them.

Proceeding southward, we soon found that we were closely pursued by the Federal Cavalry. Colonel Rogers ordered a halt and into line faced to the rear. Having thus formed his regiment, with two guns of Bledsoe's Battery in our center, we waited until we found the enemy had retired. We then again marched about a mile, when the enemy's cavalry again appeared in close pursuit. Colonel Rogers again formed us in line of battle facing to the rear with Bledsoe's two guns being again in our center. Here, let me say a word concerning this gallant command, especially of its brave Captain, than whom no more gallant man ever left that State, Missouri, from which none but brave men ever came within my knowledge. Captain Bledsoe was about six feet three, bony, swarthy, resolute, in fact seemed not to know the meaning of the word Fear. As our regiment supported this battery for about twelve months, I had occasion to know this man and equally brave men. Captain Bledsoe did not on this occasion leave the handling of these guns to any other, but took personal command of the two guns. We were formed on a high ridge, overlooking a depression between this and another ridge over which we had just passed. The intervening space was densely covered with black-jack brush. From the top of one ridge to the top of the other was about 200 yards on a straight line, while going down one and up the other would be at least 300 yards. We could plainly see a grave yard that we had passed on the hill where the enemy was forming. Forming on this ridge, the Federal Cavalry dismounted and ran down the hill to a spot of about two acres that was more thickly set with brush than any other. Captain Bledsoe, seeing the enemy run for this thicket, double-shotted his two guns, putting 50 pounds of buckshot in each, and pointing them to this thicket. Colonel Rogers ordered us to fire when Captain Bledsoe gave the command. I shall never forget Bledsoe's appearance at this time. Awaiting quietly the assembling of the enemy in the brush to which he had himself sighted his guns, he drew from his pocket a plug of tobacco and filled his mouth by tearing off apparently half of it. Returning his tobacco to his pocket, his eyes were all the time fixed on the movement of the enemy. As soon as he saw they were within range of his guns, as he had sighted them, he commanded "Fire." At this command, the infantry being ready, a volley from the rifles of the infantry and a discharge from the two cannons simultaneously filled the air with the roar of cannon and rattle of rifles. After the first volley the men, having reloaded stood at ready. Colonel Rogers, whose position would not permit his seeing the conditions of things in front, commanded "Continue firing!" I repeated this command when my Orderly Sergeant, L.J. Burch, said "Captain, we can see nothing to shoot at." The enemy had disappeared. Colonel Rogers then sent his Adjutant to the rear to ask our Cavalry to pursue the fleeing enemy. There were four lines of cavalry formed in our rear. Reaching the first of these lines, the Adjutant called upon the commander to charge. He refused. The second and third lines failed likewise to respond. Coming to the last line, commanded by the brave Colonel McCulloch of Missouri, he at once put his men in pursuit on a run. Having chased the Federal Cavalry until they came to the main column of the infantry, Colonel McCulloch returned to us.

. . . As a result of the fire of the infantry and Bledsoe's two guns, I was afterward informed that forty new graves were filled in the cemetery, with Yankees that were killed by that one volley. Having dismounted at the graveyard, when they advanced again to this place they buried their dead in the graveyard.[30]

The Second Texas, having survived the battle of Iuka almost unscathed, proceeded on to Saltillo, Mississippi, to rendezvous with Confederate General Van Dorn's forces who were planning an attack on Corinth.

4

The Battle of Corinth

. . . Suddenly we saw a magnificent brigade emerge from the timber into the open in our front. They were formed in two lines of battle. The sun glistened on their bayonets as they came forward at right shoulder shift in perfect order, a grand but terrible sight. At their head, in front of their center, rode the commander, a man of fine physique, in the prime of life, quiet and cool, as though he were taking his brigade on a drill. . . . Then we learned who it was — Colonel Rogers, of the 2nd Texas, commanding a Texas brigade.

John Crane of the 17th Wisconsin
Regiment at Fort Robinett.

The armies of Generals Sterling Price and Earl Van Dorn rendezvous on September 28, at Ripley, Mississippi, uniting to form the Army of West Tennessee, with command given to Van Dorn over the protests of Price. The Army is organized into three divisions commanded by Brigadier Generals Hebert, Lovell and Dabney H. Maury. Maury's Division, which will bear the brunt of many of the upcoming battles, is composed of the brigades of Brigadier Generals Phifer, Cabell, and John C. Moore. Moore's Brigade, in turn, contains the following regiments: 42nd Alabama, 15th Arkansas Regiment,

35th Mississippi, 23rd Arkansas Regiment, Bledsoe's Battery (artillery), and the 2nd Texas Infantry.

With new units being recruited daily for service in this army, and with the return of exchanged prisoners, the rolls of the Army of West Tennessee swell to about 22,000 effective troops. One of the new units assigned to Hebert's Division is the 40th Mississippi, characterized as a regiment of extremes. It carries with it a mountainous conglomeration of luggage and personal household goods, and its colonel uses a camel to transport his personal gear. Furthermore, it boasts of having the tallest soldier and the largest soldier in the army. The tallest soldier, a slender man, is judged to be seven feet; while the largest is a lad no more than eighteen years old weighing more than three hundred pounds.[1]

The battle plan for the army developed by Van Dorn evolves into a surprise attack on the Federal garrison at Corinth, under the command of General Rosecrans. Federal troops in that city number 15,000 with the remainder of the garrison stationed in the nearby villages of Rienzi, Burnsville, Jacinto, and Iuka, with an aggregate strength of about 25,000 troops. The plan is to move the Confederate Army north from Ripley to Pocahontas, threatening an attack on the Federal garrison at Bolivar, Tennessee, to the north of Pocahontas, and then rapidly veer eastward twenty miles to surprise Corinth before it can be reinforced. The feint at Bolivar is planned to immobilize the 8,000 troops there under General Hurlbut and prevent their movement to reinforce Corinth. With a rapid movement eastward on Corinth, Van Dorn hopes to find General Rosecrans's 15,000 troops unreinforced and therefore outnumbered. By the time reinforcements from the outlying villages arrive, Van Dorn feels that Corinth can be captured, and its huge supply of stores destroyed.[2] General Price does not favor the plan, wishing at least to postpone the attack until the arrival of more reinforcements from Jackson, Mississippi. Van Dorn overrules Price, and pushes to conclude preparations for the attack. It is reported that General Price, in a private letter written after the battle, stated, ". . .

every General was opposed to making the fight save one, . . ." but this assertion cannot be verified.[3]

The object of the attack, Corinth, had been fortified on three separate occasions in the last seven months. Confederate General Beauregard had built a line of light defensive entrenchments two and a half miles from Corinth that extended around the city from the northwest to the east in an arc. After the Union occupation of this city in May, General Halleck had constructed another line of trenches one- and a-half miles from the city, extending from the west to the south, to supplement the so-called "Beauregard line," and a strongly built inner system of breastworks and siege gun emplacements was constructed on the western periphery of the city by General Rosecrans in August. The key to this inner line of defense lay in the two gun emplacements known as Battery Robinett and Battery Williams, less than a mile from Corinth in a northwest direction, straddling the Memphis and Charleston Railroad tracks. Battery Robinett contained three 20-pound siege guns, and Battery Williams's emplacements were four 24-pound siege guns and two 8-inch howitzers trained on the western approaches to the city.

In addition to these potent defenses, the Confederates would be plagued by the problem of finding an adequate supply of drinking water. Northern Mississippi was in the grip of a heat wave with daily temperatures rising above 90°. What little potable surface water that existed had dried up, and the only means of resupply was to capture the few 300-foot deep draw wells outside of Corinth.

The Army of West Tennessee breaks camp on August 30 and proceeds toward Pocahontas, arriving there early on the morning of October 1; Lovell's division, in advance, repairs the Davis Bridge over the Big Hatchie River. The army then swings east, crosses the river, and begins the advance toward Corinth. Van Dorn, fearing an attack on the Confederate rear by the Federal forces in Bolivar, Tennessee, stations a cavalry regiment to guard the Davis Bridge and parks the Confederate supply wagons on the east side of the river, under guard of the First Texas Legion, commanded by Colonel E.R. Hawkins.

The element of surprise is weakened for the Confederates when, on October 1, a rumor reaches Rosecrans that the Rebel Army at Pocahontas is 40,000 strong, and he reacts by recalling all troops from the environs of Corinth for reinforcement. The concentrated Union Army of 25,000 men behind solid defensive lines now outnumbers the Confederate attackers. The only remaining unknown for Rosecrans is the location of the attack. Thinking that the Confederates might possibly be feigning an attack on Corinth, he sends the Divisions of Generals Hamilton, Davies, and McKean to man the right, center, and left, respectively, of the Beauregard line in order to probe the Confederate strength. At 10:00 A.M., October 3, the Confederates form a battle line to meet this challenge, and the battle for Corinth begins.[4]

The Confederates approach Corinth from the west, roughly along a line that parallels — and is astride — the Memphis and Charleston Railroad bed. General Lovell's division attacks south of the railroad and Price's Corp north of the railroad. General Maury's Division forms the right flank of Price's line of attack, with Moore's Brigade flanking on the railroad. Throughout the day Moore and his veterans battle the three brigades of General McKean with bullets and bayonets. Action begins when the Second Texas encounters pickets of the 14th and 18th Wisconsin of Oliver's Brigade. The Texans place Companies F and K in front, as skirmishers to cross a corn field. Firing begins in the woods on the other side, and Major William Timmons, commanding the skirmishers, takes a severe wound in the arm and must retire from the field. Captain John Muller, of Company F, is appointed acting major, and the advance continues. The Federals fall back 300 yards to the old Beauregard line and determine to make a defensive stand there. This portion of the Beauregard line is in the rear of a 300-yard opening chopped from the woods, and the felled trees are used to form an extensive abatis. Behind this clearing are rifle pits that front and flank a hill crowned with two field artillery batteries. The men from Illinois, Michigan, Missouri, and Wisconsin pour fire into the clearing at the Texans, who recoil and regroup for a charge. With blood-curdling Texas yells a wave of attackers race across the clearing with gleaming bayonets at the fore. From the rifle pits a hasty volley is delivered and the Yankees retreat up the wooded hill, scrambling to locate better defensive sites. Behind the crest of the hill an effective fire is poured into the ranks of the Texans who move slowly upward to their objective. The left flank of Moore's Brigade, manned by the Forty-second Alabama, comes under heavy fire but advances in a flanking movement. The fight continues until the Alabama Regiment succeeds in flanking Oliver's Brigade, which is now in danger of being encircled. Accordingly, at noon the Federals withdraw from this hill to the east. McArthur's Brigade has formed a defensive line east of the hill and, reinforced by the retreating Federals of Oliver's Brigade, prepares to receive Moore's Confederates. Streaming over the captured hill, Moore's troops regroup and form a second battle line. A second bayonet charge is ordered and delivered by the Rebels on the extreme right flank of McArthur's Brigade, which dissolves under its ferocity. McArthur, realizing that he is about to be flanked, orders a countercharge on the Confederate attackers which is delivered by the 7th Illinois. The Second Texas refuses to yield to the Yankee attackers and hurls itself against the oncoming line of blue uniforms, cutting the line of charge in the center and rolling up one side of the line. The Federal troops on this side of the encircled line surrender and are taken to the rear.[5] The Forty-second Alabama, in their eagerness to come to the aid of the Second Texas, mistakenly fires into the ranks of Company K, killing Lieutenant J.M.B. Haynie and six privates.

To avoid being flanked on the right and encircled, McArthur retreats a short distance to the east and re-forms another line of battle facing to the north to avoid another flanking movement by the Confederates. In this retreat, McArthur abandons the camps of the 17th Wisconsin and the 21st Missouri which Moore's men occupy.

Confederate General Lovell, who is south of the railroad and advancing toward Corinth, states in his official report of the battle, "On our right front was a strong redoubt, well flanked with infantry and with an abatis of felled timbers half a mile in width extending around it in one direction but with no obstructions to the north." [6] General Maury orders Moore's Brigade, now north of the redoubt, to cross the railroad to the south and attack the fortress at its weakest point. This redoubt is Battery F next to the intrenched division headquarters, and main camp of General McKean's Division, perched on a hill that gives a commanding view of the battleground. This camp contains a commissary that will later supply the Second Texas with captured rations and afford them their first meal of the day. General Lovell attempts to shell this redoubt from a hill to the west, but his batteries are quickly silenced by the 1st Minnesota Battery occupying the redoubt. At 3:30 P.M. Moore calls for reinforcements from General Cabell, whose brigade is being held in reserve. Cabell responds by sending the 19th and 20th Arkansas Regiments to Moore's assistance, and the assault on the armed camp begins. From the brow of a ridge seventy-five yards south of the railroad, concentrated volleys of fire are poured into the ranks of the oncoming Confederate assault by the 15th and 16th Iowa. The Iowans are firing from two lines, the first in a prone position and the second standing. Fortunately, the Confederate advance is masked by thick underbrush, allowing some cover. Behind this ridge McKean's division headquarters and Battery F are being evacuated hastily, for General Lovell is also massing Confederate troops to the south for an attack on this emplacement. The firefight between Moore's Brigade and the Iowa troops continues for almost an hour until the evacuation of artillery is completed from the redoubt. As the Iowa Regiments withdraw, Moore's men charge, capturing a few prisoners, General McKean's camp, and a large supply of foodstuffs. At this juncture the men pause to enjoy Yankee hospitality that includes bread, butter, cheese, crackers, and most importantly, water — and a chance to refill their canteens. It has been a sultry 90° day, and the dusty, perspiring men are exhausted from the rigors of the battle. Moore's Brigade unites with General Lovell's Division at this point, and they continue the sweep toward Corinth, arriving at dark, on a wooded hill overlooking the city.

The Confederate assault on the outer defenses of Corinth has been successful on all fronts, and darkness of October 3rd finds the besieging Rebel Army drawn in a battle line outside the inner defenses of Corinth. However, General Van Dorn is unhappy with the progress and wants to press the attack against the retreating Federals. But darkness, the exhaustion of the men — and more importantly their empty cartridge boxes — are convincing arguments against a renewal of the battle. The men bed down to sleep on their arms in the woods, and Van Dorn telegraphs Richmond that "We have driven the enemy from every position. We are within three-quarters of a mile of Corinth. The enemy are huddled together about the town, trying to hold the position. So far all is glorious, and our men behaved nobly. Our loss, I am afraid, is heavy. It is near night. Lovell's and Price's troops have our thanks." [7]

Van Dorn, however, has not correctly estimated either the size of the Federal troops nor their will to fight. Only the divisions of McKean and Davies have been heavily engaged by the Confederates on October 3rd. Rosecrans withdraws these were weary troops during the night from the key Union defensive locations and replaces them with the fresh divisions of Generals Stanley and Hamilton. The redeployment of troops during the night gives the Confederates the impression that Rosecrans has been reinforced. The Federal positions facing Confederate troops on the defensive line west of the city are now manned by the divisions of McKean on the left, Stanley in the center, Davies on the right, with Hamilton facing north to intercept any possible flanking movements. The remainder of the troops are placed east of Corinth as a reserve to counterattack against any possible breaks in the Federal line.

Against these forces, General Van Dorn plans to attack McKean with the division of General Lovell; General Maury will strike Stanley in the center, and General Hebert's Division will attempt to flank Davies on the Federal right. Van Dorn plans a sunrise attack, to be initiated by General Hebert.

The Confederates are awakened at 4:00 A.M. by batteries in their rear shelling the defenses of Corinth. Several houses in the town are hit and demolished. At early dawn Federal artillery locates the position of the Confederate gun emplacements and silences them.

The sultry dawn signals the beginning of a hot, still day in which temperatures of 94° will be reported. The grimy, dust-covered Texans begin to look about them and appreciate the formidable Yankee defensive positions they must attack. Directly in front of them lies a clearing about 400-yards wide, in which the felled trees have been arranged — and the branches interlaced — to form what one Confederate veteran will later describe as "the most obstructive abatis that it was my misfortune to encounter, or to see, during the war." [8] To their east behind this abatis is Battery Robinett, fronted by a steep earth wall six feet high, directly in front of which is a ditch five feet deep. This redoubt is armed with three 20-pound siege guns. Slightly to the southeast of this battery, on a hill, is Battery Williams, placed so as to train its firepower in the front of Battery Robinett. This second battery contains four 24-pound siege guns and two 8-inch howitzers. On the crest of this hill, Battery F of the 2nd U.S. Light Artillery, is located with six field artillery pieces trained on the clearing, and stationed partly down the front slope is the 47th Illinois, armed with the new long-range Springfield rifles so dreaded by the Confederates. Manning the breastworks that flank the two redoubts is the 43rd Ohio, and directly behind Battery Robinett the 11th Missouri is stationed. To the right of Battery Robinett, and stationed behind breastworks is the 63rd Ohio. Slightly north of these armed breastworks lie two field batteries of the 8th Wisconsin, supported by the 27th Ohio.

Maury's Division will be ordered to attack a virtual armed *cul de sac*. With a premonition of the danger facing him, Colonel Rogers dons an armored vest and pins a short note on his clothing on which is written his name, age, rank, command, and the address of friends.[9] Colonel Rogers, acting apparently at the rank of brigadier general, will lead the Second Texas, the Sixth Texas, the Ninth Texas, a portion of the Thirty-fifth Mississippi, and a company of the Forty-second Alabama against Battery Robinett, their objective.[10] Captain George Foster, leader of the company of Alabamians assigned to Rogers, challenges the Texans to a macabre footrace for possession of the battery: "They shan't beat us to those breastworks," he declares, and when the charge is sounded, will draw his sword and cry, "Forward Alabamians." [11] This temporary brigade crouches in a forward position anticipating the signal to attack from General Van Dorn. While in this forward position, in the early light of day, a company of Federal skirmishers strays too far from Corinth on a reconnaissance mission and encounters the attackers. A brief fight ensues and their leader, Colonel Joseph A. "Fighting Joe" Mower of the 11th Missouri, is captured after receiving a severe wound in the neck. Mower will later be recaptured from the retreating Confederates, and before the cessation of the Civil War will rise to the rank of major general.

The sun has now risen, and General Hebert's Division has not launched their attack as planned. After a lengthy delay, Hebert suspiciously reports to General Van Dorn that he is sick and cannot lead his troops into battle.[12] General Martin Green assumes command of the Confederate left flank and must be briefed on the battle plan, causing additional delay. From their advanced positions, within four or five-hundred-yards of Battery Robinett, Rogers's Brigade is taking heavy fire from the Federals. "We were discovered at dawn, and Fort Williams, Robinette, and College Hill opened a terrific enfilading fire of shot and shell upon us. We lay flat on our faces, and the shells passed a few feet over us (we thought these feet were only inches), doing but slight damage. We re-

mained in this position, hugging the ground, for four mortal
hours before the signal gun was fired and the order to charge
was given." [13]

It is now 10:00 A.M., and the signal gun is finally fired to
advance the attack, but the left flank of Confederates does not
lead the attack according to plan; only Maury's Division in
the center assaults the Federals. Led by their intrepid commanders, Generals Moore and Phifer, two brigades strike the
Yankee center between Stanley and Davies. H.C. Dial, a Confederate veteran of this charge, will later write, "Gen. Phifer
was a brave officer. Well do I remember his passing me after
I was wounded, hat in hand, cheering on his men to victory or
death." [14] One of Stanley's Brigades recoils in horror from the
gleaming Rebel bayonets and stampedes from its defensive
position, literally knocking down and running over the reserves placed behind. Moore and Phifer have broken the Yankee Center! Battery Powell, north of Battery Robinett, is captured, and Moore leads his men into Corinth, fighting from
house to house. Moore urgently calls for reinforcements
against the expected counterattack, but none arrive. Cabell's
Brigade, held as a reserve, has been placed by Van Dorn
north of Maury's Division and cannot respond in time. The
victory, teetering in the balance, now falls toward the Federal
side. The remnants of the Confederate charge advance
through the city, taking the Corinth House, General Rosecrans's headquarters, and approach the Tishomingo Hotel on
the square, when they are struck by a mighty counterattack
from Rosecrans's reserves. Led by the 10th Ohio, the 5th Minnesota, and supported by the 1st Missouri Artillery, which
salvos grapeshot into the Confederate ranks, the counterattack builds up momentum. Volunteers from Stanley's Brigade, who had run from the field earlier, rejoin the surge of
blue-uniformed attackers. Seeing the approaching onslaught,
some Confederates surrender and a few, taking horses tied at
the hitching posts, gallop from town. The ragged remainder of
the attackers stream from town in front of a wave of Union soldiers that moves to regain their original positions. Cabell's

Brigade finally arrives in time to meet the counterattack head-on, drawing heavy fire and casualties.

In the meantime, while all Yankee eyes are riveted on Moore's and Phifer's attack, four columns of men, forming Colonel Rogers's Brigade, appear from the woods west of Battery Robinett and move toward it with a slow, steady step. Captain Oscar Jackson of the 63rd Ohio, facing these columns of attackers remembers,

> In my campaigning I had never seen anything so hard to stand as that slow, steady tramp. Not a sound was heard, but they looked as if they intended to walk over us. I afterwards stood a bayonet charge when the enemy came at us on the double-quick with a yell and it was not so trying on the nerves as that steady, solemn advance. I could see that my men were affected by it.[15]

Attention is now shifted to Rogers's men and fire is concentrated on them. The columns become disorganized as the men scramble around the trunks and stumps of the fallen trees and hack their way through the interlaced limbs of the abatis, while overhead shrapnel shells explode. Through the abatis the men re-form in columns, and the advance continues while Battery Robinett changes from shells to grapeshot and cannister which cut swaths through the advancing columns. Thomas Hagan will write home to his father in Missouri, "We advanced through open hilly ground on which there was not a single bush to screen a person from the terrible storm of shot and shell from their heavy siege guns, which were in full view for over a mile, and looked like if [*sic*] hell had been let loose. Shells bursting all around you; round shot plowing the ground everywhere; grape and cannister sweeping down the hill almost by the bushel; it is a miracle how anyone escaped." [16]

The Second Texas and other brigade units have now advanced into rifle range, and a murderous fire from the hill commences upon the Confederates by the 47th Illinois armed with their Springfield rifles. The guns at Robinett now change from grapeshot and begin to fire whole bags of buckshot into the ranks of the oncoming troops. Captain Oscar Jackson of the 63rd Ohio continues his narration:

The column was then in full view and only about thirty yards distant. . . . "Boys, give them a volley."

It seems to me that the fire of my company had cut down the head of the column that struck us as deep back as my company was long. As the smoke cleared away, there was apparently ten yards square of a mass of struggling bodies and butternut clothes. Their column appeared to reel like a rope shaken at the end. . . . The enemy were stopped, but deploying their column, returned the fire, and, a fine thing for us, fired too low, striking the ground, knocking the dirt and chips all over us, wounding a few, not one in my company. We got ahead of them with the next volley which we delivered right in their faces. At this close distance we fought for perhaps five minutes, when the enemy gave back in confusion.

The thinned ranks fall back, out of range of the withering fire. The Second Texas has taken casualties, and Matt Conklin of Company C writes home later, ". . . Adj't Mangum and Col. Rogers' son (Halbert) were both wounded in the first charge. Young Rogers was wounded in the mouth, the ball coming out at the shoulder. I took them off the field in my blanket." [17]

Captain Jackson of the 63rd Ohio, continuing his narrative of the battle writes,

When I saw the enemy retreating in such confusion, I remarked to a comrade that we would not have to fight these men anymore today, as I thought it would be impossible to rally them again, but strange to say, in some forty minutes I saw them reformed and coming at us again with that slow, steady step, but they made a change in their tactics, for as they came over the banks, or rather out of a ravine, in front of us, they came at us with a yell on the double-quick. Our men stood firm with loaded guns and fixed bayonets and gave them a volley that threw them somewhat in confusion, slaughtering them fearfully, but pressing on, and firing at us rapidly, they dashed themselves against us like water against a rock and were a second time repulsed and gave back.

The colors of the Second Texas fall to the ground as the fourth color bearer of the day is shot to death, and Colonel Rogers seizes them and rides back to rally his troops for another assault. Waving the regimental colors from horseback, Rogers asks the men if they are willing to follow him again, and with a shout of approval, the columns re-form for a third try. Colonel Rogers leads the column on horseback, gauging his pace to match the steps of his men, and carrying the colors aloft. The columns reach the ditch of the battery, and Colonel Rogers jumps his horse over the ditch, dismounts, and dashing up to the side of the battery plants the colors squarely upon the fort. The men yell their approval and move quickly to the attack, as they swarm around the fort and over the top. The 63rd Ohio, north of Battery Robinett, is met with the bayonet and, after a bloody struggle, they fall back from the fort. South of the battery the 43rd Ohio is struck by the Confederate assault and retreats, leaving its leader, Colonel J.L. Kirby Smith, behind, mortally wounded. In front of the fort, Confederates crouching in the ditch for refuge are the targets of hand grenades lobbed from the fort.[18] The fuses burn too slowly, and they are tossed back into the fort before they can explode. Crawling up the steep embankment into the battery, many of Rogers's men are shot and fall back into the ditch dead. William Bryan of Company C is shot through the head as he scrambles into the fort, but the men continue over the top and drive the Union gunners from their emplacements.[19] Thirteen of the thirty-six men who serve the guns of Battery Robinett will be either killed or wounded in this desperate struggle. Their leader, Lieutenant Robinett of the First United States Infantry, is likewise wounded.

Suddenly firing ceases, and Battery Robinett is in the possession of the Confederates from Texas, Alabama, and Mississippi. A group of about thirteen jubilant Confederates stand upon the parapets of the redoubt talking to Colonel Rogers and Captain Foster, when suddenly, from over the brow of a slight inclination to the east, they catch the first sight of a massive sea of blue uniforms moving toward them. The Confederate attackers are themselves being counterattacked by the dauntless men of the 63rd Ohio, the 43rd Ohio and the 11th Missouri. The troops of the 43rd and 63rd Ohio, driven from their entrenchments by the fierce Confederate attacks, simply will not abandon their positions to the enemy. About seventy-five yards to the rear of Battery Robinett they are rallied by their officers and, united with the 11th Missouri, return with a vengeance. Realizing the hopelessness of the situation, Rogers and Foster wave handkerchiefs to surrender their troops.[20] Other Confederates about the fort, however, do not see the surrender sign and fire into the mass of Union soldiers. Massive fire is returned on the Confederates at very close range, and Colonel Rogers falls with eleven wounds, never to rise again. Captain Foster of Alabama is slain, and of the remainder that are not killed by the volley, a few escape, and some throw up their hands in surrender. The remainder of the attacking Confederates fall back, bringing with them their most prized possession, the Regimental Flag. Sources vary as to who saved the flag that day from Federal capture. Charles I. Evans credits Private Ben Weed of Company I from Gonzales County for the rescue,[21] while another source credits Private John Lloyd of Company E who was from Taylor, Texas.[22]

The remainder of Maury's Division reenters the woods west of the city, and within a short while General Van Dorn calls off the Confederate attack on Corinth. Maury's Division is cut to pieces; of the four thousand men that form this unit, over two thousand have been killed or are missing. Tears fill the eyes of General Price as he views the pathetic remnants of his prize division, and tears also fall in Texas when the long casualty reports of the Second Texas Infantry are published. In part, this casualty report will state:

> Col. Rogers was killed Saturday, the 4th, on the enemy's breastworks while waving a flag of truce. The gallant Capt. John Mueller, the bravest of the brave, was killed some twenty steps from the breastworks of Battery Robinett, by a discharge of grape from a 24-pounder, while gallantly leading his regiment. He was acting major at the time. The brave and chilvalrous Wm. Bryan, of Co. C, also fell, pierced thro' the brain after he had reached the top of the fort — "Battery Robinett." Capt. Ed. Daly also fell at the breastwork, shot through the thigh with a

grapeshot, which, I learn from a paroled prisoner, so shattered the bone, that amputation was necessary. Thus will one of the bravest officers be lost to the army.[23]

Captain Fly of Company I and Captain Goff of Company K are among the soldiers captured and paroled by the Federals. Of the 324 men of the regiment that marched on Corinth, only 124 will muster for dress parade on October 18. Only 11 of the 33 men in Captain Foster's Alabama Company answer to roll call the next morning. The Sixth Texas, Ninth Texas, and the Thirty-fifth Mississippi suffer grievous casualties. The Federal losses among the defenders of Battery Robinett are also high; total casualties for the 43rd Ohio and the 63rd Ohio are 50% and 53%, respectively.

Newspaper correspondents at Corinth telegraph dramatic eyewitness accounts of the daring Confederate assaults on Battery Robinett to both Northern and Southern newspapers in unanimous praise of the bravery of Colonel Rogers and the Second Texas Infantry. One Northern correspondent writes:

> It is the concurrent testimony of all who witnessed it, that the charge made by the head of the rebel column on our breastworks, on Saturday, has no parallel in this war for intrepid, obstinate courage and none to equal it in history. I have conversed with many officers of all grades, who express this opinion, and make no attempt to conceal their admiration for the men and the discipline that could face the murderous leaden storm of our forts and batteries; sweep across the field with closed ranks, despite the yawning gaps made by every discharge of our guns; and actually mount our works and plant their banners there, in the agonies of the death struggle.
>
> The 2nd Texas infantry, under Col. Rogers, lead the charge, and the Colonel himself fell on our breastworks, with the colors of his regiment in his hand. . . . After the battle but four of his entire regiment was left alive, and three of these were wounded and all taken prisoner. An officer who witnessed it declared that he scarcely knew which to admire most: the daring bravery of the rebel troops, or the steady valor that repulsed and scattered them despite their determined and obstinate attack.[24]

General Rosecrans, while on an inspection tour of the defensive perimeter around Battery Robinett, discovers the body of Colonel Rogers and asks his men to uncover the face so that he may see it. With admiration, Rosecrans tells his troops, "He was one of the bravest men that ever led a charge. Bury him with military honors and mark his grave so that his friends may claim him." [25]

General Van Dorn praises the bravery of Colonel Rogers in his official report of the battle:

> . . . I cannot refrain, however, from mentioning here the conspicuous gallantry of a noble Texan, whose deeds at Corinth are the constant theme of both friends and foes. As long as courage, manliness, fortitude, patriotism, and honor exist the name of Rogers will be revered and honored among men. He fell in the front of battle, and died beneath the colors of his regiment, in the very center of the enemy's stronghold. He sleeps, and glory is his sentinel.[26]

Rogers's daughter in later years will remember him with pride and write, "Col. Rogers left to his children the legacy of an unsullied name, and a fame that will live while a Southern heart throbs with love for, and pride in, this sunny Southland of ours." [27]

The Confederate Army, with sorrow, turns its back on its fallen comrades and retreats from Corinth by 1 P.M. Strangely, the Union Army does not pursue the same day, but waits until the next day to chase the fleeing Confederates. This decision by General Rosecrans will save the Confederates from being trapped on the Hatchie River, as another Federal division bears down on Corinth with reinforcements from the west. The division of General Ord, rushing from Bolivar, Tennessee, eastward to reinforce Corinth, will collide with the westward moving columns of Confederates at Davis Bridge on the Hatchie River. After camping at Chewalla on the night of October 4, Van Dorn's army moves toward Davis Bridge to cross the Hatchie River with Maury's battle-riddled division leading the line of march, and the lightly engaged division of Lovell forming the rear guard. Thus, Van Dorn remains more concerned about potential attacks from the pursuing army of Rosecrans than the reinforcements that must surely be marching from Bolivar. By 7:30 A.M., October 5, the Mississippi Cavalry of General Wirt Adams intercepts Ord's Division at Metamora, a short distance west of Davis Bridge, and relays a warning to General Van Dorn.

The Confederate Army is now in grave peril. If Davis Bridge is captured by the Federals, Van Dorn will be trapped between the Hatchie River with Ord's Division on the west bank and the pursuing army of Rosecrans, which after great delay, has been organized and put in pursuit of the fleeing Confederates by General McPherson. In addition, the Confederate supply train of wagons, parked slightly east of Davis Bridge, is now under threat of immediate capture by Ord's advancing troops. The First Texas Legion, under Colonel E.R. Hawkins, whose assignment has been to guard the wagon train, has now rushed across Davis Bridge uniting with Adams's Cavalry to slow the Federal advance. The weary remnants of Maury's Division is marched at the double-quick toward Davis Bridge for reinforcements, and the wagons are moved from the point of danger, eastward. The Confederate traffic, flowing both east and west along the same road, becomes ensnarled, slowing the arrival of further reinforcements. The 360 men of the First Texas Legion form a battle line east of the river, and watch to their amazement as the Federal Army of twelve regiments begins to deploy a battle line that stretches as far as can be seen in either direction. From a ridge that commands the crossing, Federal artillery is placed, and several batteries form directly in front of the Texans to support Federal troops. Just in the nick of time, Moore's Brigade, now numbering no more than 300 men, arrives and begins to file across the bridge, aligning on the right flank of the First Texas Legion. The Federals spot the arrival of reinforcements, and a terrific bombardment is focused from the ridge on the troops crossing the bridge. Most of Moore's units cross the river as the firing increases in tempo, but the Second Texas, placed in the rear of the brigade, arrives at the river to cross the bridge and is met by a hail of shell fire and cannot cross.[28] The small Confederate force west of the river is no match for Ord's Division, and Moore's Brigade on the right side of the line of battle is quickly flanked by the 14th and 15th Illinois Regiments who pour a galling fire into the side and rear of the Confederate battle line. The Confederates must either retreat or be cut off from the bridge by the encircling Union regiments. In the resulting confusion, a pocket of more than 400 Confederates is trapped in a bend of the river, and the men are left to fend for themselves. Some throw up their hands and surrender, while others abandon their rifles and swim the river. The Second Texas forms a battle line on the east side of the river and supports the trapped Confederates hiding under the river banks as best it can by volleys fired into the advancing Federals. Many of Moore's brigade are captured in the river bend, and most of those that cross the river are without arms.

The Second Texas and those remaining troops that have returned to the east side of the river hold the bridge until the arrival of Cabell's and Phifer's brigades, which assume excellent defensive positions for an expected Federal crossing. The Federal attack is not long in coming, as General Ord orders his regiments across the bridge to the east side. The Federal regiments, when reaching the east side, are ordered to position themselves by regiments alternately north and south of the bridge. However, a bend in the river north of the bridge forces the regiments posted north of the bridge into a small open position with no cove, which results in heavy Federal losses.

Regiment by regiment, the Union soldiers race for the bridge in platoon fronts, meet a murderous Confederate fire while crossing the Hatchie River, and are boxed in by a crossfire on the east bank. Colonel E.L. Stirman of the First Arkansas Sharpshooters would remember that on the east side of the river:

> Our men would lie down and could not be seen until the enemy were within 75 yards of our line. We would allow them to approach until we could see the whites of their eyes, then without

exposing ourselves in the least we would pour volley after volley into them, cutting them down like grass. No man on earth could stand such a fire. Our men were all fine shots and nearly every shot must have taken effect. I never saw such a slaughter in my life. They fell by the hundred, then recoiled, re-formed and rushed to meet the same result. It was impossible to drive us from the position by direct attack.[29]

The brave Union soldiers refuse to abandon the attack, and, in spite of fearful losses, gain secure positions on the east side of the Hatchie River. General Ord is shot down on the bridge by a Confederate sharpshooter and retires from the field with a severe wound. General Hurlbut assumes Federal command and moves to reinforce the troops on the east side of the Hatchie River. Confederate ammunition is running low, and it begins to appear certain that Van Dorn and his forces will be trapped between two Federal armies.

In a masterful stroke of luck, the Seventh Tennessee Cavalry discovers a second crossing on the Hatchie about six miles below the Davis Bridge. A dam has been built to impound water for Crum's Mill, and, with some engineering, it is widened to support the crossing of wagons and artillery. The Confederates commence to retreat from Davis Bridge toward Crum's Mill by 3:30 P.M. The Federals, suffering from the fearful losses taken in crossing Davis Bridge, fail to follow through on their attack and break off action. By 1:00 A.M., October 5, the remains of Van Dorn's army has completely crossed to the west side of the Hatchie River.

5

The Campaign
of Vicksburg

. . . I eat two meals of mule *today the first in my life. A new
way to celebrate the forth of July, or rather a new dish . . .*
From July 4, 1863, entry in the
Vicksburg diary of Major Maurice Simons.

The Second Texas, in its rearguard position, crosses the
makeshift bridge over the Hatchie River at Crum's Mill by
9:00 P.M., October 5, 1862, completing the exodus of the
Confederate Army. The Confederates move to Holly Springs,
Mississippi, and then south of there twelve miles to Lump-
kin's Mill. Captain Nobel L. McGinnis of Company H, by virtue of his seniority, assumes temporary command of the regiment. His senior officers are absent from the regiment;
Lieutenant Colonel Ashbel Smith has traveled to Texas on a
mission to recruit and train conscripted replacements, and
Major William Timmons is on medical leave recuperating
from a wounded arm received in the battle of Corinth.

Cool autumn nights are a reminder that winter is approaching, and it will be one of the worst, some say, in many
years. The regiment is unprepared for the winter campaign. A
newspaper correspondent with Price's Army reports,

This little band of heroes [the Second Texas] are in very sad condition; at least one-third of them are actually barefooted, one-half are without blankets, and all are without tents. Will Texians permit the noble sons of Texas to remain thus? I trust not. Those who have ever had a sympathizing heart and open purse for our brave soldiers will not permit this to be the case long. The nights and mornings this early in the season are very cold indeed and winter has not yet arrived. When it does come, our poor boys will suffer indeed. But there is no murmuring among the boys. All you ever hear from them in reference to their condition is that when the war is over and peace declared, how they are going to enjoy themselves. Each has his own peculiar idea of what perfect enjoyment will be. One says he'll "sleep the first six months"; another "will sleep in a place where he won't have to get up two or three times during the night to warm" . . .[1]

A later visitor to the winter quarters of the Second Texas writes home to urge speedy aid,

I do sincerely hope the good people of Texas will go to work at once and make up warm underclothing for our soldiers up here. The Government is now making several hundred thousand warm, serviceable uniforms; but it will be some time before the men up here can be supplied. The 2d Texas is bad off for underclothing. Please call on the ladies of Texas to knit socks and make up warm overshirts. Let subscriptions be raised to make up 1,000 pair shoes at once, and foreward [*sic*] them immediately. We are having very cold weather now and will no doubt have a very cold winter. Therefore it behooves the good people of our "Lone Star State" to take this matter in hand at once, and do all possible to relieve the sufferings of our soldiers, away from home battling for their rights and our own.[2]

No aid is forthcoming. The men of the regiment, with no tents and few blankets, must now survive the rigors of a cold winter as best they can. A heavy snowfall makes construction of shelters imperative. Caves are dug in the sides of gullies for shelter with great fires built in the openings to keep the Texans warm. Rations are low; the Second Texas is forced to survive on voluntary contributions of food from the populace of the countryside. Mississippians willingly contribute a portion of what little quantities of food they have, including mainly sweet potatoes, pumpkins, cushaws, cornmeal, and some meat and bacon. Charles I. Evans wryly comments that the most certain way to die of heartburn is to attempt to subsist for a week on a diet of sweet potatoes.[3]

The Federal Army, flush with success from its defensive victory at Corinth, plans to take the offensive in the fall of 1862. General Grant masses troops at Grand Junction, Tennessee, halfway between Memphis and Corinth, for a movement into northwestern Mississippi. The Federals plan to move southward along the Mississippi Central Railroad, capturing the Mississippi towns of Holly Springs, Oxford, and Grenada. With Grenada captured, the Yazoo delta region of Mississippi will be isolated from reinforcement, and Vicksburg, the key to the Confederate defense of the Mississippi River, can be threatened. Control of the Yazoo River is important; it is believed that the Confederate Navy is constructing several ironclad gunboats there.

The Federal Army feigns an encircling movement on Confederate troops and forces a Confederate retreat from Holly Springs to Abbeville, Mississippi. While on this movement, Charles I. Evans relates, "At one place where the regiment stopped to camp for the night, the old gentlemen who lived near by came into camp and said: 'Boys, it's awful cold; just pitch into that fence there and burn all the rails you can to-night.' It was generally thought that he knew the boys were going to do that anyway, and he intended to put a good face on the matter by inviting them. But all doubts of the genuineness of his hospitality was removed when he further told them that there was a house full of sweet potatoes up in the yard, and for them to come up and get all they wanted." [4]

The retreat continues, until the Confederate Army reaches Grenada, Mississippi, on December 5, 1862. The Second Texas again constructs dugouts to protect themselves from the rigors of the winter, and camp life resumes. Picket duty and parade ground drills become a part of camp life again. The monotony is occasionally shattered by clashes between Federal cavalry and Confederate pickets. The Confederate Army has been reorganized under the leadership of General John Pemberton, who replaces General Earl Van Dorn as commander. Van Dorn had been censured by Southern newspapers for the loss of Corinth, but is acquitted of wrongdoing in the plan and execution of the battle by a military court-of-inquiry. General Pemberton, born in the North, is not popular with the troops, and his continued retreats since taking command are viewed with suspicion. General Sterling Price retains his universal popularity among all troops of the army. To emphasize government support for the Mississippi campaign and quell reports of dissension within the army, President Jefferson Davis visits the army in Grenada, Mississippi, and reviews the troops on Christmas Eve. Charles I. Evans reports that the President and his staff are received by the troops in silence, while the appearance of "Old Pap" Price brings loud cheering and hurrahs.[5]

While the Confederate Army is camped at Grenada, a new round of promotions is approved for the Second Texas. Ashbel Smith, still away in Texas on a recruiting mission, is appointed colonel. William Timmons, having recently returned to duty and still enfeebled from a wound, is appointed lieutenant colonel. Nobel L. McGinnis is appointed major, and the following captains are approved to fill vacancies: Lieutenant Andrew Gammel to captain of Company D, Lieutenant Jackson McMahan to captain of Company F, and Lieutenant Thomas S. Douglass to captain of Company H.

However, a very important promotion fails to be confirmed by the Confederate Senate in Richmond. Using his political support, General William Hardee, a foe of the Second Texas Infantry since Shiloh, has the Senate motion of the confirmation of John C. Moore's rank as Brigadier General squelched. General Moore, in a letter written from Grenada on December 18, 1862, to Adjutant General Cooper[6] states,

I have the honor to acknowledge the receipt of a copy of a Report made by Genl Hardee respecting the conduct of the 2nd Regt Texas Infantry at the battle of Shiloh. This was received some two days since endorsed by his Excellency the President with the remark that unless I gave some satisfactory explanation, action would be taken in my case. As I was not in command of the Regiment on the 7th April 1862, and as no charges are made against me as an officer, I am at a loss how to proceed with a defense. If action in my case means that my conduct at the battle of Shiloh will be investigated, I can assure the President that I know of no more speedy way of obtaining justice than by *prompt action.* The parties who are prosecuting this matter seem decidedly foggy on several points, but none astonishes me so much as when the Genl. speaks of detailing the officer to Gen'l Little to whose Brigade he says the Regt belonged telling him to say to me if I have any explanations to make, he would be pleased to receive it. The Regt never was attached to Genl Little's command and he never did report to me the conversation nor would I have made any explanation if he had, as I conceived none due to Genl Hardee, not belonging to his command. These are points of no great importance but merely show the evidently confused state of the parties which is in keeping with what followed the attack on Monday at Shiloh. Capt Close says when Genl Hardee ordered the Regiment to take positions in line of Battle, it moved with slowness and Gen'l Hardee remarked so. The line of battle was formed under the orders of Genl Withers to whose Division we belonged and before Genl Hardee and staff came up. I presume that Genl Hardee does not know me, even when he sees me, nor that I was in command of a Brigade on the 7th April, and not of the Regt which was then commanded by the late Col W.P. Rogers who died so gallantly at Corinth than whom no braver man has fallen during this war. That the Regt was repulsed and fell back in great confusion is set forth in my report, but this was not confined to the Regt, but extended to the whole line; and why the Genl singled out this Regt and pronounced its members "cowards" he can best explain. Though nominally in command, Genl Hardee and Staff took personal direction of the Brigade, led it into action, and it was repulsed with the result detailed in my report. If he had other troops in action except, perhaps, one in batteries which were near us, I did not see them. The enemy were attacked in their position on this part of the line by our Brigade alone. That censure may not be attached to someone I will not say but if I am that one, then let it come, but come in the light of justice with open manly dealing and not as the assassin's blow delivered at the back of his intended victim under the cover of night, from a want of those qualities that lead the humble to attack face to face in the light of day. Neither Genl Hardee nor any other officer as far as I know has openly charged me as wanting in the discharge of my duty on that occasion. That I could not rally the troops at once I am free to confess and that Genl Hardee and Staff failed in the same undertaking I think I can find officers to testify. But I saw enough on that morning to satisfy me that the advance and the attack of our Brigade was a bungling ill-managed affair. I learn that when my name was presented to the Senate for confirmation as Brig Genl an Honorable Senator stated that he was authorized by Genl Hardee to say that I and my Regt ran at the battle of Shiloh and this defeated the ratification of my appointment. From the Genl's Report it seems that he has no recollection of this, but I am led to strongly suspect that he is fond of *"using the cats paw in raking* the chestnuts *from the fire"* I know nothing of Genl Hardee except from his high position as an officer, but as such I had supposed that he had too much of the high toned gentleman in his composition to take advantage of my absence and prostitute his influence to the accomplishment of so low an end. But why should not so noted a leader be skilled in the art of attack and defense whether in assailing the stronghold of the enemy or the good name of a brother officer. The Genl says he did not make a report of the battle of Shiloh. I hope he will pardon me for saying that unless he was more successful on other occasions than on Monday morning I think the omission can be easily accounted for. I am well aware, Sir, of the unequal contest between Genl Hardee and myself when considering the might of influence he can bring to bear from his position as an officer, but, I believe that I can dare to hope that I have sustained a good name with those of my commanding officers who know me most intimately and in their judgment and testimony I am willing to stand or fall. I have the honor to enclose herewith copies of my Reports for the information of the President on this Subject. If consistent with the rules governing that body I would be pleased if this communication be presented to the Senate, should my name be again presented for confirmation as Brigadier General.

I am General

Very Respectfully

Your obt servt
Jno. C. Moore
Brig Genl Cmdg. Brigade

General Moore retains his rank of brigadier general in the Provisional Confederate Army, but fails confirmation of this rank in the Regular Confederate Army. His rank in the regular service remains at captain. The Moore-Hardee controversy will not die, and continues to unjustly discredit General Moore throughout the remainder of the war.

Two days after Christmas, the Second Texas is transported by rail to Vicksburg, Mississippi, arriving at 11 P.M. on December 29. The city is alive with activity, as news has been received that Union General William T. Sherman is attempting an amphibious landing of Federal troops from transports at Chickasaw Bluffs, north of Vicksburg. The regiment is immediately ordered to march northward seven miles to reinforce Confederate General Stephen D. Lee who has been engaged with the Federals since December 26. Rain and heavy mud cause widespread straggling. At daybreak only eighty Texans arrive to take up positions in the rifle-pits that front on the Yazoo River. The complement of troops is brought to its full regimental strength of three hundred men by noon with the arrival of the muddy stragglers.

The Second Texas positions are a part of the rifle-pits and batteries that form a defensive arc around the county road leading from the swamp at Chickasaw Bayou to Vicksburg. Near this swamp is the only solid ground that fronts the Yazoo River, and General Sherman has chosen this location to disembark his army from a flotilla of river transports and gunboats. He plans to flank the Vicksburg defenses to the north and join up with Grant's Army for a coordinated attack on Vicksburg. But General Grant, now headquartered at Oxford, is plagued by two cavalry raids that cause the Federal offensive in northern Mississippi to grind to a halt. The first, led by General Nathan Bedford Forrest, in mid-December moves into west Tennessee and wreaks havoc. Grant's only supply line, the Mobile and Ohio Railroad, is cut in several places along a sixty-mile path of destruction. Telegraphic communications between Grant and the outside world are interrupted for more than two weeks as Federal engineers struggle to repair the extensive damages caused by Forrest.

Having planned for such a contingency, Grant has stockpiled a huge store of supplies at Holly Springs, which the army will consume while repairs are completed on the Mobile and Ohio. However, on December 20, General Earl Van Dorn executes a daring cavalry raid on the supply depot at Holly Springs and destroys over a million dollars worth of Federal supplies. With no communications, supplies, or hopes of resupply, Grant has only one alternative — retreat. Grant, unknown to Sherman, evacuates Oxford on December 21, leaving Sherman's troops in an extremely vulnerable position.

Sherman's troops, now at Chickasaw Landing, discover that they must cross the swamp on a long, narrow sand spit that is covered by Confederate crossfire, to reach a steep twenty-foot river bank. Confederate defensive positions line the top of this bank where the county road begins, which in turn is dominated by hills on which are placed field batteries. Sherman realizes that the county road can only be reached by a direct frontal assault into this *cul-de-sac*. Brave Union soldiers obey the orders to attack, and many are killed in the attempt to scramble up the steep river bank. The 16th Ohio takes 311 total casualties and the 54th Indiana counts 264 killed, wounded or missing. The daring attack makes a slight inroad into the Confederate defenses, but is finally repulsed with many Federal casualties. The Federal attack has subsided by the time the Second Texas Infantry arrives as reinforcements on December 29. The Federal Army is stalemated on the landing and is unable to break through Confederate defenses to the road. Fierce Confederate bushwhacking costs the Federals additional casualties by the hour. With no other alternative operations possible, Sherman begins to reembark his troops on transports by January 2. The Second Texas, placed in the advanced position of sharpshooters, uncovers the evacuation plan and hastens to attack the Federal rear guard.

As the river was approached a line of battle could be seen drawn up on the bank, and a large number of steamboats crowded with blue uniforms and about a dozen gunboats were in the river. When within about one hundred yards of them the command was given to "Commence firing!" Until then not a shot had been fired by the enemy, but they all looked on at the advancing skirmish lines as if it were drilling for their entertainment. After firing a few shots the two regiments of infantry on the bank marched off by the right flank down the river at double-quick, and the decks of the steamboats were cleared with great rapidity. The gunboats began pouring their broadsides across the field, and for better protection against their fire the Texans rushed forward and took positions behind the levee just on the river bank and behind a very large and tall pile of bales of hay. From these positions they poured a deadly fire into the immense crowds upon the steamboats as they hurriedly cut their cables and passed out of range around the bend of the river. A great many men were seen to jump into the water from the top decks of the boats as they could not get down the narrow stairways fast enough. When the steamboats were out of sight the Texans turned their attention to the gunboats, and soon became so proficient at shooting into the port-holes that they could not fire a shot as they passed up and down the river.[7]

The alertness of the Second Texas has not escaped the notice of General Stephen D. Lee, Commander of the Confederate defenders, who wrote in this official report, "This most gallant regiment [The Second Texas] with a dash rushed almost up to the boats, delivering their fire with terrible effect on their crowded transports. Never had I seen so sudden a disappearance from crowded vessels nor vessels move off so hurriedly. The gunboats at once opened on the skirmishers with about twenty boat-howitzers from their upper decks and with rifles from their plated decks. The Texans remained until their troops disappeared, and as nothing was to be gained by firing on their ironclads, they withdrew." [8] But there was a price to be paid for such gallantry. Lieutenant Colonel William Timmons, newly returned to duty after recovery from a wound in the arm at Corinth, is struck in the ankle by a minié ball while leading the charge on the river bank. The ankle is shattered by the ball, and the foot must be amputated. He is rushed back to Vicksburg and placed in the home of Mrs. Holt.[9] By lantern light surgeons amputate Timmons's foot, but a second severe wound in such a short time is more than his enfeebled constitution can bear, and he lapses into shock and dies. The regiment mourns the loss of such a noble spirit, and a state of sadness grips the city of Houston when it receives word of his passing. The *Tri-Weekly Telegraph* of Houston publishes this tribute to his memory:

> It is with sincere regret that we have to announce the death of this gallant officer. He was well known to our citizens and much beloved. Early in the present contest he took a prominent part in raising and drilling a company of young men in this city. Our citizens well remember the perfection in drill attained by the Confederate Guards, and their proficiency in the manual. When the 2nd Texas was made up, the first infantry regiment in point of fact raised in Texas, Capt. Timmins with his company volunteered *en masse*. They have been with the regiment ever since. Col. Timmins was always at the post of duty, and was twice wounded, the last time at the Battle of Vicksburg, from the effects of which he died.[10]

In the same article appears a testimonial written about Colonel Timmons by the officers of the regiment.

> On this, the 26th of January, 1863, Lieut. Col. Wm. C. Timmins bid adieu to his world. His death was the result of a wound through the ankle joint, received in the battle of Chickasaw Bayou, while gallantly charging the enemy with his regiment, on the 2nd day of the present month.
>
> Now, whereas it has pleased Almighty God to take from the regiment, within a short period of time, another of its gallant commanders, we have to express on this sad occasion our profound respect and admiration for the gallantry of the deceased on the field of battle, our high appreciation of his manly virtues, his affectionate social qualities, and our sense of the great loss we, his brother officers, the regiment and the service, have sustained in his death.
>
> We beg here permission to tender to the family of Lieut. Col. Timmins our deep sympathy with them in this their great bereavement.

To fill the gap in the rank of command created by the death of Timmons, Nobel L. McGinnis is promoted to the rank of lieutenant colonel, Captain George Washington Lafayette Fly from Company I is promoted to the rank of major, and Lieutenant James McFarland is promoted to captain of Company I.

The Second Texas remains at Chickasaw Bayou for two months, camping in a beautiful grove of walnut trees known by the men as Camp Timmons.

At this location Major Fly receives a great surprise. A courier from Vicksburg informs him that his wife has arrived at that city. Major Fly rushes to her hotel to find the reason for her visit. G.W.L. Fly, having been captured in the attack on Battery Robinett by the Yankees, is reported by the Texas newspapers as having been killed in the battle of Corinth. Mrs. Fly accepts the reports of Major Fly's death as true and grieves greatly. All letters sent from Mississippi to Mrs. Fly are miscarried, so she remains convinced of his death. But about six weeks after the report of Fly's death, a discharged soldier who has returned to Gonzales County sees Mrs. Fly dressed in mourning and approaches her to offer respects. When the object of her mourning is announced, the surprised soldier reports having seen Major Fly alive long after the battle of Corinth. Mrs. Fly is greatly disturbed (but happy) by this news and decides to travel to Mississippi to discover the truth about her husband. The trip overland from Texas through Louisiana to Mississippi is extremely hazardous at this time of the war. Friends and relatives attempt to dissuade her, but to no avail. Mrs. Fly, with her three children of the ages six, four and two years, with two Negro slaves, sets out in a two-horse wagon for Mississippi. After many harrowing experiences, the family crosses the Mississippi River at Rodney, Mississippi, and completes the journey to Vicksburg by rail. The family is happily reunited, and Major Fly arranges to board them in a private residence near the regimental camp.[11]

While the 2nd Texas is at Camp Timmons, Colonel Ashbel Smith returns from Texas with about 150 conscripted soldiers to serve in the regiment. Colonel Smith's assignment has been odious to him, for he has little patience with men who will not volunteer for military service.

From Sabine Parish, December 27, 1862, Colonel Smith (enroute to Mississippi) writes Major A.G. Dickinson of his troubles with his conscripts:

My dear Major

. . . My situation for the last two weeks have been as you may well imagine, excessively disagreeable. I have with me ten or twelve good men and true — the rest of my little command is made up of the most pitiful slinks and invalids: — and among them I am informed, an unmistakable abolitionist. The Provisional Serg. Gray whom I permitted to accompany Major Gaines to assist in arranging his papers, I have since learned is a notorious mutineer, and disloyal abolitionist.

I have already furloughed indefinitely over 50 of the Tyler crowd — I cant call them soldiers and four out of five of the balance are importuning me to be furloughed and half of them ought to be discharged for physical inability. The Tyler detachment when I received it was more like the cleaning out of an old hospital than anything else to which I can liken it — nearblind, one-eyed, lame, [?], rheumatic, consumptive, bursten, men complaining of piles, kidney worms, spinal disease, rotten shins, fits, double joints, and every other disease almost that curses the human family. I would stand the ailments of which they suffer, and commiserate the sufferers; but their pitiful, mean, disloyal spirit is more contemptible than their diseases are disabling. Upward of 20 of the most able bodied has deserted.

I have tried to cheer, in spirit I arouse them by an occasional remark, a few have responded nobly and are really afraid the fights will be over before we reach the seat of war — but the majority are so mean that they say they dont want to fight. — I have so tempered uniform good temper with firmness that I suppose I am at this moment the "damnedest amiable gentlemen" of your acquaintance . . .

. . . My letter or scrawl is dry because my brain has but one pleasant idea in it — it is that I am on the way to my regiment.
Very faithfully yours
Ashbel Smith[12]

Ralph Smith recollects that the conscripts were viewed by the regiment with suspicion:

> Conscripts and volunteers being actuated by different motives, interfere and hinder each other like a Team composed of a lazy mule and a spirited horse, when combined in the same regiment. Our conscripts never amalgamated with the "boys" as the Colonel always called the remnant of the original volunteers, which was no doubt rather our fault than theirs, for we considered ourselves their superiors, an opinion even in which our officers shared, . . .[13]

As for the new regimental commander, Colonel Ashbel Smith, it didn't take "the boys" long to find a quaint flaw in his personality. As Ralph Smith remembers,

> . . He was quite an athlete and his temper was somewhat inflammatory and when enraged he cut such fantastic capers before high heaven as made the angels smile. These bursts of anger soon passed off but while they lasted the Colonel danced, swore, jingled his sword and denounced the object of his wrath in words that burned holes in the surrounding atmosphere. . . . Owing to his eccentric movements when he had a "spell" on we had given Colonel Smith the name "Jingle Box." Though, of course, we did not use that pet name when addressing him he was fully aware of it, having heard us use it in a thousand different indirect ways without taking notice. . . .[14]

In March, the Second Texas Regiment boards the steamer, *John Walsh,* at Snyder's Bluff and proceeds up the Yazoo River to man Fort Pemberton at the junction of the Yalobusha and Tallahatchee Rivers, near Greenwood, Mississippi. To relieve the monotony of the trip, the high-spirited men of the regiment play a prank on Colonel Smith the second night out. "Someone had during the night disfigured the mane and tail of the Colonel's black charger to such an extent that we were unable to recognize him. The resulting "crazy spell" was one of the most excruciating that we had ever succeeded in bringing on the Colonel. He charged up and down the deck, beat the floor with his sword and swore that if the dastard who did this unholy deed did not come forward to be hung immediately he would throw the whole regiment in irons and make the last one of them draw for a black bean and shoot the man who got it for an example." [15]

With heavy spring rains and Yankee treachery the Tallahatchee River has risen to flood stage. In fact, the entire countryside is inundated with water.

With the failure of Sherman's amphibious operation at Chickasaw Bluffs, Grant continues to search for a route by which Federal troops can be moved into a location near Vicksburg. Colonel James H. Wilson, Chief of Topographical Engineers, develops plans for such a route and with General Grant's approval begins to implement the plan, known as the Yazoo Pass Expedition,[16] by February 1863. An ancient channel of the Yazoo River, which intersects the Mississippi River across from Helena, Arkansas, is to be reopened to navigation. A levee across this channel had been built to protect the low-lying Yazoo delta country which was in some places eight and a half feet lower than the level of the Mississippi River. Colonel Wilson sets to work on February 2 using 500 men armed with picks and shovels to interdict the levee. A large black-powder mine is detonated on February 4 which forces an opening in the levee that widens to 75 yards by the eroding force of the large torrent of water rushing through the gap. The current is so swift in the opening that no navigation through it can be attempted for several days. However, by the end of February, an invasion force is assembled that consists of two ironclad gunboats and twenty-two light transports, carrying forty-five hundred Federal troops. Colonel Wilson's plan is to enter the Coldwater River after negotiating the Yazoo Pass, and proceeding down this river, enter the Tallahatchee River. From there the Yankee armada is to proceed to the confluence of the Tallahatchee and Yalobusha Rivers which forms the Yazoo River near Greenwood, Mississippi. When the expedition reaches the Yazoo River from this route, Federal reinforcements are to be sent through the same passage, and an army is to be concentrated that will threaten Vicksburg.

Almost immediately after the interdiction of the Yazoo Pass Levee, Confederate officials get wind of the plan and defensive actions are initiated. Forces are dispatched to harass the fleet and impede its movements. While the Coldwater River is quite deep, it is very narrow and numerous large trees line the banks. These trees are felled, so that they fall into the water, blocking passage until they can be cleared. Removal of the trees from the channel is accomplished by hawsers manned by entire Federal regiments. As one tree is lifted free of the channel, the distant sound of chopping and the crashing of trees into the water can be heard from up ahead. The delaying tactics buy time which the Confederates need to complete Fort Pemberton, an earthwork and cotton bale fort built near where the Tallahatchee and Yalobusha Rivers meet to form the Yazoo River. Under the command of General W.W. Loring, the fort is constructed in a strategic location to control access to the Yazoo River.

Upon arrival at Greenwood, the Second Texas finds construction still proceeding on Fort Pemberton, manned now only by Waul's Texas Legion. A portion of the Second Texas is divided into squads which are sent into the countryside to impress Negro laborers. These laborers complete the earthwork fortifications of Fort Pemberton and extend rifle-pits to both sides. To impede Federal navigation of the river, the steamboat, *Star of the West,* is sunk in the channel opposite Fort Pemberton, and chain cables are extended across the river.

On Wednesday, March 11, 1863, the Federal fleet is sighted, and the battle for the Yazoo River begins. The Federal ironclad, *Chillicothe,* commences firing on the fort and immediately receives a return fire. Within a short time, the *Chillicothe* has taken two hits from the fort — one on the main turret by a 32-pounder — and the second amidships from an 18-pounder rifled solid shot.[17] The gunboat is reversed up stream to a bend in the river about 1,200 yards from the fort, and with only its bow guns exposed, continues to shell the fort ineffectually. By 4 P.M., the ironclad, *DeKalb,* rounds the bend upstream with smoke pouring from her stacks to challenge the fort, and a furious exchange of firing takes place, ceasing only at nightfall. The next

morning the Confederates find that Federal forces are constructing a land battery about 700 yards upriver, consisting of a 30-
pound Parrott Gun. The position is reinforced in the next two
days with another Parrott Gun and an 8-inch ship howitzer.

By Friday morning at 10 A.M. a sustained bombardment
of the fort begins with the massed firepower of the land battery, the ironclads, *Chillicothe* and *DeKalb,* and a 13-inch mortar. Fort Pemberton is struck by an 11-inch shell from the
Chillicothe which passes through the parapet and ignites a
powder magazine. A pyrotechnic display results from the hit
and fifteen Confederate artillerymen from the Pointe Coupeé
Battery are burned by the magazine ignition. Another shell
explodes over a confederate battery, killing one man. Federal
troops are disembarked from the transports in a vain attempt
to flank Fort Pemberton from the land side. However, the
lands around the fort are completely inundated from the
breached levees on the Mississippi, and the only points above
water are on the immediate river banks. Troop movement by
land is impossible for the Federals; only a direct assault on the
fort from the ironclads in the river will carry the position. By
Friday evening the Federal attack has bogged down, as many
hits have been made upon the ironclads by well-placed Confederate artillery fire. The Second Texas covers the right flank
of the fort from rifle-pits and consequently does not suffer
from the intense fire directed on the fort. The Texans have a
low opinion of the design of the fort and refer to it as "a
slaughter pen." [18]

Lieutenant Henry of Company A supervises the construction of canoes, by which squads of men from the Second
Texas are ferried over to the river bank to observe and report
on the activities of the Federals. Rather than remain as pas-
sive spies, the men keep up a constant bushwhacking on the
Federal ships. However, the rifle fire directed upon the gunboats is often returned in the form of a broadside from the
ship's guns which "cut wagon roads through the canebrakes,"
but fail to injure any Texans.[19]

A weak, ineffectual fire is maintained upon Fort Pemberton until Monday, when a grand assault is attempted. The attack is led by the ironclad, *Chillicothe*, as the *DeKalb* has been disabled by the fight on Friday. From 1,200 yards up river the *Chillicothe* pumps iron at Fort Pemberton only twenty minutes before it takes a direct hit from a heavy Confederate battery and is so badly disabled that the assault is postponed. During the five days the fort is under attack, the *Chillicothe* takes fifty-two hits from Confederate batteries, a pounding which renders her incapable of further service. Union forces remain in their positions until Friday without firing another battery and then return up the Tallahatchee River in retreat. The retreat continues only a short distance up the Tallahatchee River until a juncture is made with the Union relief force commanded by Brigadier General I.F. Quinby steaming down the Tallahatchee. Quinby assumes command of the combined forces which return to renew the attack on Fort Pemberton.

Federal reconnaissance patrols are sent out in force to locate a land route over which an infantry attack can be made on the fort. One of these patrols clashes with Company B of the Second Texas in an incident described by Lieutenant Daniel Smith.[20]

In compliance with orders, I would respectfully communicate that on Monday the 23rd inst. Co. B in company with 2nd Texas Regiment was ordered on outpost to meet the advance enemy and take position on the banks of the Tallahatchee River after being encamped at what is known as Fort Texas for a short time. Co. B was ordered out and placed under the command of Maj. G.W.L. Fly to proceed across the Tallahatchee River and take position in or near Tindale's Farm under cover of the woods and fire into the enemies transports as they passed down the river. Having arrived at this place too late to do the enemy any effectual injury Maj. Fly ordered the command to fall back and leave a picket in an old field near the river bank, placing the reserve in the houses attached to the farm where they stayed until the morning of the 24th when the reserve consisting of 21 men, three men and a non-commissioned officer having been ordered to guard the boats at the landing; were ordered to take positions at the old Gin House. About 12 noon the enemy cavalry made a dash on our outpost capturing Private Callahan. I immediately formed my company to receive the enemy. While waiting for their advance on me an order came from Maj Fly. I having dispatched a messenger to the opposite side of the river, informing him of the approach of the enemies cavalry ordering me to fall back with my company to the position occupied by the reserve the night before. While making my retreat the advance of the enemy made a charge on me. I immediately ordered my men to give them a running fight, which we did emptying two saddles and causing the enemy to about face and retreat in double quick order. I then fell back to the houses and while forming to receive the second onset of the enemy, I discovered that they were being heavily reinforced.

Not deeming it prudent to attempt to hold our position, having nothing to cross the river in but an open flat boat and knowing that the enemy could surround me, and in case they should do so, could pick off my men in the open boat, they having the protection of the heavy timber which lines the bank of the river. I ordered the crossing of the river before the enemy should attack which I did with safety with the loss of not a single man with the exception of Private Matthew Callahan above mentioned who was taken prisoner. . . .

Quinby fails to find a flanking route around the fort, and because of dwindling rations and ammunition and a fear that receding flood waters will trap the flotilla in the Tallahatchee, another retreat is ordered. The Yazoo expedition to attack Vicksburg is called off.

The Second Texas returns to Camp Timmons and will remain encamped at this site until May 1. The weather turns a bit warmer, but the men continue to suffer, as usual, from neglect and improper rations. Colonel Ashbel Smith writes home,[21]

. . . The 2nd Texas has been healthy until quite recently. Diarrhea with some scurvy are now disabling our men. Our surgeons say that a supply of vegetables would prove a complete restorative. There are too, at some few miles distant from camps, in the country, sufficient supplies of vegetables. Money would get them. They cannot however be got by infantry soldiers acting individually. You may judge how difficult it is for us to effect anything by individual exertions, when field officers below the rank of Brig. General are not allowed to go beyond brigade lines without a written pass. And in regard to sending a quartermaster, concerted action among the men to contribute the necessary funds seems impracticable. I should have preferred, for my own opinion, that a portion of the munificent sum which we learn has been raised in Houston for our regiment, should have been appropriated in this way. But the men, the rank and file, in their generosity, wishes that the families of the dead and of the poor from among us should be provided for [and] voted to leave the entire sum in Texas to be appropriated to the support of these families. We could easily have anticipated the funds here by checks on the fund in question. We must wait, however. In a few weeks there will be green apples, green peaches, green grapes, and these articles, though green, were found last year to put an end to the same diseases as are now prevailing among us. On the whole, the health of the regiment is tolerably good. No fatigue or exposure hurts them; they are, too, in excellent spirits and discipline.

The Second Texas is moved twelve miles south of Vicksburg to the little deserted town of Warrenton, Mississippi, on the Mississippi River. From this location, the southern routes of attack on Vicksburg can be defended.

The duties of the regiment are to guard the road leading from Grand Gulf to Vicksburg and man a battery to attack the Union warships and transports that ply the waterway. No rations are supplied for the regiment and the men must forage to survive. But these enterprising men find a food supply quickly. The ditches in and around Warrenton are teeming with crayfish which the men discover are quite delicious. ". . . It was an everyday occurrence to see forty or fifty men coming into camp with gunny sacks filled with the fish [*sic* — crustaceans] swung on a rail or a pole carried on the shoulders of two men." [22]

This added ration supplies a welcome protein supplement to the monotonous diet of corn dodgers. Further foodstuffs are unwittingly discovered by Federal ironclads. During the daily shelling received by the battery at Warrenton from Federal warships, the top of a large cypress tree is cut by a shot and falls behind the ramparts of the defenses. The limb is

hollow and bees have filled it with honey. With a little explo-
ration, the men find a great many bee trees in the swamp
around Warrenton, and with the services of a crosscut saw the
camp is soon supplied with honey. The regiment will affectionately refer to their encampment at Warrenton as "Camp
Crawfish and Honey." [23]

The Union Army, under Grant, initiates its spring campaign in April, 1863 with a daring troop movement through
swamps and bogs around Vicksburg from the west side of the
Mississippi River. With the help of the Federal Navy — under
Admiral Porter who runs a fleet past the Vicksburg batteries
— Grant's army is transported to the east side of the Mississippi River at Bruinsburg on April 30.

Grant pushes his forces inland and after a few minor engagements captures Jackson, Mississippi. The Federal Army
has now interposed itself between Pemberton's Vicksburg defenders and the army of General Joseph E. Johnston, sent to
reinforce Pemberton. With the Stars and Stripes flying over
the capitol at Jackson, the Federal Army turns west and
moves into position to attack Vicksburg. The strategically important city of Vicksburg holds the final key to complete control of the Mississippi River, an important Northern objective.
Located at a hairpin turn in the Mississippi River atop a 200-
foot high bluff, its defensive position controls river traffic and
permits a steady flow of supplies and men across the river
from the Trans-Mississippi Region. Confederate military engineers have constructed an arc of defenses on the landward
side of the city that terminates at both ends with the river.
However, Grant's troop movement has caught the Confederates by surprise, and not enough rations and ammunition
have been stored in Vicksburg to support a lengthy siege.
Other supplies are scarce also. Major M.K. Simons, on a supply trip from Warrenton to Vicksburg, reports on May 8, ". . .
I went to Vicksburg this morning . . . I bought me a pair of
pants that would in ordinary times cost six or eight dollars, for
which I had to pay sixty dollars . . ." [24]

By May 17, the Federal Army moves to within striking

distance of Vicksburg, and the Second Texas Infantry is summoned from Warrenton to aid in its defense. The regiment is positioned initially on the extreme Confederate right flank which borders on the river, but later in the day is moved into a position on the defensive periphery between the Baldwin Ferry Road and the Alabama and Vicksburg Railroad. By 2 A.M. new marching orders are received, and the Second Texas Infantry is roused from sleep and sent to replace the 42nd Alabama Infantry, which mans the fort commanding the Baldwin Ferry Road. This fort is the key to defenses along the southern portion of the Vicksburg line, and must be manned by battle-tested veterans. The fort, by its association with the regiment, becomes known as the Second Texas Lunette, due to the half-moon shape of its design. Placed on a hill, it commands the Baldwin Ferry Road as it curves to enter the Confederate defenses. Two embrasures for cannon, with a traverse between them, form the main outlines of the floor plan for the lunette, which is protected by a parapet four- and one-half feet high on the inside. The superior slope of this earthen fortress is fourteen feet thick and protected in the front by a ditch six feet deep. The lunette is placed somewhat forward of the regular line of defense and can hold only four companies of the regiment. Two companies of the regiment are stationed in rifle-pits that protect the right flank of the fort. The remaining four companies, under the command of Lieutenant Colonel Nobel L. McGinnis, are placed on the left flank of the fort and separated from it by an open space of 100 yards, through which the Baldwin Ferry Road passes into the Confederate lines. The fort is difficult to defend because the hilly topography of the area offers almost as much cover for the attackers as for the defenders. Several hills close to the fort are of a higher elevation and provide excellent vantage points from which murderous plunging fire can be poured into the lunette. On the morning of May 18, Colonel Smith immediately sets to work to improve the defensive posture of the fort before the Federals encircle Vicksburg. A squad from the regiment is sent forward to remove all obstructions from the line of fire of the fort, burning several houses and chopping down trees to accomplish this purpose. Other men with shovels deepen the parapet about the fort to six feet, so that a rifleman can fire from within the walls with a minimum exposure to enemy fire. Rifle-pits are dug behind the fort to serve as a second line of defense in the event of Federal capture of the fort. Each Texan is issued five or six additional smooth-bore muskets loaded with ball-and-buck cartridges to improve the short range firepower, and the stage is set for what all anticipate to be a massive Federal attack.[25]

By May 19, the companies of Captains Christian and Debord, acting as skirmishers under the command of Major Fly, encounter a force of Federal troops in front of the fort and are driven back into Confederate lines. Vicksburg has been encircled. Soon every hilltop and open area has been mounted by either a siege gun or a field battery, which begins to fire shells into the defensive works and over the heads of the troops into the city itself. Houses in the suburbs begin to burn from direct hits by Federal shells, and the citizens of Vicksburg desert their homes for the safety of caves dug in the hillsides. By nightfall, Admiral Porter brings the Federal fleet, consisting of gunboats and mortar boats, in range of Vicksburg, and commences to throw shells into the city. Porter's bombardment of Vicksburg will become a nightly occurrence. General Moore writes in his official report of the siege, "Some idea may be formed of the artillery fire to which we were exposed, when I state that a small party sent out for that purpose collected some two thousand shells near and in rear of the trenches occupied by our brigade. This was soon after the siege began, and was but a portion of those that failed to explode." [26]

More flaws are discovered in the design and construction of the Second Texas Lunette as it receives its baptism of Federal fire. Elongated shells fired from rifled Federal siege guns penetrate the upper parapets of the fort, killing several men. Two more feet of earth are added to the inner walls of the fort, strengthening them enough to withstand the continued pounding. From elevated positions, Federal snipers pour minié balls into the rear of the fort and its approaches making movements to and from the fort perilous. Covered walkways are built to hide movements within the fort, reducing mortality rates from snipers' bullets. The two artillery batteries within the fort become a target of intense Yankee shelling, and are dismounted, putting them temporarily out of service. So much rifle fire enters the fort from the cannon embrasures that Colonel Smith, in the latter days of the siege, will order them filled with cotton bales.

On May 20 and 21, Confederate positions continue to absorb a steady diet of field artillery shells by day, and huge mortar shells from the river by night. After dark, shells thrown into the city can be detected by trails of sparks left in their wakes from burning fuses. Incendiary shells of Greek fire explode in the air with resulting sheets of red, green, and blue flames. In the midst of these pyrotechnics, the Texans attempt to sleep as well as they can and calmly await the infantry attack that is soon expected. The first attack occurs on May 22. Dawn's first light on this day filters through the smoke from Federal campfires drawn in a semicircle about Vicksburg. A signal gun from General Grant's headquarters fires a shell to initiate another round of artillery bombardments on the defenses of Vicksburg, continuing until 10 A.M. At this time all Federal firing ceases. An eerie silence falls over the besieged army which is suddenly broken by a cry from Private Brooks of Company C, "Here they come!" The flash of glittering bayonets is seen in front of the Texans as five regiments of Federal troops break from the valleys in front of the Second Texas Lunette and rush toward the fort. The brigades of Federal Generals Burbridge and Benton, armed with ladders and scaling tools, form a sea of blue uniforms that close upon Confederate lines shouting, "Vicksburg or hell." [27] The 33rd and 99th Illinois strike the right flank of the lunette; while the 16th and 18th Indiana and the 23rd Wisconsin charge directly for the ditch in front of the lunette. In an act of singular bravery, Thomas J. Higgins, the color-bearer for the 99th Illinois, races toward the lunette, far outdistancing his comrades. Proudly waving the Stars and Stripes, this one man army rushes to the breastworks at the right flank of the lunette and attempts to plant the regimental colors as a guide for other Federals. The men of the Second Texas are impressed by this act of bravery, and shouts are heard among the Texans, "Don't shoot him. He is too brave; capture him alive." [28] Corporal Charles I. Evans, the regimental biographer from Company G, takes the flag from Higgins's hands and marches him to the rear as a prisoner. In the meantime, the Second Texas pours deadly fire from their many muskets into the advancing ranks of Federals, which falter and begin to retreat in confusion. Many Yankees find protective cover from the hail of lead in the deep ditch in front of the fort and crouch there to await reinforcements. A second Yankee charge fills the ditch with men who attempt to scale the superior slope of the fort to the parapet. Reaching the right cannon embrasure, they fire into the fort with telling effect. Inside the lunette, the situation has become critical. One of the two cannons bursts when fired, creating several casualties for Company K. Zack Oppenheimer and Wright Wiseman are torn to pieces by the explosion and die, while Abraham Gisler loses a leg and Davey Burnett has three fingers severed from his right hand.[29] The second cannon cannot be fired because its gunners are in an exposed position and are shot by Federal troops in the moat when they attempt to service the cannon. The fort begins to fill with smoke and burning cotton fibers that drift through the air, threatening to ignite the ammunition boxes. Revetments for the lunette have been constructed from cotton bales, and the incessant hail of minié balls from Yankee guns has dislodged the fibrous material which drifts throughout the inside of the fort, ignited by the muzzle flash of the defenders' rifles. Colonel Smith orders the men to extinguish the burning cotton and organizes a force of reserves to counterattack the Yankees who are scaling the parapet. At the cannon embrasure on the right flank of the fort, Federal troops have organized to enter the fort. At Colonel Smith's command, "Volunteers to clear that embrasure," [30] Sergeant William T.

Spence of Company B and Privates T.E. Bagwell, A.S. Kittridge and J.A. Stewart of Company C, rush forward to engage the Yankee troops. From a distance of less than five paces, murderous fire is exchanged. The Yankees are hurled back into the moat, but Private Bagwell is slain, and Sergeant Spence is mortally wounded and dies a few days later. Since flanking fire cannot be brought to bear on the Yankees in the moat, the men of the Second Texas improvise their own artillery. Using spherical case shot from the field artillery as hand grenades, the Texans light the fuses on these cannon balls and roll them over the top of the parapet into the moat below. Federal troops cannot penetrate strong Confederate defenses around the lunette, and the attack fails. By 3 P.M. the moat has been cleared of Federal troops, and Texans experience a lull in the battle. However, the Union attack on Confederate defensive positions 400 yards south of the Second Texas lunette has been more successful. The Federal brigade under Brigadier General Michael Lawler[31] has driven the 30th Alabama from rifle-pits fronting the Railroad Redoubt, a fort constructed to defend the railroad tracks from Vicksburg to Jackson, and threatens capture of this fortification. Charles I. Evans reports that from the Second Texas Lunette three Federal regimental battle flags can be seen fluttering from the crown of the fort. Thus by 3 P.M. the Corp of Union General McClernand has made some headway against the defensive positions around Vicksburg, while the Corps of Generals Sherman and MacPherson have been repulsed in their attacks on Confederate positions on the Jackson Road, north of the Second Texas Lunette. However, General McClernand has committed all of his reserves to the attack and does not have the manpower to improve on the position he has taken at the Railroad Redoubt. Several times during the day McClernand requests aid from General Grant who responds by ordering the Corps of Generals Sherman and MacPherson to renew their attacks on the Confederate defenses as a diversion to relieve McClernand's Corp. By 5 P.M., Federal troops mass again for another attack on the Second Texas Lunette. Union

General Sanford's Brigade, summoned as reinforcements, attacks the lunette. Moving down the Baldwin Ferry Road, Federal soldiers flank the lunette on the left and threaten to attack it from the rear. A field gun of the Chicago Mercantile Battery is pushed into position on the left of the fort by Yankees and commences to fire at the parapets and embrasures. From the fort, Colonel Smith orders Company G, stationed to the right of the lunette, to counterattack the Yankee forces that have massed on the left. The regiment concentrates its firepower on the left, but the Federal troops hold their ground and will not retreat. Federal soldiers are now within the Vicksburg defensive lines, and Colonel Smith issues a request for reinforcements. Confederate General Martin Green, responding to Smith's appeal, counterattacks by moving up the Baldwin Ferry Road from Vicksburg. His brigade of Arkansas and Missouri troops dislodge the Yankees from their positions, and they fall back in confusion. With the Federal retreat a silence falls over the battle lines around the lunette, and in the twilight of day, Texans begin to observe the carnage that has taken place during the battle. From the front of the fort back two hundred yards, the ground is littered with the crumpled bodies of dead and wounded Federal troops. Major Isaac H. Elliott of the 33rd Illinois Regiment, one of the attackers, would later estimate that the three Federal brigades that attacked the Texans on May 22 had suffered casualties of 600 killed and 1,200 wounded around the lunette.[32] However, the official casualty list posts 111 killed, 535 wounded, and 11 missing. Rifles, canteens, and other equipment cover the ground in abundance around the fort, and the regiment rearms itself with about 200 new Enfield rifles abandoned on the field by the Yankees. To the south, the climax of a spirited battle is being fought that results in the recapture of the Railroad Redoubt by the Confederates. To the amusement of the Confederate troops, the soldiers of Waul's Texas Legion put on a demonstration of cowhand skills, and toss lariats over the Yankee battle flags that have been planted on the redoubt, pulling them down.[33]

Under cover of darkness, Major Fly leads a reconnaissance to the front of the fort and discovers that several holes had been dug in the earthworks by Yankees hiding in the moat as protection from Confederate rifle fire. "Major Fly had these holes filled, and, to prevent their being opened again for a like purpose, he had buried in them 27 Yankee carcasses." [34] The dead and wounded Federals soon begin to create problems for the Confederates. During the night, dead and wounded soldiers are removed by the Federal medical corps from the more remote areas of the battlefield. By day, though, it can be seen that due to their close proximity to Confederate lines, many dead and wounded can only be safely removed by the declaration of a temporary cease-fire. The Confederate leaders await a request from General Grant for such a cease-fire, but none is forthcoming. The hot sun beams down on the wounded, and the groans and pleadings for water increase. A brave boy from the Second Texas volunteers for a mission of mercy. Charles I. Evans remembers that:

> With the acquiescence of his captain, he mounted the breastworks with a canteen of water and a haversack in one hand, and waved his handkerchief to the enemy. They cried, "Come on," and the Texan advanced to the ravine where the wounded man lay, and handed him the food and water, for which he was very grateful. He talked with him a few minutes, and ascertained that he was a lieutenant in the Eight Indiana Regiment, and that his thigh was broken. The Texan bade him good-by, and started to return to the trenches, when nearly every Union soldier who could see him fired at him. His clothes were cut in many places, but not a shot broke the skin. . . .[35]

As the day progresses, the cries of the wounded grow fainter and finally cease. The stench of rotting corpses grows unbearable, and finally on May 25, General Pemberton offers General Grant a temporary cessation of hostilities to remove the remaining casualties. At 6 P.M., May 25, soldiers of the Blue and Gray mix freely for two hours on the battlefield, exchanging newspapers and conversation while the dead are buried. Major Maurice Simons records in his diary on May 25, the following entry:

... At 2 PM we sent a flag of truce to the Enemy requesting them to come and bury their dead, that have become so offensive that it is imposible for our men to stay in the trenches, the enemy accepted the offer for armistice, which was to last till 8 1/2 oclock PM: all were delighted to have an opportunity of walking and looking around once more without his head being endangered to the Enemys sharp shooters and they seemed to enjoy it as much as our men it looked realy strange, to see these of both sides, walking up and shaking hands, and drinking together (the latter always having to come from the Yankees as our men are not supplied with much of it) they joke each other at a great rate, our boys giving them the worst of it, as a general thing. They ask the Yanks why "they don't come in[to] Town?" "Why they turned back the other eavening?" This is the right road to Vicksburg and the nearest, when are you coming to see us again and pointing to the dead Yankees (that were laying in great numbers around & in front of our fort (occupied by 2nd Texas) these friends of yours deddent make the trip; the Yankees looked mean I thought especially when our men would ask them geeringly [*sic*] if they had all gotten negro wives yet & how they liked them. The Yankees got through with their unpleasant job about sunset, having buried they say some 300 including those that they had previously gotten off under cover of the night & some 20 that our boys buryed by crawling out after night when the Yankee sharpshooters could not see to shoot them. The dead were the most horrible sight that I ever beheld, having [been] on the battlefield four days; — about dusk each party returned to their own works; which are not over two hundred yards, apart in some places. It was a great recreation & a very pleasant one it felt to me like Sunday, everything being so quiet after a constant fireing for eight days and nights; none can conseave [*sic*], who have not experienced it, the pleasant feelings that this short paws [*sic*] produced.[36]

Just how intense was the barrage of projectiles that the Federals loosed upon Vicksburg during those eight days? All the veterans of the Siege of Vicksburg agree that the shelling was the most intense that they experienced throughout the entire war. The reader can appreciate the horrors of this early battle of "modern warfare" by examination of a few entries from Major Simons's diary.

Wednesday (May) 20th The morning was most beautiful but the roaring of cannon has continued all night, & still the deafning sound of shot and shell of every conceivable shape are continually hissing through the air; their sound is as varied as their shape . . .

Thursday (May) 21st . . . The Yankees have closed their lines around our works, and their sharpshooters are continually poring a shower of minney balls into or rather at our brest works, which renders it quite hazzardas! Yes almost certain death for any one to look over the parripat [parapet] quite a number of our men have been killed — some eight or ten of the 2nd Texas have been picked off. Co K has so far escaped, for the past three days the firing has been without intermition minney balls, are whialing [wheeling] by us at the rate of several hundred per hour; everyone is dodging them we must be near a mile from the enemy yet they come so thick that one would suppose they were only a few hundred yards off . . .

Friday (May) 22 At daylight this morning the cannon opened their fire with unusual fearceness & though we thought on yesterday that, the cannonading was sevear it was not to be compared with that that is now going on, the Enemy are surely preparing to assalt our works: the cannon are roaring all round us, I have just been counting the number per minute and find it to average from *ten* to *forty* per minute, it has been one continuous roar all day, the sound of musketry is entirely lost though from the number of minney balls that are continually hissing by our ears we know that there must be a fight now progressing. Our quarters are between two high hills which pertects us prety well yet there has been hunders of shot & shell fallen all around us. One shell entered the ground right at the door of our tent . . .

Saturday (May) 23 . . . It is now 9 oclock PM the Mortar Boats are now hard at work shelling us they are throwing most tremendous shell they come at the rate of about 2 per minute they explode in the air the fragments flying for miles round and occasionally one of those pieces comes rushing through the air fearefully near us. . . .

Sunday (May) 24 All night the shelling process of the Enemy was carried on without intermition; it seemed realy strange to lie down to sleep while such monsters of shells were bursting over our heads every five minutes, & fragments flying in every direction; I was awakened once by a piece of it [that] was driven by my bed with the speed of lightening but soon I was again lost to all around me. There is no place of escape, so we must take our chances; it is now 5 PM & still the shelling continues at the rate of one every minute. I mean one of the 15 in. leaving out of the question those of smaller dementions; which come over us from the oppeset [*sic*] direction; . . . it seems almost out of the question to be sitting here writing while those miserable shell are bursting around, yet it is not worthwhile to dodg them, as one cannot tell from what direction they come; yet one will dodge & theres no use trying to brace ones self against it.

After the disastrous Union attacks of May 19–22 on Confederate defenses at Vicksburg, General Grant realizes that the city cannot be taken directly without prohibitive casualties. No more orders for troop assaults are to be issued. Vicksburg is to be taken by the use of the ancient strategy of siege. Union troops have encircled the city, and Admiral Porter controls the water routes from the Mississippi River. With no opportunities to resupply the garrison of 31,000 troops, the Vicksburg defenders will rapidly deplete their rations and ammunition and must hand over the city or starve. The Rebels remain optimistic though; Confederate General Joseph E. Johnston is organizing an army to lift the siege and is expected on any day to attack the Federal Army from the rear. These two combined Rebel armies now outnumber the Federals, and Grant works persistently to reinforce and resupply his troops. Every day more cannon are seen by the defenders to crown the hills that surround the city. Shelling of the city becomes so intense that both civilians and soldiers dig caves in the sides of the hills for protection. Major Simons writes on May 26, ". . . After breakfast the Ball was again opened and now cannon and small arms are booming away at the usual rate — I have some men at work digging me out a cave in which to sleep & sit when the shell are falling, these have become so common that there's not a hill, that has not [a] number of inmates: the fact is, the inhabitants of Vicksburg are now all living underground 'in these dens.' I will try mine tonight. . . ."

The exploding shells have killed large numbers of horses, mules, and other livestock, and their carcasses litter the streets of Vicksburg, creating a health problem. Animal remains are hauled to the bluffs overlooking the Mississippi and tossed over the side. Only a few of the carcasses are carried away by the river, however, and the vast majority line the banks, soon rendering the river water unfit for human consumption. Sufficient drinking water soon becomes a serious problem, and the Texans dig shallow wells in the hollows behind the lunette. This poor-quality water in limited quantity is used for cooking and drinking, and Colonel Smith posts a guard over the wells so that the water can be rationed for consumption only.

The contrast Union shelling of Vicksburg increases in intensity, and the men of the regiment begin daily to suffer more casualties. A fragment from a bursting shell strikes Captain Tom Douglass of Company H, fracturing his skull and injuring an ear. Not long afterwards a minié ball strikes Lieutenant Francis Marion Parks of Company H in the back of the neck, and the two lifelong friends from Burleson County spend the remainder of the siege in the hospital as ward mates.[37] Another large, bursting shell kills William Sims, Eli Obery, and L.G. Thurmon, all of Company K. Of the five Obery brothers from Jackson county who joined up and proudly marched away to serve the Confederacy, only one now remains alive. He is hospitalized with a broken leg which occurred as the result of a house falling in upon him. On May 30, Lieutenant Sterling Fisher is struck by the fragments of a bursting shell that mangles his right ankle and severely lacerates his back and hip. His right foot is amputated, and he lies in a very serious condition in a hospital tent. Major Simons writes in his diary that in his opinion he feels that the wound will prove to be fatal; but on a visit to the hospital is surprised by Fisher's morale. ". . . He stands it like a soldier, he says he has no fear but that he will get well, . . . when I walked up to him he extended his hand saying, 'they have got me at last.' I asked him if he was much hurt — well says he, 'I am pretty badly scratched.' "

Sterling Fisher's life continues to hang in the balance

throughout the siege, but the good deeds that he has performed on another day at another battlefield will ultimately save his life. On June 14, another bursting shell takes the life of Lieutenant Kirk of Company K.

A description of these "monster shells" is given by Major Simons as a June 2 entry of his diary,

> . . . The shell that they through [throw] from the mortars are 15 to 18 inch these will weigh from two to two hundred and fifty pounds each. They are filled with small pieces or iron bullets & powder they usually burst while in the air & scatter their contents & fragments in every direction; they are thoron [thrown] at a distance of four mile, that is when they reach us, which of late has become quite frequent during last night I suppose no less than fifty of those monsters, found, their way to our "retreate," many of them entering the ground within a remarkable short distance of our tent, one within eight feet; they go into the Earth a remarkable distance probably as deep as twenty feet making a hole that one might almost ride into; when after going into the earth they explode; (which they do quite frequently) one is reminded of an earth quake for the earth seems to shake as if it was about to burst asunder, . . .

The unexploded shells are taken apart for the powder they contain, and Simons writes for June 16, ". . . The boys are now amusing themselves at a game of marbles, playing with balls taken out of a shell that did not explode the balls are of Iron the size of a musket ball; . . ."

By June 3, stocks of flour have run low, and the Confederate troops are issued bread made from corn meal and mashed peas. Flour continues to be issued to the sick and wounded, but this practice will soon cease.

Back at the Second Texas Lunette trench warfare continues daily in a style to be imitated in later wars. Neither side seems to be making much headway. Union troops have placed a field artillery piece about three hundred yards to the right of the fort, and by using small charges of powder, are firing 6-pounder shells to ricochet from the wall of the fort and fall into the trenches. The Texans quickly pounce on these live shells, whose fuses are smoking, and hurl them out of the trenches before they can explode. However, after a soldier is killed while in the act of returning a shell, the men are issued buckets of water, and the nearest man to a live shell fields it, and scrambles to a bucket to extinguish the fuse.

Union troop attacks on the Vicksburg defenses have failed because of the large expanse of open ground between Union and Confederate lines. While rushing over such distances, an attacker becomes an easy target for a defender. Grant decides to move Union lines as close to Confederate defenses as possible. If another general attack is ordered, Federal troops can then be in a position to move upon Confederate lines before massed rifle fire can be brought to bear. Grant's Corps of Engineers sets out to move Federal trenches forward, while at the same time efforts are initiated to undermine key forts on the Confederate line of defense. One of the first chosen for destruction is the Second Texas Lunette. From inside the fort the men can clearly hear picks and shovels striking the soil beneath them as the mine is moved toward its objective. Colonel Smith orders counter-mining operations to begin. Being guided by the digging sounds, a shaft twenty feet deep is constructed to interdict the Union mine. Sometime in the latter part of June the two shafts meet, and the Union miners are captured. Not all Union mining efforts are unsuccessful; the fort occupied by the 3rd Louisiana Regiment is undermined and the resulting shaft filled with 2000 pounds of gun powder. These explosives are ignited on July 1, and a breach is blown in the Confederate defenses. While the mining operations on the Second Texas Lunette are being carried out, two trenches are dug by Union troops that approach the fort from the left front and right front. To protect the diggers from Confederate rifle fire, a large roller is placed at the head of each trench. The rollers are cylinders seven to eight feet long and four- and one-half feet in diameter, constructed of woven wire with a center of cane and green saplings or cotton bales. Both trenches are dug to within twenty feet of the fort before Confederate troops develop a method to destroy the rollers. Fed-

eral troops are now in close proximity to the lunette and occupy positions that will favor any subsequent attacks.

By July 1, the Confederate hopes for holding out any
longer become bleak. The Union Army besieging Vicksburg
has now been reinforced to a strength of over 70,000 men, out-
numbering the combined Confederate armies of Generals
Pemberton and Johnston. General Joseph E. Johnston's army,
remaining mysteriously inactive throughout May and June,
has now lost the opportunity to relieve the siege. The shortage
of cannonballs and shells has forced the defenders of Vicksburg to cease any return fire, and the remaining munitions are
saved for possible troop attacks. Confederate troops are now
issued only quarter rations consisting of musty cornmeal and
peas with no beef or pork. The Commissary Department begins to slaughter mules on June 27 to feed the sick and
wounded, and by July 3, Major Simons writes, ". . . We killed
eleven mules today to issue the men in the morning, we will
have mule stake for our breakfast." With such limited rations,
the men who have endured the elements of nature and the
ceaseless Federal bombardment for over forty days while
squatting in their trenches day and night, have reached their
physical and psychological limits of endurance. On July 2,
General Pemberton circulates a questionnaire among his officers to ascertain the practicability of an attack to break out of
the siege lines. The officers respond almost unanimously that
their soldiers are not now capable of the forced marches and
fatigues necessary to carry out such an operation. With no
other options remaining, General Pemberton initiates the ne-
gotiations that will result in the surrender of the Vicksburg
garrison on July 4. A cease-fire is imposed on July 3, and the
men of the Second Texas begin to nervously joke among themselves about whether they prefer the internment camps of
Johnson's Island, Camp Chase or Camp Douglas as sites for
their new residences. Many of the veterans have already
served terms of incarceration in these Union prison camps.
However, the shells and bullets are no longer flying for the
first time in forty-five days, and the men rejoice in the blessed

silence. Confederate troops suffer from a condition that psychologists will later describe as "battle fatigue." Over forty days of round-the-clock shelling has allowed no time for relaxation. The night bombardments from the mortar boats have been particularly fierce. One such night during the height of the shelling is described analytically, in terms of ordnance, by Major Simons in his diary entry for June 26,

> All night the Enemy continued their shelling from the mortars, we counted the number of these large 15 in shells (weighing two hundred pounds each), that fell during the night which resulted as follows: from 8 oclock PM to 12 [midnight] — 130, from 12 to 4 Am — 36. Making in all from 8 oclock PM to 4 Am — 166 these shell each wigh [*sic*] 200 lbs which would just make thirty three Thousand two hundred pounds (33,200) of Iron that they fired at us on last night; exclusive, of the shot and shell thrown from there [their] land Batterys; there was nothing unusual in the firing of last night; only that we took the pains to count them for curiosity; we have been under this fire for forty days which would make (3984000) three million nine hundred and eighty four thousand pounds of Iron that the mortars have thrown at us, which would require (498000) lbs of powder. This is onely the doings of the mortars which has not been half.

As dawn breaks on July 4, the men of the Second Texas Infantry experience two new phenomena: mule meat and surrender. The former is dished up for breakfast, and Major Simons comments tersely, "I eat two meals of *mule* to day the first in my life. A new way to celebrate the forth [fourth] of July, or rather a new dish, . . ."

At 10 A.M., July 4, the Second Texas Infantry is marched outside the trenches and ordered by its Union captors to stack arms. All regimental battle flags are ordered surrendered, but somehow the Second Texas flag turns up mysteriously "missing." A soldier from Company B hides the banner on his person and later smuggles it out of Vicksburg. The flag is left in the safekeeping of a lady at Snyder's Bluff, Mississippi, who buries it. No one knows for certain what finally becomes of the banner; some say it was left in Mississippi, while others contend that it was returned to Texas. Officers are allowed to retain their sidearms, but several enlisted men illegally smuggle revolvers out of Vicksburg. Ralph Smith is among those Texans who return to Texas sporting an illegal Vicksburg revolver.

The Federal Government offers paroles to all captured soldiers and officers willing to abide by its terms. Almost all Confederate troops pledge to honor the agreement. Printing presses are commandeered by the Union Army, and the process of issuing paroles will not be completed until July 11. A copy of a typical parole is reproduced.[38]

> Vicksburg, Mississippi   July ____ A.D. 1863
> To All Whom it May Concern, Know Ye That:
> _____a _____of Co _____Reg't
>
> Vol., C.S.A. being a prisoner of War, in the hands of the United States Forces, in virtue of the capitulation of the City of Vicksburg and its Garrison, by Lieut. Gen. John C. Pemberton, C.S.A., Commanding, on the 4th day of July, 1863, do in pursuance of the terms of the said capitulation, give this my solemn parole under oath —
>
> That I will not take up arms again against the United States, nor serve in any military police or constabulary force on any Fort, Garrison or field work, held by the Confederate States of America, against the United States of America, nor as guard of prisons, depots, or stores, nor discharge any duties usually performed by officers or soldiers against the United States of America until duly exchanged by the proper authorities.
>
> Sworn and subscribed before me at Vicksburg, Miss. this _ day of July, 1863.
> _____ Reg't _____Vols., and Paroling Officer.

By evening, General Grant offers Union rations to the starving Confederates. "We now draw from 'Mr. Grant' and the boys say that they mean to injure him all they can, by eating up his supplies; . . ." [39]

Major Simons draws five day's rations for the Brigade and is astonished at the supply of food he receives, almost a month's supply for his Confederate Brigade. The thirteen hundred fifty pounds of coffee issued by the Federal Government is the first seen by the Brigade in a year. The last coffee tasted by the Confederate troops was captured from the soldiers of General Rose-crans at the Battle of Iuka.

The scene in Vicksburg on the evening of July 4 is confusion. Confederates and Yankees are intermingled, laughing and talking together. Yankee troops are plundering and pillaging the private residences with the authorities exercising very little control. There is very little friction between the soldiers that were killing each other only two days before. Occasionally a disagreement will evolve into a fisticuffs match, but only rarely. The Confederate soldiers, however, are irritated by the presence of black Union soldiers. ". . . One thing I saw today that was quite grating to my feeling, to wit negroes on guard (white man Yankees I should say) saluting them, all on an equality." [40]

The City Hospital on the outskirts of town has suffered heavily from the daily bombardments, and sick and wounded troops have been moved to tents around the city to lessen their chances of further injury. General Grant orders the seriously wounded Confederate casualties to be moved to the old Vick Mansion for treatment. Although seriously wounded, Captain Tom Douglass refuses to be moved and prefers to be issued his parole so he can leave Vicksburg with Lieutenant Francis Marion Parks. "If Frank leaves, I'm going too." [41] These men of Company H return together from the war to Burleson County. Lieutenant Sterling Fisher is still fighting for his life, trying to recover from the serious wounds he has received on May 30. Lying in a tent, he has been exposed to flies whose eggs have hatched into maggots, now in his wounds as well as in the creases of his neck and between his fingers. Nurses have been removing the maggots one by one with forceps. The three large wounds are not healing due to lack of medication and proper food. Bones are exposed in these wounds, and he must lie on them, which further aggravates their healing and intensifies the suffering. His hair and beard have both fallen out, so that his friends can barely recognize him. His friends of the Second Texas assemble for a last good-bye before they change camps, and tears show unashamedly on many a weatherbeaten face. A small supply of coins is pressed into his hands, and with a hushed, "God bless you," the men file out of the tent with an air of gloom and finality.

Hardly has Fisher been moved into a ward at the Vick Mansion before a Union soldier posted on guard duty demands to know if any of the inmates belong to the Second Texas Infantry. When Fisher feebly acknowledges his regiment, the soldier thrusts a worn memorandum book before his eyes, asking him to identify the names written on the page. Through bleary eyes Fisher recognizes one of the names as his own, written in his own hand. With Fisher's acknowledgment of his name and subsequent questions from the guard, it becomes established that the two men had met before — on the battlefield at Shiloh. On April 6, 1862, after the attack on the Hornet's Nest, the Second Texas had halted to rest in a ravine. Fisher and a comrade, Dan Smith, were sent to the rear carrying canteens to fill with water when they passed three wounded Federal troops, a captain and two enlisted men. The men were suffering intensely from their wounds, and their groans pricked the conscience of young Fisher. Fisher and Smith had hastened to their aid, preparing beds of leaves in the shade, and they had placed the Union soldiers in comfortable positions on these hastily constructed pallets. Fisher had then brought the men canteens of water and some haversacks filled with rations, that had been abandoned on the battlefield. A gold watch chain was removed from the captain's neck and placed in his pocket for safekeeping from plunderers, and a Confederate ambulance hailed to pick up the men. Fisher, in a later description of the incident, writes, "The three were profuse in their expressions of gratitude, and asked us to write our names in their memorandum-books, which we did. In returning their books and on their reading our names with that of our regiment '2d Texas Infantry,' they looked at us in astonishment, and asked if we were really Texans. When we assured them we were, they said they were astonished, for they had prayed not to fall into the hands of Texans, as they believed that if they did, they would be shown no quarter, and would certainly be butchered like beasts." [42] The possessor of one of these memorandum books is now Fisher's guard. "You saved my life and that of my captain and comrade, and I have hunted for you or some of your command on every battlefield since, that I might prove myself as true as you . . ." [43] The guard disappears, but soon returns with the Federal surgeon in charge of the hospital (a colonel) and other officers, and repeats this story to them. Soon tobacco, canned fruit, and other delicacies are heaped on Fisher and the other men of his ward, and fresh sheets, new blankets, and pillowcases replace the other bedding. Sterling Fisher recovers from his wounds, due in no small measure to the kindness that has been reciprocated by his Union captors.

Back at the camp for the paroled Confederate prisoners, things are not going well. General Pemberton attempts to hold his Confederate Army together as a unit and move it to Brandon, Mississippi. This army, once exchanged, can then continue resistance as an organized fighting unit. However, the morale in the army is bad, and soldiers begin to leave for their home states without permission, rather than wait out the exchange period in camps. Since Pemberton has no arms with which to enforce his orders, he is powerless to stem the tide of desertions. The men of the Second Texas are no exception, and the ranks shrink daily as men return to Texas to see their loved ones again. In a single evening, all of Company K find transportation across the Mississippi River and desert. The Texans do not feel that they have abandoned the army, but that they will visit their homes and families rather than spend this time in a paroled prisoners' camp. When exchanged in October, they will return to duty. Many valuable regimental records are lost during this period of confusion, and at least one important document is found blowing across the ground by troops of other commands.[44]

Powerless to stop the flight of his men, General Pemberton reluctantly agrees to furlough them for a period of forty days. On July 17, 1863, Colonel Ashbel Smith receives the following order while in camp at Brandon, Mississippi:[45]

"Col. Ashbel Smith of 2nd Texas Regt of Volunteers will proceed immediately to the State of Texas, collect and organize his Regiment. He is authorized to take with him Capt. Wm. Christians [*sic*], Lts. Hostis and Coates of Company D, Privates A.S. Kittridge, Dudley Ward, and ——— Denzer to aid in the execution of this order. As soon as he collects and organizes this Regiment he will report with it at Demopolis, Ala. at such a time parole of army be designated. For this purpose a leave of absence of forty days is granted. By Order of Gen'l Pemberton"

The Second Texas returns home.

Colonel William P. Rogers

William P. Rogers, as he might have dressed when lecturing on the law at old Baylor University, Independence, Texas.

— *From private collection of the Author*

Colonel Ashbel Smith

Dr. Ashbel Smith, physician, scientist, diplomat, and politician who served Texas from the days of the Republic. Dr. Smith was the first chairman of the board of regents of The University of Texas.

Private Sam Houston, Jr., physician, writer, and poet, eldest son of the General.

— *Humanities Research Center, UT*

Private Ralph Smith, "the sometimes Private," who wrote a humorous account of his service with the Second Texas Infantry.

Major George Washington Lafayette Fly, college president, legislator, and successful attorney from Victoria, Texas.

Captain Clark Owen, dressed in a military uniform of the Republic of Texas. Captain Owen served Texas from the days of the Republic as senator and colonel in the army.

The Federal gunboats *Lexington* and *Tyler* that shelled the Confederate Army from the Tennessee River during the Battle of Shiloh.

— Library of Congress

The Federal ironclads, *Chillicothe,* top, and *Baron de Kalb,* bottom, which battled the Confederate defenders of Fort Pemberton, on the Tallahatchie River, north of Greenwood, Mississippi.

Private Sam Houston, Jr.'s bible, pierced by a bullet while being carried in his knapsack during the Battle of Shiloh.

— *Sam Houston Museum, Huntsville, Texas*

The Tishomingo Hotel, Corinth, Mississippi, used as a Confederate hospital after the Battle of Shiloh.

— *U.S. Military History Institute*

View of the rear of a portion of the Federal defenses northwest of Corinth, Mississippi. To the left of railroad cut is the outline of Fort Williams, and to the right is seen a portion of the breastwork of Fort Robinett. From the woods in the background Confederates massed for the attack on Fort Robinett, October 4, 1862.

— *Chicago Historical Society, Clark Street at North Avenue, Chicago, Illinois 60614*

Aftermath of the attack on Fort Robinett, October 4, 1862. The fort and its Federal defenders seen in background. Felled trees, cut to form an unobstructed fire zone, and a portion of the limbs used to form an abatis are seen in the foreground. The body of Colonel W.P. Rogers lies in the center, and his horse to the right.

— *Library of Congress*

Confederates killed in the attack on Fort Robinett, October 4, 1862. The body of Colonel Rogers, propped up by a stump, is seen left front. Rogers, singled out for his heroism, is buried in a single grave, while the remainder are interred in a mass grave.

— *Library of Congress*

A portion of an armored vest taken from the body of Colonel Rogers at Fort Robinett. The vest is exhibited at the Wisconsin Historical Society Museum, Madison, Wisconsin.

— *Jon Harrison, McAllen, Texas*

Confederate Cemetery at Hazlehurst, Mississippi, resting place of many of the soldiers of the Second Texas Infantry.

— From private collection of the Author

The Texas Hospital Cemetery at Quitman, Mississippi, containing over 200 headstones of Texas Confederates hidden in the underbrush.

— From private collection of the Author

Typical headstone in Texas Hospital Cemetery, placed by WPA in 1930s.

— From private collection of the Author

Remains of the mineral water baths that formed a portion of the Texas Hospital in Quitman, Mississippi. The Texas Hospital was burned by the troops of General W.T. Sherman in a devastating raid through Clark County in early 1864.

— From private collection of the Author

The Old Soldiers Graveyard at Enterprise, Mississippi, final resting place of many soldiers from the Second Texas.
— *Mrs. L.B. Buckley, Enterprise, Mississippi*

The old Presbyterian Church at Enterprise, Mississippi. This building served as a hospital which ministered to the needs of sick and wounded Texas soldiers. A solid structure, it still remains standing.
— *Mrs. L.B. Buckley, Enterprise, Mississippi*

6

A Regimental Postscript

I joined the service in 1861; was a member of the Second Regiment of Texas Infantry; and expected to continue in service 'till the war should end, but three years absence from home has produced many changes. The Wolf is at my door & I have but *one Leg* with which to repel him.

From Major M.K. Simons's letter of resignation.

Small groups of ragged, penniless Texans cross the Mississippi River as best they can and proceed generally on foot across Louisiana. The three hundred-mile trek takes about twenty days afoot, and the men subsist on what they can beg, borrow, or steal (forage), according to Ralph Smith. Henry Meyer, a private in Company B of the Second Texas, who lived in La Grange, Texas, remembers his trip back to Texas in the following manner:[1]

After the surrender of Vicksburg, picking up a canteen and a piece of blanket, all I had left, I told them that I was going back to Texas and fight them till the war was over. I started down the river marching to my own tune. I bought a skiff from a Yankee soldier for 50 cents in silver. Now I was the owner of a marine and charged four Arkansas fellows $20 apiece to put them across, which took me all day. I picked up a companion at Berwick Bay and started for New Orleans. We got along very well till we got to the mouth of Big Black (River) where we found a gunboat. Being unacquainted with United States Marine regulations I paid no attention to their signals and a shot was fired across my prow and as I did not stop others were fired and as I had no white flag I held up my oar as a signal of surrender and pulled back to the boat. I showed by parole. Was then instructed as to how to respond to signals and was allowed to go. We kept afloat till we reached Natchez where the boats got too thick and I made enquiries as to how far it was to Alexandria on the Red River. I went across there. Traveling on foot the rest of the way.

While Henry Meyer marched to his own tune back to Texas, Major George Washington Lafayette Fly had the problem of crossing the Mississippi River and returning home with his wife and three small children. Mrs. Fly, accompanied by her children, had left Gonzales County, Texas, in search of her husband, reported dead in the attack on Battery Robinett. After a happy reunion in Vicksburg, she and the children were sent to stay with her father in Starkville, Mississippi, during the capture of Vicksburg. After Major Fly's capture and parole, he was ordered by the Confederate Army to Demopolis, Alabama, and finally to Enterprise, Mississippi, where he received orders in November, 1863, to return to Texas and aid in the reorganization of the regiment. But, by this time the Federals have declared all Confederate troops to be exchanged, and he once again becomes an active combatant in the war. Major Fly, in an article written in later years, describes his journey back to Texas:[2]

> Acting upon the principal that had ever actuated me, I determined to do the best I could and leave the results to Him who rules all things. I sold my ponies and wagon, and purchased two good mules and an old ambulance. Into this ambulance I placed my wife, children, and negroes, with camping outfit and a supply of provisions sufficient for several days. On the third day out I was joined by Capt. Holder of my regiment, and a Dr. Jordan, both of whom had been ordered across to Texas. Before reaching the Mississippi, we were joined by a citizen, a Mr. Harris, of Starkville, Miss., an old friend and schoolmate of my wife. With

this company I finally reached the Mississippi River after many adventures. Reaching the river at Rodney, and finding it impossible to cross there, we remained in camp for three day, within three miles of the Federal forces at Rodney. After reconnoitering for three days, I determined to proceed at Bruinsburg, where Gen. Grant had effected a crossing. Here, taking our hack to pieces, we sent the bed across in one skiff pulled by four negro men, and the running gear across on another. In the stern of each of these skiffs sat two men, Capt. Holder and the negro in one, and Dr. Jordan and Mr. Harris in the other. These managed the mules and horses. Thus everything went over except myself, my wife, children, and negro girl. These, with our camp equipage, remained until the return of the skiffs. These were all carried by the same means. During this time, it being 9 AM when we began crossing, a Yankee gunboat lay just above us around a bend of the river, and another just below around another bend. I anxiously watched the smoke of these two enemies. Across the river, we hastily put our hack in running order and left with all possible speed. We traveled sixteen miles that evening. With varied adventures, in four weeks we reached my home in Gonzales County, . . .

Small bands of the ragged veterans of the Second Texas first begin arriving in Houston by the early part of August, 1863. A warm welcome is given the soldiers, who are boarded in private homes. New clothes and shoes are donated by the grateful citizens to replace the soldiers' rags, and the men sleep in beds for the first time in many months.

The *Tri-Weekly Telegraph* of Houston publishes a short article in August, 1863, on the history of the regiment that closes with the following words of commendation,

> These gallant men are now home on furlough and as paroled prisoners of war. We trust they will be everywhere welcomed to the homes of the people, and made to feel that they have been fighting for a people worthy of brave soldiers.
>
> But alas! where are the fifteen hundred men who left with or who have since joined this noble band? Where are our own beloved friends, brothers, sons and fellows, who come not back to us with these war-worn veterans? Mourn ye bereaved for your loved ones who lie low in distant vales, their silent beds scarce

marked enough to be found by the eye of affection that may
search for them; but ye men and women of Texas, glory in their
fame, for they fell upon the field of immortal honor and the nob-
lest cause ever fought for.

The day will come, yes is now, when to have belonged to
the Second Texas will be an honor more to be prized than any
that man can confer.

The Second Texas is declared exchanged by the Federals
in October, 1863, and is to be reorganized in Houston. The
call to reassemble is sent throughout the state and the volunteers respond to another call to arms. When the companies
align themselves on the parade ground at Camp Bee, the
thinned ranks of troops tell a silent story not only of the regiment but of the Confederacy itself. On January 6, 1864, Major
Fly reports that only three companies are available for field
duty; but on January 22, the number has increased to five
companies. By April the regiment shows a field strength of
190 men and 18 officers, with an assigned strength of 382
men. In point of fact, the Second Texas Infantry will never
again be larger than battalion strength, but continues to be
carried on the muster rolls as a regiment throughout the remainder of the war. Even with its reduced size, many of the
men that fill out the ranks are untrained conscript soldiers
and must be drilled in the manual of arms. While many of the
regiment's bravest soldiers lie in unmarked graves in Tennessee and Mississippi, many of its survivors have transferred to
other Confederate units stationed outside of Texas and continue to battle Federal forces. Curtis W. Noble of Company D
and a small group of other soldiers from the Second Texas
mysteriously escape capture at the surrender of Vicksburg
and join Company E of the Ninth Texas Regiment to fight
Sherman in Georgia.[3] Brigadier General John Moore commands a brigade in General Cheatham's Division that clashes
with Union General Hooker's troops in Tennessee at Lookout
Mountain, in what will be know as the "battle above the
clouds." [4] Other Second Texas soldiers remain on detached
duty at the Texas Hospital in Quitman, Mississippi, and at
Demopolis, Alabama.

Charles I. Evans, the regimental historian, receives a promotion to lieutenant and is transferred to H.H. Christian's battery and then to O.G. Jones's battery. While in this battery one of the guns commanded by Evans fires the last shot of the war at Palmetto Ranch near Brownsville, Texas, on May 13, 1865.[5]

The regiment is destined never to leave the state again. It is reassigned to the District of Texas, Arizona, and New Mexico under the command of General John Magruder. The regiment is first stationed at Velasco near the mouth of the Brazos River to defend against an expected Federal invasion from the Gulf, and later in January, 1864, moved to garrison Fort Caney near Cedar Lake at the mouth of the Caney River. A short time later a Federal gunboat shells Fort Caney and silences its one field piece. During the battle, a Spanish sailing vessel is driven aground near the fort, and confiscated by Confederate General Bee. The ship's consignment consists of coffee, potatoes, salt fish, calico, washbowls and pitchers, bar iron, and cases of bottles that Ralph Smith refers to as "soothing syrup." As to its effects on the men, he writes, "Meanwhile the boys had tested the various brands of soothing syrup which they found to be exhilarating in its effects. However, after continual sampling they discovered it to be overpoweringly intoxicating. In fact, by twelve o'clock at night the whole command was stretched out on the beach helplessly drunk, except [for] Major Fly, Sargeant Bill, and myself." [6]

The regiment is now under the command of Major Fly, as Colonel Smith has been serving on detached duty, first as inspector general of state troops, and then as a member of the board of examination for disabled, disqualified and incompetent officers. By August, 1864, the regiment has returned to garrison duty at Galveston, and Colonel Smith rejoins the regiment. The Second Texas is detailed to guard General Magruder's headquarters and the quartermaster and commissary stores.

Yellow fever becomes rampant throughout the city of Galveston and the garrison, and reaches epidemic stage by

September. Many of the veterans of the regiment who have survived the campaigns in Tennessee and Mississippi now fall victim to the mosquito, and die. Morale among the troops drops to a low ebb as comrades die from an unseen foe in a camp hundreds of miles away from the nearest battlefield. "This was a time," according to Ralph Smith, "that tried men's souls beyond the test of battle shouts." [7] The Confederacy reels from repeated defeats, and the men begin to sense that the end of the war is near.

Runaway inflation has driven the price of food and clothing beyond the reach of most families, and the heads of households weekly receive letters from home describing dire poverty and starvation. Some desertion takes place, but it never becomes widespread, a credit to the devotion of the men to their cause.

The garrison guarding Galveston now includes the remnants of Second, Twenty-first, Twentieth, and the Eighth Texas Regiments, the Second Texas Cavalry, Bradford's Regiment of Cavalry, the infantry of Waul's Texas Legion, and the First Texas Heavy Artillery Regiment. Lieutenant J.T. Scott, Acting Inspector General, reviews the regiments of the garrison periodically and his reports reaffirm the breakdown of morale and discipline among the troops reported by Ralph Smith and others. Lieutenant Scott's caustic reports describe an officer of one of the regiments as "utterly inefficient," and another as "absolutely worthless." On December 1, 1864, he reviews the Second Texas and reports,[8]

> The instruction of this command in company drill is deficient, and in battallion drill exceedingly so. This is to some extent owing to the fact that during the prevalence of yellow fever at this post, by which the regiment suffered severely, all drills were suspended. In the manual a greater degree of efficiency exists, although the guns are not handled with proper life and vigor. Some of the officers mess with the men, and some of the men board with families in the town at a distance from their quarters. It is stated that this cannot be avoided because of the great scarcity of cooking utensils, which to some extent is true. The clothing issued is very inferior and should not be charged as

a full issue of any particular article to the men. The blankets are of very inferior quality, and like the clothing, very deficient. The condition of arms, accoutrements, etc., cannot be excelled by any regiment of the service, The guns, especially, are kept in excellent condition, and in some companies approach a standard of perfection. While the accoutrements and equipments are in good order, they are of inferior quality and deficient in quantity. The conscripts endeavor to procure orders for detail as soon as they are assigned, and in many instances are successful. This needs attention and correction.

Reports by Lieutenant Scott on other regiments of the Galveston garrison during the same time include such statements as, "discipline lax," ". . . they have received no pay for ten or twelve months," and ". . . character of the post subject to endemic diseases."

Inadequate rations force the troops of the garrison to beg meat and bread from the citizens of Galveston. Those troops whose families reside in the city must watch with impotent anger as wives and children beg for food that cannot be purchased since no pay has been issued. The situation becomes desperate, and finally one evening a mob of soldiers and their families march on the residence of General Hawes, Commander of the defenses of Galveston, to secure provisions by force if necessary. The Second Texas is sent to aid in quelling the riot. Families are promised a share of supplies from the dwindling provisions of commissary stores, and the mob is dispersed by a volley fired over their heads from a company of the Second Texas. However, a shot is fired too low by an inexperienced soldier, and one of the troops of Waul's Texas Legion is killed.[9]

By April, 1865, with the surrender of General Lee at Appomattox, the War between the States is almost over, with the South teetering on the brink of destruction. On May 21, Colonel Ashbel Smith, now commander of the Confederate forces on Galveston Island, orders an evacuation. The troops realize that surrender is imminent and begin to collect for overdue pay that is, in some cases, two years in arrears. Wholesale looting takes place, with the seizure of arms, ammunition, and

wagons from the quartermaster and commissary stores. A disorganized band of ragged men stream off the island toward
their homes and families, and the Second Texas Infantry is no
more.

The appearance of Confederate veterans as they returned
home was well described by Lewis S. Delony[10] who wrote
about the return of his father to their Guadalupe County
home,

> I remember very well when my father returned from the
> war. I saw a bunch of men with a wagon on the road in front of
> our house. They looked to me like a bunch of wild men. They
> were bare-headed and bare-footed, and their clothes were in
> rags. My mother had been standing on the gallery every day
> looking for father. This morning she happened to be in the
> house sewing when I ran in and called her to come and look at
> the wild men. My father was walking and leading old Money,
> his war horse, and a one-legged Confederate soldier was riding
> him. Before my mother and I could get to them, they helped the
> man off and placed him in a wagon. Then my mother put her
> arms around my father and cried for joy.

7

Reminiscences

. . . Col. you cant imagine my feelings on Seeing your famil-
iar Signature. it brings a thousand thoughts Back to me
never to be forgotten. It Brings me or carries me back to the
night the yankees Run their first Gunboats by Vicksburg
when you Staid with me on out *poast* and cautioned me to
keep a *Strict look* out and you getting me to tuck your Blanket Round you when you lay down to get a little Rest. it carries me to the 22d of May 1863 when the yankees were in
our out side ditch and you fixed the fuse to the Shell whilst
I threw them over on the yanks. . . . Don't you remember it.
I do and will to my last Hour on Earth. Col. I write these
things I cant Help it. they are Sacred to me. You even feel
near to me like a father. you done all you could for the
South . . .

From a letter by H.H. Merritt to
Colonel Ashbel Smith, April 17, 1877.

This history of the Second Texas Infantry has drawn to a
close. Yet, the book fails to be complete without sharing with
the reader a brief glimpse into the lives and careers of three of
the officers of the Second Texas.

The chapter begins on a serious note with an examination of the military career of John C. Moore after his capture
at Vicksburg. Justice, long overdue, demands a public airing

of the treatment given to General Moore by his superior officers in the Confederate Army. When the facts are brought to
bear, Moore's resignation of February 3, 1864, will not appear
to be such a mystery as it has seemed to many Confederate
biographers over the years.

The soldiers of the regiment returned to their homes in an
impoverished condition after the war, only to suffer further
from the injustices of the reconstruction. The story of George
Washington Lafayette Fly's unique solution to his impoverished financial condition serves as an almost singular success
story for an otherwise bleak period of Texas history.

Finally, we shall examine the relationship that existed,
both during and after the war, between the men of the regiment and Ashbel Smith. Accounts written by Smith's contemporaries of his often unorthodox handling of military matters
give insight as to why this bookish Phi Beta Kappa graduate
of Yale came to be loved and revered by the men of his rugged
Texas regiment.

Let us begin with a biography of Brigadier General John
C. Moore, from the time of his capture at Vicksburg, to his
death.

As Moore suffered the privations of a Confederate soldier
through the war, likewise did his family, residing in the border
state of Kentucky, suffer. Major Maurice Simons gives us a
glimpse of the hardships suffered by Moore's family when he
writes in his Vicksburg diary on July 3, 1863:[1]

> On [the] last night I called on Gen. Moor I found him
> rather sad, he said that all day his thoughts were of his wife &
> children, they are in Ky she has to support her self & children
> by teaching musick, at a very low rate, he has not been able to
> send her any money for the reason that the money we have
> (Confederate) does not pass & he has not been able to procure
> any other kind. I had it in my power to loan him sixty dollars in
> gold, & I took great pleasure in doing so; he expressed so much
> grattitude, that it realy made me feel ashamed that the amount
> was so small. I thought of my own dear Lizzie & our little dar-
> ling & felt so grateful that their surroundings was so much more
> pleasent, at least they are not reminded that their Husband &

father is a "rebbell" [rebel] & I pray God that they never may be thus taunted, it is hard enough to be separated from our loved ones; but to be sensured [*sic*] on account of their conduct (& at the same time be affraid to retort) O how it must sting.

Perhaps by July 4, with the surrender of the encircled Vicksburg garrison, Moore is able to send the money to his wife. From Vicksburg, General Moore is ordered to the camp for paroled prisoners in Demopolis, Alabama, where he and thousands of other Confederate soldiers wait to be exchanged. General Moore parts ways with the Second Texas Infantry at Vicksburg, as the regiment is furloughed to Texas and he continues under orders to Demopolis with the Alabama and Mississippi regiments of his brigade. Morale is low in the camp at Demopolis as the Confederate parolees idly wait out the sultry heat of an Alabama summer, dreaming of being reunited with their families at home. Word reaches the camp on August 28, 1863, that General Hardee is being placed in command of all paroled prisoners that were captured at Vicksburg. Almost immediately, General Hardee, an enemy of Moore (see Moore's letter, Chapter 5), begins to make changes in Moore's Brigade. From Major Simons's diary entry for August 29, we read:

> Henry & I went to town after breakfast. Gen Moore came up on the cars he was very much put out on learning that the new commander Gen Hardee had split up his Brigade and especially so on hearing that his Old Redgt the 2nd Texas had been also taken away . . .

In addition to losing the Second Texas, Moore's Brigade also loses the Thirty-fifth Mississippi Regiment.[2] When this undermanned brigade is exchanged around October 1, it consists only of the Thirty-seventh, Fortieth, and Forty-second Alabama Regiments.

General Moore has apparently suspected that command of the parolees will be given to Hardee and has already initiated attempts to be transferred to another military district. As early as July 31, 1863, Major Simons writes in his diary, "Gen Moore is very anxious for me to go with him to Mobiel [*sic*]."

In Mobile, Moore is visiting General Dabney H. Maury, Commander of the Department of the Gulf, and discussing the prospects for a new military command. General Moore had served under General Maury as a plebe at West Point and in the Army of West Tennessee during the attack on Corinth. The visit bears fruit, for on September 9, General Maury sends the following communication to Richmond: "Please send me Brig. Gen. J.C. Moore. He has no real command nor important duty. His ability, skill, and experience will be most important to me at this time." [3] Richmond remains curiously silent on Maury's request for over two months, and meanwhile on October 1, Confederate troops at Demopolis are declared exchanged and are subsequently rearmed and outfitted for battle.

From his headquarters at Enterprise, Mississippi, General Hardee supervises the reorganization of the exchanged Confederate soldiers from the Divisions of Bowen, Smith and Forney. The exchanged soldiers of Stevenson's Division, made up of Alabama regiments, remain stationed at Demopolis. General Hardee has an ample supply of good arms on hand, and the troops at Enterprise are "fully supplied with most excellent new Enfield Rifles," [4] while the men of Moore's Brigade, encamped at Demopolis, do not fare quite so well. Moore reports,[5]

> My brigade was supplied with a lot of arms and accouterments that had been condemned as unfit for service and piled up in an outhouse near the railroad depot. I was assured that this was merely a temporary supply, that it would answer for drill and guard duty, and that we would be supplied with serviceable guns before being ordered to the field. These arms were of many different calibers. Most of them, however, had the essential parts — lock, stock, and barrel — but were in bad order.
> ... When we secured ammunition we found the cartridges either too large or too small for a number of the guns. When too small they could at least be inserted in the barrel and held in place by ramming leaves on top as wadding; but when a snugly fitting cartridge was inserted into a gun with a worthless lock spring the

soldier frequently discovered it had become permanently lodged in the barrel and some of those guns may remain loaded to this day.

General Moore is chaffing under the treatment that he and his men are receiving from General Hardee, and on October 21, pens this letter to General S. Cooper, Adjutant General of the Confederate Army in Richmond.[6]

General

I hope you will pardon me for addressing you this note as a private communication.

I have made efforts to be removed from my present unpleasant position. I have been placed under Lieutenant General Hardee. His former treatment of myself, of which you, perhaps remember something, renders my present position a very unhappy one to me. I believe you will appreciate my situation and will not think my present course unworthy of a soldier. Having failed to effect any change, I have been much tempted to resign, even if it brings on me the necessity of serving as a private. I would then, at least, be relieved from my present mortification.

Gen. Maury has desired much to have me ordered to report to him. If you will do this for me, General, or order me to the Dept. of Texas, I will feel ever grateful for the kindness.

I am Sir
Very Respectfully
Your Obedt Servt
John C. Moore
Brig Gen

The tension between Moore and Hardee is temporarily relieved on October 27, when General Hardee is transferred to the vicinity of Chattanooga, Tennessee, to replace General Leonidas Polk in General Braxton Bragg's Army of Tennessee.[7] Moore's relief is shortlived, however, as his brigade is ordered transferred to the Army of Tennessee, and he follows General Hardee to Chattanooga. Moore's brigade is ordered to take up positions on the eastern slope of Lookout Mountain, overlooking the Tennessee River with the Federal garrison of Chattanooga on the opposite side. General Moore would later write,[8]

We were without tents, having been ordered to leave these

in our first encampment, near the foot of the mountain. Many of
the men were but scantily supplied with blankets, as well as provisions, which consisted principally of rice and beans. During
the three weeks we occupied this position the men were frequently exposed to a cold north wind, the ground being sometimes covered with snow.

Thus Moore's Brigade receives its first assignment as an
element of the troubled Army of Tennessee. The Army is torn
with dissension among its commanders that dates back to the
battle of Chickamauga and General Bragg's failure to follow
up on his costly victory. During Moore's three-week sojourn
on Lookout Mountain, General Bragg reorganizes his army to
reduce internal strife among his staff. The newly created corps
cause considerable confusion among the staff officers as to
who commands the newly arrived troops on Lookout Mountain. Moore's brigade is finally placed under the command of
General Hardee, much to the chagrin of General Moore.
Lookout Mountain, a position of great strategic importance to
the Army of Tennessee, is very vulnerable to attack from Federal forces across the river. General Moore immediately reports the condition of his men and their inadequate issue of
arms to General Bragg, suggesting that several dangerously
exposed areas on Lookout Mountain be reinforced with defensive positions. Receiving only unfulfilled promises in return,
Moore returns to his brigade and attempts to do what he can
on his own initiative to improve defensive positions.

Under the cover of darkness, Confederate engineers begin to construct rifle pits along the perimeter of General Moore's defensive positions. Such construction efforts cannot be
continued in daylight, since the area is within easy range of
Federal artillery batteries stationed on Moccasin Point, a
mountain across the Tennessee River from Lookout Mountain. These construction efforts continue at a half-hearted
pace, and General Moore describes them as,[9] ". . . a narrow,
shallow, but worthless, line of trenches (unworthily called rifle pits) . . ." General Bragg and his staff seem to be uncon-
cerned about the grave threats to Lookout Mountain posed by

Federal troops concentrating in Chattanooga under the command of General Grant.

General Cheatham, division commander of the Confederates on Lookout Mountain, has been absent on leave for several weeks, and General J.K. Jackson, as senior brigadier general, has assumed command of the division. A plan for the defense of Lookout Mountain, the responsibility of General Hardee, has not been shown to the Confederate brigade commanders stationed on the mountain. In fact, Moore states that General Jackson, the division commander, has been seen on Lookout Mountain only once during the prior three weeks.

November 24 dawns as a cloudy day, with the upper parts of Lookout Mountain obscured. However, from the Craven house on the side of Lookout Mountain, where Moore's brigade has its headquarters, considerable Federal troop activity can be observed. Yankee troops are massing in Lookout Valley for an attack on the mountain. Moore quickly dashes off a message to Division Headquarters of what he has seen.[10] General Hooker, leading the division of Generals Geary, Cruft and Osterhaus, positions his men for an assault on the mountain. The first wave of Federal attackers strikes the pickets placed at the foot of Lookout Mountain by Generals Moore and Walthall. The pickets, a force of more than 225 men, are surprised by the rapid attack, and as their line of retreat is up the steep mountain, must surrender. Moore forms his brigade in a battle line and dispatches a message to Major J.S. Reeve at Division Headquarters:[11]

> Major: The enemy have formed line and commenced skirmishing with our pickets near the railroad-bridge crossing of Lookout Creek. Cannot yet tell their object. When shall I place my brigade in line? Walthall is now on the left with his brigade.
> > Respectfully
> > Jno. C. Moore

This message reaches headquarters at 10:05 A.M., its tone suggesting an uncertainty as to how to proceed. After the war, Moore will write that neither he nor General Walthall had ever received any instructions from Hardee's staff as to how to proceed in case of attack.

Moore and Walthall hold a quick parley and decide upon their own plan of action. General Moore dispatches a message to General Jackson, evoking the following call for reinforcements at 11:30 A.M.

> Maj. J.J. Reeve
> Assistant Adjutant General
>
> Major: General Moore, whose brigade is one of the two now at the Craven house, informs me that he has only 30 rounds of ammunition, and that his arms are very inferior. In case the attack should be made at that point, I respectfully suggest that a brigade be sent to re-enforce.
>
> I should think that any movements of the enemy could be discovered from Lookout Point very easily.
>
> I am, major, & C,
>
> John K. Jackson

Division headquarters orders Moore to occupy the rifle pits with his brigade and while moving into that position is met head-on by the remnants of Walthall's brigade rushing pell-mell to the rear. The force of Federal attackers has overrun Walthall's positions, and the men of his brigade are fleeing for their lives. Walthall's men refuse to rally on Moore's brigade and continue their flight to the rear. As they approach their objective, Moore's men find that a portion of the rifle pits have already been occupied by attacking Federal troops, who flee at the sight of a Confederate counterattack. Moore's brigade holds the rifle pits until 3:00 P.M. despite heavy Federal attacks. Two Federal color-bearers are shot down while attempting to plant their colors on the embankment of the Confederate-held rifle pits.[12] The Federal attackers finally succeed in turning the Confederate left flank, and Moore's brigade, which is dangerously low on ammunition, is forced to retreat to the rear.[13] To Moore's surprise, he encounters the brigade of General Pettus in a stationary line of battle about three hundred yards to the rear of the rifle pits. General Moore's pleas for reinforcements have been ignored. Had General Pettus been ordered to advance and reinforce Moore's left flank, the rifle pits could have been held by the Confederates.

A dense fog collects around the mountain at the elevation of the battle, and vision is diminished. Moore and Pettus hold a new line of defense despite spirited Federal attacks until 2 A.M. of November 25, when they are ordered to retreat off the mountain.

The morning of November 25 finds Moore's brigade on Missionary Ridge adjacent to Lookout Mountain, now in Federal control. Little is recorded in detail of their activities during this day, except that they are heavily engaged by Federal attackers. By dusk the Confederate Army of Tennessee, driven from their defenses around Chattanooga, is ordered to begin the retreat from Tennessee to Dalton, Georgia.

The Army of Tennessee, wrecked physically and in low morale, assembles at Dalton, Georgia, after one of the most disastrous defeats of the Civil War. Richmond removes Braxton Bragg from command and appoints William J. Hardee as his successor. From Dalton, General Moore writes his official report on December 3, 1863, on the battles around Chattanooga. In his usual forthright manner, he lets the chips fall where they may.

He points out the lack of planning and leadership of General John K. Jackson during the battles of November 24 and 25 and states that General Jackson was absent from the battlefield throughout both days of the conflict. Moore writes, "Had General Jackson been on the ground and given proper orders for the disposition of his command, I feel assured that the result would have been different." [14] Finally, Moore brings to the attention of the entire Army his plight with inadequate arms by stating, "My own command acted much better than might have been expected under the circumstances, as they fought during the engagements of the two days with arms that had been condemned as unfit for service, and which were received while at Demopolis, Alabama, to be used only for drill and guard duty."

Moore's criticism of General Jackson is aimed over Jackson's head and directed at the leadership furnished by General Hardee. General Moore has now had an opportunity to serve under General Hardee's leadership on two occasions, at Shiloh and at Lookout Mountain, both of which ended in rather disastrous circumstances. General Jackson, in his official report on the battle of Lookout Mountain, attempts to counter General Moore's criticism, but his ineffectual defenses only add a new luster of truth to the charges made by General Moore. General Hardee fails to file an official report on the battle of Lookout Mountain, as duty requires, so we know little of his plans and thoughts on the defense of Lookout Mountain. General Hardee, it may be remembered, also failed to file an official report on the Battle of Shiloh.

General Moore soon finds relief for the gloomy prospects of continued service under General Hardee. General Maury's request for Moore's services and Moore's personal letter to General Cooper on October 21 appear to bring results. Special Order Number 276, issued from the Adjutant and Inspector General's Office in Richmond on November 23, contains the following:[15]

> XXXII Brig. Gen. John C. Moore will proceed without delay to Mobile, Ala. and report to Maj. Gen. D.H. Maury, Commanding, &C, for assignment to duty.
>
> By Command of the Secretary of War:
> John Withers
> Assistant Adjutant-General

General Moore proceeds to Mobile, Alabama, for his new assignment, which is given in Special Order No. 117 from Headquarters, Department of the Gulf, December 10, 1863.[16]

> II. Brig. Gen. John C. Moore, Provisional Army, C.S., having reported at these headquarters in accordance with Special Orders No. 278, Paragraph XXXIII, dated November 23, 1863, Adjutant and Inspector General's Office, Richmond, is hereby assigned to command of eastern division, Department of the Gulf (General Clanton's Command) and that portion of the Department of the Gulf lying west of Dog River (including Hall's Mills). Commanders of troops within the above-mentioned districts will report to him without delay. He will estab-

lish his headquarters at Mobile or wherever he may deem proper.

By command of Major-General Maury.

Special Order Number 117 appears to confuse the Adjutant General's Office in Richmond, Virginia, as to the type of command General Moore is supposed to fill. After a telegram from Richmond to General Maury on December 19 requesting clarification (the telegram has evidently been lost) of General Moore's assignment, Maury telegraphs Richmond on December 20 the following: ". . . General Moore has never been applied for by me for artillery duty. I write by mail." [17] Maury's letter of December 20 states that General Moore has neither been applied for, nor assigned, as chief of artillery — but has been assigned to an important command within the Department of the Gulf. General Maury reiterates his original request for General Moore's services that he made on September 9, and comments on the long length of time required by Richmond to respond to this request.[18]

Adjutant General Cooper responds on December 23 with the following tersely written order:

Order Brigadier-General Moore to rejoin his former brigade in Lieutenant-General Hardee's command, and retain Brigadier-General Shoup for artillery.[19]

Has the Adjutant General in Richmond made an honest error, or is this new duty assignment and subsequent cancellation, a deliberate effort by General Moore's enemies to embarrass and frustrate the General? One must remember that General Moore's enemies have earlier taken steps to deny his Senate confirmation as brigadier general. It is possible that this cancellation of transfer is a ruse to embarrass General Moore.

Having been placed again in the personally distasteful position as subordinate to General Hardee, General Moore takes the only step left to a gentlemen. From General Moore, we read a letter[20] sent to Adjutant-General Cooper in Richmond:

Hdqts Moore's Brig., Cheathams Div.
Near Dalton, Ga., Jan. 15, 1864
General

I have the honor to tender my resignation of the appointments of Brig. Gen. C.S. Provisional Army. My reasons for this step were explained in a communication addressed to you on October last.

When ordered to Mobile, I hoped the difficulty in the way of my serving in the present position had been removed, but that order having been revoked by direction of the President, I see no alternative left me but resignation.

Hoping the President will appreciate my motives and accept my resignation, I have the honor to be

Very respectfully
Yr Obed't Servt
John C. Moore
Brig. Gen.

Thus it appears that President Jefferson Davis has apparently intervened directly to order the removal of General Moore from Mobile. While President Davis may have had sound reasons in making his decision, it seems quite likely that political pressure has been applied in General Moore's case.

The resignation is declined on January 28, 1864, with a terse explanation written by General Cooper, "The reasons given for this resignation are not deemed sufficient."

General Moore travels to Richmond and is granted an interview with President Davis on January 30, but can find no remedy to his present situation as Davis refuses to relent on his decision. Faced with the same bleak prospect, General Moore pens a second letter of resignation to General Cooper that next day.[21]

Richmond Va.
Jan 31st 1864
General

I tendered my resignation a short time since on which you endorsed the remark "the reasons given for this resignation are not considered sufficient."

I appreciate most fully, General, the compliment you

thus pay me in showing a desire to retain me in my present position.

I saw the President, yesterday, and he seemed disposed to sustain your decision. He spoke so kindly on the subject that while in his presence I resolved to return to my command and endeavor to submit to my unpleasant and mortifying position; but it is a matter on which my mind has dwelt so much that I feel confident that I can never discharge my duties there with satisfaction to myself or, perhaps, my command.

I therefore beg of you most earnestly to remember my case, and accept this my second tender of resignation. If accepted, I return to my former position as Captain of Arty. in the regular service, and respectfully ask that I be ordered to report to Col. Gorgas, Chf. Ord., for duty where I feel I can still be of service to our cause.

> I am, Sir,
> Very respectfully,
> Yr. Obdt. Servant
> John C. Moore
> Brig. Gen. PACS

General Moore's second letter of resignation is accepted to the regret of his brigade, and he is ordered to report to Colonel Gorgas. Moore is immediately promoted to the rank of lieutenant colonel and assigned to the command of the Savannah Arsenal in Georgia. The Savannah Arsenal includes a foundry, laboratory, magazine, warehouse, carpenter shop, blacksmith shop, gunsmith shop, and machine shop.[22] Moore continues in this capacity until September, 1864, when he is transferred to the command of the Selma Arsenal in Selma, Alabama. The Selma Arsenal is equipped with machinery for the manufacture of arms, ammunition and equipment,[23] and employs some 4,000 workers.[24] In April, 1865, Moore receives a twelve hour advance warning of a Federal cavalry raid aimed at the arsenal in Selma.[25] In great haste, ordnance stores, and the most valuable machinery are loaded onto two steamboats and shipped down the Alabama River to safety in Mobile. On the heels of General Moore's departure, Federal

General James H. Wilson's cavalry rides into Selma and burns the arsenal along with most of the town. Moore spends only a few days in Mobile, until orders are received for all Confederate forces to evacuate the city under imminent threat of capture by Federal forces. Moore tarries in the city too long, attempting to reship the Selma Arsenal machinery and is captured on April 24 by the Federals as they occupy Mobile. Moore spends the short remaining duration of the war as a paroled prisoner.

After the cessation of hostilities, John C. Moore brings his family from Kentucky to settle in Texas. Moore will continue his career in education and teaching throughout the remainder of his life. One of his first teaching assignments is a position for 1869–1870 at the Coronal Institute, a private college formed in San Marcos, Texas, in 1868. General Moore is listed as professor of mathematics and serves in this capacity at least one term. Other former Confederates listed on that faculty are Major D. Trueheart, (Stonewall Jackson's former Chief of Artillery) as professor of natural sciences, and Colonel G.H. Snyder as professor of history and literature. The Coronal Institute was founded by Orlando Newton Hollingsworth, a former member of the Third Texas Cavalry which fought dismounted as infantry in the battle of Corinth as an element of Maury's Division. Hollingsworth was wounded in the knee, probably in the attack on Battery Robinett.

General Moore served in the schools of Galveston and Kerr Counties in various capacities, and was later instrumental in opening the first public school in Mexia, Texas, in 1884. Mrs. Alma C. Harris,[26] a member of the first graduating class in 1888, wrote these fond reminiscences:

> It was September 1884 that the first Public School of Mexia opened in the fine new building on Sumpter Street with General John C. Moore as Superintendent. . . . I remember General Moore with great respect, I would almost say with reverence. He was a tall man, very erect and dignified. He had grey hair and a neatly clipped grey beard. He impressed me as a fine cultured gentleman of the old school, with a kind and courteous manner to all. That he was a man of ability is proved by

the fact that he graded and organized the school and had it running smoothly and efficiently from the first. He laid the foundation of the present school system. Those who followed builded thereon. . . . All honor to this School Board and to General John C. Moore as founders of the Mexia Public Schools.

General Moore resigns from the Mexia School System in 1887 and finishes his career in education as Superintendent of Schools in East Dallas, and in his last position as a school teacher in Coryell City, Coryell County. General John C. Moore dies on December 31, 1910, in Osage, Texas, Coryell County, at the home of his daughter, and lies beneath a simple marker beside his wife in the Osage Cemetery.

The Second person I should like to discuss is Major George Washington Lafayette Fly and his life after the Civil War. Major Fly and his family reside at Big Hill, about six miles from Gonzales, Texas, in early 1866. In Major Fly's own words:[27]

> . . . Pressed by the necessity to make a living, in January, 1886, I said to my wife, "My father left me $20,000 of property and an education. The Yankees have taken my property; they cannot take my education. I must rely upon that for a support. She asked, "What will you do?" I answered, "Teach school." She asked, "Where?" I answered, "Right here." She thought it a doubtful undertaking, but consented. This was Friday night, after we retired. The next morning I mounted my horse and, visiting my neighbors, told them I would open school the next Monday in a certain house on my land. I asked no one to send to me. Monday morning came, and I found myself a pedagogue with nineteen scholars. The next Monday I had thirty-five. At the end of five months I closed with a two-day examination and exhibition. I announced that I would open again on September 1st. I built a house of stone with two large rooms and advertised for boarders. I continued for four years, running an independent boarding school with from forty-five to seventy-five students, from ten to fifteen of whom boarded with us. Stonewall Institute, as I named it, was soon known throughout the State. I had boarders from the banks of the Brazos, from the banks of the Rio Grande, and from intermediate territory. I loved the work and am now gratified to know that those educated at Stonewall have

distinguished themselves in almost every honorable vocation of
life, especially as physicians, lawyers, and judges of various
courts one now being on the Court of Civil Appeals and another
present Justice of the Court of Criminal Appeals. The difficulty
of securing servants to assist my wife with the boarding house
caused me to abandon this work which was suited to my taste
and by which I was enabled to pay off an indebtedness of $4,000
contracted before the war.

Thus the Stonewall Institute, named for General T.J.
"Stonewall" Jackson, flourished for four years under the direction of Major Fly.[28] In 1870, Major Fly moved to Gonzales,
Texas, took up the study of law, and was admitted to practice
in 1871. From 1873 until 1875, Major Fly interrupts his practice of law to become president of Gonzales College. In 1875,
Major Fly resumes his law practice which he will continue until his death. By 1880, Major Fly writes in a letter to Ashbel
Smith, ". . . at present I am a candidate for Legislature with
fair prospects of election as I have no opponent and not much
probability of having one." [29] In the same letter, Major Fly
modestly discusses his qualifications, "While I feel my inability and lack of qualifications I have confidence to believe that
those who know me would accord to me honesty of purpose
and sincerity in what I might say and this I know has more influence than well rounded sentences or flashes of oratory."
Major Fly is elected to the 17th Legislature and serves with
distinction.

In 1886, Major Fly moves to Victoria and continues his
successful law practice. In Victoria, Major Fly is instrumental
in the organization of the William R. Scurry Camp of the
United Confederate Veterans, and is one of its charter members. Major Fly dies on January 27, 1905, and is laid to rest in
the Masonic Cemetery at Victoria.

This chapter would not be complete without some remarks about that distinguished Texan, Colonel Ashbel Smith.
Colonel Smith's life and achievements have been the subject
of many articles and books;[30] therefore, what I wish to add in
these few concluding pages will deal only with Colonel
Smith's association with the Second Texas Infantry during

and after the Civil War. The incidents in Colonel Smith's military career that I will relate are not generally found in other readily accessible sources.

Colonel Smith organizes the Bayland Guards in April, 1861, and although he had no previous military training, begins a scholarly study of the martial arts, and can soon drill the company with the expertise of a seasoned veteran. Colonel Smith's scholarly knowledge of warfare, however, is soon put to a practical test. Flavia Fleischman[31] relates the incident:

> . . While his (Smith's) company was still down on the bay in a formulative stage, one of the neighbors organized a cavalry company. The two captains had many spirited disputes as to the relative value of cavalry and infantry. Captain Smith quoted Caesar and spoke learnedly of hollow squares. The cavalry captain did not know who Caesar was or anything about him, but he did have faith in the men and horses. After arguing for some days they determined to put the matter to a practical test. The Bayland Guards were formed in a hollow square near the bayshore, while the cavalry company formed a line on the prairie and charged them. The infantry stood their ground very well until they saw that the cavalry men were in dead earnest, and then, not having guns with bayonets or anything else to repel the attack, they turned tail and fled into the bay.
>
> I don't know anything about that cavalry company or what it accomplished during the war, but I do know that if that story was true it was the only company in existence that ever made the Bayland Guards literally "take water."

By March, 1862, Captain Ashbel Smith has served proudly in the military for over a year, and feels that this experience entitles him to a larger command. As the Second Texas Infantry moves from its training grounds in Houston to the battlefields of Tennessee and Mississippi, Smith pens a hurried message.[32] Addressed from "Mississippi River near Lake Providence, March 28, 1862, Head Quarters 2d Reg T.V. on board 'Magnolia,' " the message is sent to General Hebert, Commander of the Military Department of Texas. Scrawled across the front of the letter is the apologetic postscript, "written amid the confusion of a steamboat cabin."

Dear Sir

We, that is the 2d Reg: T.I., are proceeding rapidly and without accident thus far, on our way to Pocahontas the point where we are ordered to rendesvous.

I have written today to Gov Lubbock on behalf of Capts McGinnis and Muller and myself, of the 2d Reg: T.I. asking of the Governor that in the officering of the 15 Regiments called for from Texas, the commands of three of these regiments be given to us. We have written with the full consent of our Col. J.C. Moore. We ask these commands, because modest as is our estimate of our capacity for the post, we believe that we are more competent to fill them than any men now and hitherto remaining at home, not entering the service until the fear of the draft compels them to do so. It is most clear that we, Captains N.L. McGinnis, John Muller, and Ashbel Smith, having been now nearly a year in camp, doing daily duty, and having conducted our respective companies over a long land route, must possess a knowledge of drill, a superiority in discipline and command and much experimental knowledge to which newly appointed field officers can lay no claim. We do not so much put foreward any rights of our own, as we hold that we cannot postpone the right of the State to the best service of every man, to the pretensions of county court politicians and grocery demogogues now loitering behind and bringing up the rear of the grand levee which every state of our Confederacy is now forced to make. . . .

Ashbel Smith's qualities of leadership were as individualistic as was the man himself. To many of the men in the regiment this highly educated Yale graduate, whose speech was interspersed with Latin and French phrases, appeared to be out of place and his eccentricities made him a prime target for practical jokers and imitators. One of the soldiers of the regiment would later write, "My recollection of him personally is that he was rather small of stature, was an awkward rider, and when passing along at a trot the rattle of his sword and canteen and spurs, perhaps, made such a comical noise that his men gave him the pet name of 'Old Jingle,' and that was what the 2d Texas always called him." [33] While the men of the regiment could smile at Smith's antics during a fit of temper, few ever questioned his ability to lead, and none ever questioned his personal bravery and devotion to duty. Smith gained the respect of a fellow officer from the regiment by the application of his personal theory: "There are certain State occasions when a controversy involving a man's honor can be settled only with a pair of pistols at ten paces." [34] The Reverend James M'Neilly relates the incident:

> . . . And I was told by one of the regiment of an incident that illustrated his theory. He had given an order against which one of his subordinate officers protested as foolish and refused to obey it. The Colonel kindly warned him that refusal subjected him to severe punishment. But the officer, who was a large man and a bully, became very offensive and insulting, intimating that the Colonel was simply showing his authority to humiliate the men and that only his rank protected him from assault. The Colonel's answer was to thrust his card into the hand of the officer, saying: "We settle this man to man. My friend will call on you in a few minutes." The bully knew that the Colonel was counted a dead shot, and he tendered an ample apology and afterwards always obeyed orders.[35]

Colonel Smith's lifelong love of books and learning was pursued, even throughout the harrowing circumstances of the campaign in Mississippi. From the muddy rifle-pits at Fort Pemberton shortly after the battle for control of the Talla-hatchie River, the bachelor colonel writes a young lady friend:[36]

> . . . The planters on the river have removed their families black and white to the hills and have dismantled their houses of furniture: and books as well as agreeable people are as scarce as their silver plate. You know that a soldier can scarcely take with him his personal baggage — luggage for a traveller baggage for a soldier — much less can he be encumbered with books — except two which I never leave behind me. It was therefore quite a *treasure trove* to stumble on "Horace" the other day in Latin, "Horace whom as a boy I hated so" as Byron wrote. When a boy I read Horace as a task and have scarcely looked at him since till now. Reading Latin with almost as much ease as English, I confess to being profoundly moved with the bounding songs of this old Roman. There is however an underlying sad-

ness in his most exhilarating strains which show that his soul belied the mirth of his intellect — but such things are not for you. . . .

James A. Stevens of the regiment remembers Colonel Smith's ability to become engrossed in reading during distressing circumstances,[37] ". . . During the man y weeks' siege (Vicksburg) Colonel Smith was often seen sitting in the trenches or at his tent or dugout door calmly reading a copy of one of his favorite classics — 'Vergil,' I believe it was — while the shells would be bursting overhead or in the rear, so passionately devoted was this singular character to literature and so accustomed do men become to the dangers of war. Colonel Smith was too brave a man to affect this unconcern."

As the regiment showed devotion to their leader, Colonel Smith reciprocated the trust placed in him by his men and always did what he could to ease their sufferings. Among an army of expert foragers in Mississippi, the Second Texas had won the laurels for being able to "locate" foodstuffs and provisions when other regiments returned empty-handed. Among the camps in Mississippi, the frequent cry, "Look to your camp kettles men; the 2d Texas is coming!"[38] often heralded the approach of the Texans. Many a hog was shot in "self-defense," while trying to attack one of the regiment, and its carcass partitioned for the mess.

Operating along the coast of Texas by 1864, the regiment was used to guard the rich agricultural area along the Brazos River from Federal attack. It was on one of these defensive expeditions that the half-starved men of the regiment, eager to gain parity for their complaining stomachs, plied their expert foraging skills on a large potato patch. The punishment for theft of civilian property by a soldier could be severe, but Colonel Smith masterminded a clever defense to protect his starving regiment from prosecution.[39]

City of Houston

April 9, 1864
Brig: General Slaughter
Chief of Staff

General,

Further reflection of the letter addressed by the overseer Harris to the Major Gen. Comdg., charging the troops under my command with taking potatoes at the plantation of W. Ewing, has induced me to make a more full communication than I could do in the indorsement on the letter in question referred to me.

. . . In order to obey *fully* the order to move my command to the Mouth of Caney, I reached the Bernard River, Churchill's Ferry in the night, where there was no water, that of the Bernard being salt. The next morning, crossing the men before the train, I moved the men to the *first* water, Cedar Lake, Ewing's plantation, and there halted them till the coming up of my wagon train.

Seeing many of my men eating raw potatoes I inquired where they got them and was answered that they bought them of the negroes. Seeing numbers of negroes passing to and fro, and other men there not of my command eating potatoes, it attracted no further attention from me, knowing that on plantations belonging to kind masters the negroes are allowed to have their own potato patches, and generally their own poultry.

At the moment when the head of my wagon train was coming up and before the arrival of the whole train, I was told by the overseer that my men were taking potatoes out of the potato banks. I ordered the assembly to be sounded immediately, and in *five* minutes, every man was in the ranks.

I then informed the overseer that the potatoes would be paid for on the account being presented. I now state that no account nor demand for payment has ever been presented to me, nor to my knowledge to any other person in any form whatever. The overseer stated to me once in the road when leaving the plantation, verbally, that 150 bushels had been destroyed. I told him politely to present his account. I heard no more of or from him till the letter sent to the Major Gen. Comdg.

As for the quantity of 150 bushels, it is simply absurd: — 600 pecks — it is nearly a *peck* to *every* man, suffering *every* man to have had a share. The head of the wagon train arriving only as the assembly sounded, it was scarcely possible to put potatoes in the wagons without my knowledge.

My present belief is, considering the officers of known probity whom I saw eating potatoes, and the numerous negroes passing about, that most of the potatoes actually taken were bought of the negroes. But for the certain ascertainment of the facts, I must wait for [unreadable] from men in my command. From the deliberate falsehoods stated in the overseers letter, his word does not weigh a feather with me. Indeed his letter appears to me to be a trick to cover up his malfeasance from the scrutiny of his master.

> I have the honor to be
> General
> very respectfully
> Your ob: serv:
> Ashbel Smith
> Col 2d Texas Infantry

Of the remarks made thus far about the Civil War experiences of Ashbel Smith, none better summarizes his military career or his qualities for leadership in a better fashion than the following letter from an old regimental comrade-in-arms:[40]

> Sour Lake, Jeff. Co. Apr. 17, 1877

Col Ashbel Smith
    Austin.

My Dear Old Col.

    I have just received the paper you sent me and have just read your speech on Gen. Rusk's portrait. Col. you can't imagine my feelings on seeing your familiar signature. it brings a thousand thoughts back to me never to be forgotten. It brings me or carries me back to the night the Yankees run their first gunboats by Vicksburg when you staid with me on out poast and cautioned me to keep a strict look out and your getting me to tuck your blanket round you when you lay down to get a little rest. it carries me to the 22d of May 1863, when the Yankees were in our out side ditch and you fixed the fuse to the Shell whilst I threw them over and on the Yanks. It carries me on through that long and bloody day — when you stood out on the hill and encouraged the Missourians and Arkansas troops on to our assistance. I can see you now. There you stand in full view of the assaulting columns. I can hear your voice come on my brave Missourians. Come and help my boys. I can see the shot and shell tare the ground at your feet. I can see the bullets pierce your clothes. I can hear the shouts of our supporters as they come up the hill, the charge in the road and the yanks going fleeing down the slope. Col, all these scenes are before me now. Even back to Shiloh when you were in front of our camp, shouting them on when we were charging that battery on the hill, where you were wounded and Sgt. Finney fell. And further on through the fall back to Corrinth. through the mud and the rain. the little logg house you were in when we boys went to see you whilst you were suffering with your wound. the hunger and thirst of that march I never shall forget. Up comes Fort Pemberton before me where I went to you to get permission to go up the river with the scouting party the advance of the enemy, the fight with the Cavalry at the corn crib. You met us at the river with reinforcements. Back to Vicksburg the surrender. Back to Texas down the gulf, Old Caney, Mud Island, and last Galveston. When you asked me to stay with you to the last. our last meal together at the Planters House. Escorting you to the steamer to take you to the blockade. Our last parting on the bow of the steamer, the last press of your hand. Dont you remember it. I do and will to my last hour on earth.

Col. I write these things I cant help it. they are sacred to me. You even feel near to me like a father. you done all you could for the South you done well, better than thousands of others. You have done well for Texas you are still doing well for Her. The people on [of] the Democratic party seems to forget what you have done for her. Why did not [they] nominate you for Gov. instead of Judge Robberts who is Judge Robberts. I never heard of him during the war. Have we old Rebs got to be ruled by his sort if so I shall stay away from the poles [polls]. I was glad when I saw your name announced for the Legislature. but say that every true Texian and old Rebel had rather have you for Gov, Col. I am glad the people have found in you a true statesman. I know you are of the truest. W.W. Merritt, my kindred friend, says to me in his letter, I like the old Col he is such a square old Reb. . . .

H.H. Merritt, Co I, 2d T.V.I.

Colonel Smith retires to his plantation, Evergreen, at the close of the war, vowing to, "abstain from all public life henceforth, not even voting." [41] His retirement is short-lived, however, and at the urgings of friends and neighbors, runs for and is elected to the State Legislature. This lighthearted biography of Colonel Smith appears in *The Southern Intelligencer* of October 25, 1866:

Col. *Ashbel Smith*

Was born in Hartford, Connecticut and is descended from the first settlers of America, the Seymours of New York and the Adams of Massachusetts. He was raised in North Carolina, and educated in New Haven and Paris. . . . Although offered by the Great Chief of the Comanches, Mukewarrah, his beautiful daughter, in marriage, but the colonel respectfully declined the distinguished alliance and has lived thus far, the life of a bachelor. We have not been able to learn the colonel's age, either from himself or others, he from very particular reasons being very reticent on that item; but from the most reliable information which we have been able to obtain, we are of opinion that the Colonel was born in the year 1775, old style, and is now about ninety-one years old, yet he is in appearance much younger. However, as to his age, we speak not from the card, nor have we any authentic information on that point, and would not injure his matrimonial prospects, if he has any, for the world.

He is still in the enjoyment of vigorous health, has a splendid constitution, and were he married to a buxom daughter of old mother Eve, might become the father of Smiths no less distinguished than celebrated John who jilted Pocahontas, the famous Georgia Smith, who followed the fortunes of Prince Eugene, and gallantly won the quarterings of his shield (three Turk's heads) before the walls of Belgrade, or the political economist Adam, or the renowned Sir Sidney who crossed the destiny of the great Napoleon before the memorable battlements of Acre.

Ashbel Smith's last great public efforts were dedicated to the advancement of education in Texas. Smith served as president of the board of trustees of Texas Medical College, and served as a Commissioner to locate the site on which the present Prairie View University now stands. Smith was instrumental in establishing The University of Texas, and served as the first chairman of its board of regents. With his characteristic energy and purpose he strove to recruit a first class faculty for the University, making several trips throughout the country to locate the best qualified professors.

Ashbel Smith's public duties continue to absorb his thoughts, and he writes less frequently in the late years about his old regiment, which he once described as "the bully regiment of this army." [42] However, in 1880 a small controversy is stirred up with an article written by "Sioux," an old soldier of the regiment. "A Tribute to the Memory of the Late Col. T.M. Jack," appearing in the *Galveston Daily News* of August 29, 1880, states that Ashbel Smith was promoted over William P. Rogers to the rank of colonel after the battle of Shiloh. The response to this error is printed in the August 31 issue of the same paper by J.H. Rogers (Colonel Rogers's son, Halbert, who was wounded at Corinth) who writes a bristling reply:

> W.P. Rogers was never major of the regiment, nor was Capt. Ashbel Smith ever promoted over him. . . . Having been a member of the regiment, Sioux ought to know better. I hope a treacherous memory is alone responsible for the mistake. He should be careful how he relies upon memory in giving historical facts.

In a letter written to the Galveston paper on September 12, 1880, Colonel Smith writes a modest disclaimer to correct the error and soothe frayed tempers. In the last portion of this letter, he writes this memorial to his old command:

> . . . It was the first regiment organized in Texas for permanent service, and for the war. Its first action was in the battle of Shiloh, it held one of the two most advanced positions of the lines in the siege of Vicksburg, and a special objective point of attack. It was with the last of all Confederate soldiers to be disbanded after the surrenders of Lee, Jos. Johnson, Richard Taylor, and Kirby Smith. It is not the place here to enumerate the many hard fought battles in which it bore a conspicuous part. The regiment knew no repose from severe duty throughout the long, dreary years of the Civil War. Yet, so far as I know, it has never had even an occasional newspaper correspondent to tell its deeds. It has never had one of those thrilling reunions properly got up by surviving members of other commands when privations are recounted, battles fought over again, and reminiscences of the past hallow the memory of the dead and warm and strengthen the friendships of the living. The drill and discipline

of this regiment, inaugurated under the personal supervision of Col. John C. Moore and the tactical instruction of Maj DeBray, now Gen. DeBray, were most thorough, and their stay and steadiness in battle would all have done credit to the best veteran warriors of any army. And the Second Texas maintained unimpaired these eminent characteristics of a true soldier to the last hour of the Confederacy. When service demanding great trust and steady valor was to be done, the Second Texas was sure to be assigned to it. I could cite numerous conspicuous instances of this fact, but I must stop. My only object in extending these remarks has been to do an act of grateful justice to a most gallant regiment, whose praises have not been sung over much, and to one of the gallant commanders, Col Wm. P. Rogers . . .

In less than six years from this date, the Second Texas will lose its last great commander — Colonel Ashbel Smith will cross the river on January 21, 1886, to rejoin his many comrades that he left behind in Mississippi and Tennessee.

APPENDIX

Personnel of the Second Texas Infantry

The muster roll that appears in this appendix was developed from three sources. The first source, regimental returns from the date of February 28 to April 31, 1862, were supplied on microfilm by the National Archives. These are the earliest dates for which a complete muster roll could be obtained and was chosen for transcription into this appendix because it identified those men who volunteered for service in the regiment. Later, new personnel in the regiment will be conscripts, placed there by the Conscription Act.

The second source of information, a set of ten rolls of microfilm, contained the compiled service records of the men of the regiment as developed by the National Archives.

Mr. Albert Blaha of Houston, Texas, kindly loaned the author his personal set of microfilm to complete this study. From this source additional names were added to the list, and much of the casualty information was obtained.

Finally, casualty reports from the *Tri-Weekly Telegraph*, Houston, Texas, published during the war, were used.

The reader should observe that the poor handwriting, often in faded ink, and the outright bad spelling that appears on these handwritten documents may have resulted in errors on this roll. Names could have either been misspelled, or in some cases, entirely omitted from the rolls. The author herewith apologizes for any mistakes that appear.

The symbols appearing beside some names are as follows:

k — killed, w — wounded, m — missing,

c — captured, S — battle of Shiloh,

C — battle of Corinth, V — siege of Vicksburg.

The large number of casualties suffered by the regiment mutely testify to the hardships of the war fought in Tennessee and Mississippi; but they also speak of the courage, discipline, and devotion to duty that was exhibited by these men who followed the Lone Star banner of the Second Texas Infantry.

COMPANY A

The San Jacinto Guards, from Harris County, raised by Major Hal G. Runnels.

Personnel

Captain Wm. A. Christian
1st Lieut. John B. Tucker
2nd Lieut. Joe Smith
D. Gallaher cS, Camp Chase,
    Ohio
B. Henry kV
1st Sgt. John Gillespie wS
Joe M. Wright POW
2nd Sgt. J.C. Murphy
3rd Sgt. Joe Herman wS, wC,
    died Quitman, Miss., Nov. 5,
    '62
4th Sgt. J.R. O'Neal died
    Corinth, Miss., June 2, '62
1st Corp. L.S. Ward
2nd Corp. John Ransom
3rd Corp. Thos. Church
Drummer Edward Folk wV

Privates

T.J. Bartlett
Robt. Basby
Chas. Bond
Barney Budder mS
John A. Budder wS
D. Callahan cC, wV
James Carter wS
John Cassady
James Cates
Wm. Clark captured Natches,
    Miss., died Camp Morton,
    Ind., Jan. 16, '64
Wm. R. Cravey wV
John Cronan
Samuel Darney died in hospital
    Nov. 5, '62
N.M. Davis mC
James Dougherty mC
J. R. DeCordova
Wm. R. Desan
T. J. Ewell
Patrick Gambrick kS
John Goldie
H. O. Graves
James M. Hall died in Miss., Nov.
    5, '62
Richard S. Henry kV, died at the
    rank of Lieut.
S. Hid
James Holland

J. H. Hughes
M. Hyde
Wm. Jones wS
Nicholas Kost cS, Camp Douglas,
    Ill.
Thos. J. Long wS, died Third St.
    Hospital, Cincinnati, Ohio,
    June 7, '62
David Lynch wS, wC
D. Mahaney
Pickney Martin cS, Camp
    Douglas, Ill.
John Massy
Wm. A. Matthews wV
Frank J. Melcher mC
F. J. Milaker
Lewis Miller
John Miner kS
J. Montgomery
J. W. Moore
Newell Morse wV
John Muir died in Miss., April 24,
    '62
Frank McCan mS
M. McCormick mS
W. McCreary wV
J. R. O'Neill died in Miss., June
    2, '62
Chas. Parthary
Peter Phelps wS
Martin Polinski cS, Camp
    Douglas, Ill.
John Rap
Joseph Richey
R. W. Roache
Levi Sala
Frank Schwaller
D.W. Smith
E.A. Taylor wV
J.E. Teal
John M. Teal died Okolona,
    Mississippi
Harrison Tims
Robt. Watson
S.M. Webb died in hospital,
    Vicksburg, Miss., Jan. 28, '63
Davis White died Okolona, Miss.,
    May 12, '62
John White dC

Oliver White kS
Wm. Wilson
J.M. Wright mS

COMPANY B

The Confederate Guards, from Houston and Harris County, raised by Maj. William C. Timmons.

Personnel

Captain Wm. C. Timmons wC, wounded Chickasaw Bayou, Miss., died Vicksburg, Miss., Jan., '63
1st Lieut. James W. Mangum
2nd Lieut. James D. McClery
2nd Lieut. Andrew S. Muir
1st Sgt. Ambrose J. Hurley
2nd Sgt. James B. Cates
3rd Sgt. Osmond J. Conklin
4th Sgt. Samuel W. Allen
5th Sgt. Wm. H. Tison
—— Loett wC
1st Corp. Wm. G. Wood mC
2nd Corp. Thos. H. Brooks wC, kV
3rd Corp. Phillip Heubner wV
4th Corp. Henry D. Domellan
Drummer Phillip Angus wV

Privates

Nicholas Albars
John Ames mS
Almeron Ammerman
A. Anson wV
McGilbray Barrow
James T. Bell
John F. Bertchiger
Henry Betner
Henry Black
Adolphus P. Blanton
John Bougot
Thos. P. Bryan
Matthew Callahan POW
Nicholas Castillo wV
Wm. Cheeney mS
Wm. Christian
George A. Christie
Horace J. Church wV
John Clark wS
Wm. H. Clark

J. Cogkin mS, died City Gen. Hosp., St. Louis, Missouri
Matthew D. Conklin
John Conway kS
Timothy Crim
Alexander Cunningham
C. S. Daly wV
Nelson T. Davis
Michael Doogan, cS, Camp Douglass, Ill.
Charles S. Doty captured Davis Bridge, wV, wounded at Caney Creek, Texas, Feb. 6, '64
Henry Drier cC
James Duncan
James Farney kS
Sterling Fisher wV
Chas. Finkleman
E. A. Flower died Aug. 6, '63, Vicksburg, Miss.
Wm. Foster wS, mC
Fredrick Gehrman
Milton Gilreath
Joseph Glaspiel
John R. Glass
James C. Hart wV
Geo. Haslip died Houston, Tex., Feb. 11, '62
William Hasting
Henry Hartman
Geo. J. Hazlett kS
Daniel Heubner wV
Robt. Hoffman
James B. Hogan
Wm. E. Jones wS
Wm. W. Jones wS
John Jones mS
Theodore Keller wounded Caney Creek, Tex., Feb. 19, '64

S. Kilion wV
John Kirk
Louis Klein
James Lambert
Joseph Leduc
Thomas Lillie died Enterprise,
    Miss., June 18, '62
Wm. A. Little
Joseph Made died Enterprise,
    Miss., June 20, '62.
William Maxwell kS
Wm J. Meeks
Anthony Merkel
Henry Meyer
Joseph Michels
Henry L. Miller
John Miller died at Vicksburg,
    Miss., Aug. 6, '63
——— Morrison kV
Michael McCarty kV
Matthew M. McClain wC
Jas. A. McCorkle captured 6 rifles
    at Shiloh
George A. Newell kV
Geo. W. Northrup wS
Malcom Patterson kS
Thos. A. Pather

A. T. Paull kS
Chas. Perry
Fredrick Reineman died
    Columbus, Miss., July 1, '62
Anthony Reiter
Peter Rhean
Henry P. Roberts wV
William Rothman POW
Charles Schott
Addison B. Seale mC
Alexander Senneschal mC
Franklin Shaw
E. Simmons wV
Daniel C. Smith
Wm. T. Spence wC, kV
Edward A. Sprague POW
Wm. E. Stokes
Wm. H. Tison died Aberdeen,
    Miss., Aug. 2, '62
Arthur Tolsen
Ernst Trinks
Jas. A. Wharf POW
James H. Wherry
John J. White
Otis E. Williams
Edward H. Wilson
Chas. L. Worg
William T. Wright

COMPANY C

The Bayland Guards, from east Harris and west Chambers
Counties, raised by Dr. Ashbel Smith.

Personnel

Captain Ashbel Smith wS
1st Lieut. J. R. Harrell
2nd Lieut. P. M. Woodall wC
R. I. Haden
J. D. McFarland
S. S. Ashe kS
3rd Lieut. M. A. Lea
1st Sgt. T. S. Reeves
2nd Sgt. E. M. Wasson
3rd Sgt. W. S. Alger kV
4th Sgt. C. M. Owen
R. D. Baden
J. W. Barnes
Wm. Alleyn kV
M. Olgiers kV
W. H. Bryan kC

1st Corp. Henry Love
3rd Corp. C. L. Wasson
Jim Hagerman
Lance Corp. J. N. Blasgrave
John Alfson
T. Anderson wV

Privates

Wm. Alger wV, died Enterprise
    Miss., Sept. 18, '63
Thos. Armstrong wV
Alex Autry kV
J. S. Bagwell kV
Moseley Baker
O. R. Baker
Amos Barron
Hiram Bartlett cS, died Camp

Douglas, Ill., May 6, '62
James Beatty wS
C. H. Belich kS
R. C. Bellamy wS
George Blackman wS, died Camp
  Douglas, Ill., June 7, '62.
G. L. Blasgrave wS
E. Blasgrave, missing, battle of
  Iuka
Jefferson Boyd kV
Charles Brooks, died Houston,
  Texas
J. Brooks
G. H. Brown
S. S. Brown
M. Carmoody
P. Casey
Barton Clark
Alex Coy
Daniel Duncan
James Dutton wS
L. J. Ellidge
Wm. Epperson
John P. Evans wS, wV
W. W. Evans
G. W. Ferrand
W. J. Field, died of diseases,
  Vicksburg, Miss., Dec. '63
A. Fisher
Sol Fisher
F. M. Fitzgerald
G. Freeman kV
W. H. Goodrich mC
Wm. Grant mV
S. A. Haddon
N. G. Haddon wS, died
  University, Mississippi
C. E. Hammatt wS, POW, U.S.
  Gen. Hospital, Keokuk, Iowa
L. J. Harper
R. L. Harris
Ed Hartman
Wm. Heffermann mS
Geo. Henshaw wS, POW
J. W. Herbert, captured May 21,
  '62, at Yazoo City, Miss.,
  Hospital
John Holby mS
John Holtz wS, captured, Camp

Douglas, Ill., wV
R. H. Horton mV
Sam Houston, Jr. wS, Camp
  Douglas, Ill.
C. E. Jones wS, died May 9, '62,
  Camp Dennison Gen.
  Hospital, Ohio.
S. E. Jones
N. T. Judd wV
T. H. Kendall, died Grenada,
  Miss., July 1, '62
Sol Lawrence
Benj. F. Lawson wC
A.J. Love wS
S.B. Malone cS, Camp Douglas,
  Ill., kV
A.J. Martin
Daniel Matthews, died Columbus,
  Miss., Dec. '63
Wm. Matthews, wV
J.P. Meeks, died Camp Churchill
  Clark, Miss., May 23, '62
Chas. Miers, missing around
  Corinth, Miss., May 29, '62
Aaron Morrell
J.M. Newsome, died Oct. 30, '64,
  Houston, Tex., yellow fever.
Henry Onge mS
Isham Palmer
H. Parnell
C.L. Pevesly
G.W. Pounds
P.L. Reaves
J. Reeder
James A. Rhea cS, died while a
  POW
Henry Roffey, died Houston,
  Tex., March, '62
Otis Ruah
T.M. Rundell, died Houston,
  Tex., Dec. 1, '63
Albert Smith
M. B. Smith
Wm. Stevens cS, Camp Douglas,
  Ill.
J. A. Steward wV
Wm. Stolls
J. W. Tarver wV
W. A. Terrell

A. J. Thomas, died Corinth
  Hospital, May 23, '62
J. P. Thomas, died Corinth
  Hospital, May 23, '62
Rufus Thomas, wS, died Corinth
  Hospital, May 14, '62
G. W. Timmons
Richard V. Tompkins wS
J. B. Vanhouten
A. G. Voortman
E. P. Wasson wS, died in Corinth
  Hospital, April 17, '62
John Waters, captured May 31,
  '62, near Corinth Miss.,
  Camp Chase, Ohio
F. A. Westerlage mS
Wm. White mS, died Gratiot St.
  Prison, St. Louis, Mo.
James Wilburn, died Vicksburg,
  Miss., Dec., '63
Sol Williams
A. K. Woodall kS
N. K. Woodall, died Houston,
  Tex., March '62
D. Wright wV

COMPANY D

The Confederate Grays, from Harris County, raised by Edward
F. Williams.

Personnel

Captain Edward F. Williams mS
Lieut. Andrew F.Gammell kV,
  while at rank of Captain
Edmond F.Daly wC, while at
  rank of Captain, died Iuka,
  Miss. Jan. 18, '63
Jas. E. Foster
Sgt. John B. Coates
John W. Bergin
Henry Reily
Henry Freeman
Michael Flick, captured near
  Vicksburg, Miss., May 20,
  '63, Fort Delaware, Del.
J. M. Bell wV
Corp. Andrew Ritchie kV
Chas. Bond
John Banks
Drummer Harry C.Downs

Privates

J. F. Bailey cV, died New
  Orleans, La., July 27, '63
Wm. P. Bergin kC
John Billingslea kS
James Blackey kS
Wentzel Blossom
J.S. Brade wV
Geo. K. Brashier, died Gen.
  Hosp.,May 26, '62
James Brockley kS

Chas. Broddick kV
Richard Brooks
Graves T. Brookshire
William Brown
Chas. Calhoun
Chas. A. Callais cC
Patrick H. Carlin wV
Lawrence T. Carpenter cS, Camp
  Douglas, Ill.
William H. Craddock kS
Michael Crane
Geo. T. Crook cS, Camp Douglas,
  Ill.
J. W. Crowley wV, captured May
  17, '63, died U.S. Military
  Hosp., June 1, '63
Geo. W. Davis cV, May 19, '63,
  Fort Delaware, Del.
James H. Davis
Daniel Delaney
T. Despauch wV
Ambers W. Downs kV
Geo. S. Downs kV
Perry Driscol
John Duclant died Galveston,
  Tex., Nov. 5, '61
John J. Duncan died in hospital,
  May 8, '62
Charles T. Favors
John A. Ford wS, kV
J. E. Foster wC

Louis Frieling

Samuel A. Garner

William George captured near Vicksburg, Miss., May 20, '63, Fort Delaware, Del.

Daniel Gorman captured Champion Hill, Miss., May 19, '63. Fort Delaware, Del., escaped!

John M. Gray

J. M. Hall died Grenada, Miss.

Edward H. Harriman

F. L. Hazelett died Camp Timmons, Miss., Feb. 1, '62

Alonson Hewitt, died Gen. Hosp., May, '62

John Hockley kV

J. J. Jones wS, recovered 5 Yankee rifles at battle of Shiloh

Wm. B. Jones captured Water Valley, Miss., Dec. 31, '62, died Feb. 1, '63, Alton Military Prison, Alton, Ohio.

John Jordon

John Kelley

Henry Kennerly wV

Thomas Keongh

Henry Knocha kV

Frank Lindley

Joseph Little mS

E. Joseph Marshall wV

Bernard Morrisey

Patrick Mullins

John McGrew died Oct. 20, '62.

G. W. Nash died Grenada, Miss.

Curtis W. Noble

Otto Page died Nov. 8, '61, Galveston, Tex.

Peter Paska died in the Gen. Hosp., May 5, '62

Wm. Pennyfeather captured Oxford, Miss., Dec. 2, '62, Alton Military Prison, Ohio

John Plunket

Francis E. Ravona

Parry E. Robinson

James A. Rickey kV

H. Chas. Selinger wV

Geo. Slaughter died Vicksburg, Miss., Jan. 20, '63

John Smith wS, captured Edwards Depot, Miss., May 16, '63, died Camp Morton, Ohio, Aug. 29, '63

Wm. Smith kS

Henry Somerville mC

Larkin B. Sweeney wV

Wm. Veasey kS

Silas M. Ward kS

William Weary kS

Antone Webber wC, died Iuka, Miss., Oct. 20, '63

James Welch kC

COMPANY E

Raised in Robertson and Brazos Counties by Dr. Belvidere Brooks.

Personnel

Captain Belvidere Brooks kS

1st Lieut. John H. Feeney kS

2nd Lieut. George W. L. Green dC

3rd Lieut. John L. Arnett died Camp Priceville, Miss., Sept 4, '62

1st Sgt. David J. Sloan died Guntown, Miss., June 1, '62

2nd Sgt. William Holder

3rd Sgt. John D.S. Gillis captured near Nashville, Tenn., Dec.

16, '64, Fort Delaware, Del.

4th Sgt. John L. Killough

5th Sgt. John Lloyd

1st Corp. Alexander Frazier

2nd Corp. John L. Yardley

3rd Corp. Wm. E. Gay died Okolona, Miss., May 11, '62

4th Corp. James C. Lawrence

Drummer Francis S. Manning

Privates

Simon Aanonson wV

William Allen
J. Posey Anderson died Holly
Springs, Miss., June 1, '62
John M. Bondurant wS, died May
15, '62
Robert Brazile died Okolona,
Miss., May 18, '62
Silas Brown mC POW
William Brown
Eldridge C. Buford died in Miss.
John Burnley died Okolona,
Miss., May 5, '62
Henry C. Burnley
L. Francis Burrows
William Byport wV
Davis W. Castle
Silas O. Cobb died Grenada,
Miss., May 15, '62
John P. Coleman died Grenada,
Miss., May 22, '62
W. Francis Coleman died Camp
Rogers, Miss., Nov. 9, '62
John Copeland died Camp
Church Hill, Miss., May 24,
'62
Isaac Copeland died in hosp.,
Columbus, Miss., July 17, '62
Andrew J. Copeland wC
Thomas B. Collins wC
John Crane wV
John Cummins captured at Fort
Pemberton, Miss.
W. Cunningham captured July 4,
'63, Vicksburg, Miss., died
Camp Morton, Ind., Aug 15,
'64.
John G. Duncan wV
Richard A. Eaton cS, Camp
Douglas, Ill., wV
Thos. F. Farmer died Enterprise,
Miss., June 20, '62
Chas. Frazier capturd Vicksburg,
Miss., May 22, '63, Fort
Delaware, Del.
Louis W. Ferguson wV
Fielding Galloway
Osburn P. Garrett died in
hospital, May 16, '62
John A. Georgon

William Gustavus cC, died Oct.
21, '64, Galveston, Tex.,
yellow fever.
James M. Hardin died Oxford,
Miss., June 12, '62
William C. Hardin died Okolona,
Miss., May 8, '62
Joseph A. Hawkins
E. Francis Hubbell died on march
from Corinth June 7, '62
Thos. H. Hudspeth wV
Wm. Jetton died Okolona,
Miss.,May 9, '62
Charles Kellogg
Martin Kiefer died Columbus,
Miss., July 8, '62
John Killough wS, died Gen.
Hosp., Meridian, Miss., June
10, '62
Jacob W. Lamb died Columbus,
Miss., May 17, '62
Oliver Leferre
Curatius M. Lefevre died Canton,
Miss., June 18, '62
Thomas C. Lefond
John Lindsey wV
Henry B. Lloyd
Thos. J. Lynd died Okolona,
Miss., May 10, '62.
Samuel B. Maffett wS
Henry B. Manius wS
Joseph Marshall
William McCheney kV
Henry S. McClendon mC
John L. McDonald
William McHenry kV
John A. McMurry died Guntown,
Miss., June 5, '62
Wiley B. Moon
Rufus B. Moore died near
Columbus, Miss., Feb. 13,
'63
Martin V. Moore
Patrick Murphy mC
Geo. W. Nash died Grenada,
Miss., June 3, '62
Roland F. Nash
David Crockett Nevill died
Okolona, Miss., May 18, '62

Thos. J. O'Hanrahan wS
Leonidas H. Parrish
Coursey Penves died Gen. Hosp.,
    Houston, Tex., Jan. 6, '63
Jacob N. Pruett died Ripley,
    Miss., Oct. 28, '62
James J. Pruett wC
John R. Pruett
James M. Reed died Grenada,
    Miss., May 29, '63
Richard C. Reed died Guntown,
    Miss., June 4, '62
Elisha P. Rice died Guntown,
    Miss., June 1, '62
Benj. Sample wS, captured, died
    Post Hosp., Camp Dennison,
    Ohio, Apr. 21, '62
Drury R. M. Sample
William Sample kS
Thos L. Saxon wS, captured,
    Alton Military Prison, Ill.
Joseph Scott wS
Darwin G. Seeley wS, captured,
    died Gen. Hosp., Camp
    Dennison, Ohio, Apr. 21, '62
Geo. B. Singleton kS
Wm. C. Sparks

Stanford Strambler died Camp
    Maury, Miss., Feb. 26, '63
John Suit
Wm. R. Syprett wV
Peyton Taylor
Patrick Tamney
Elijah W. Thompson
Eugene Vasbinder, wS, captured,
    died City Gen. Hosp., St.
    Louis, Mo., July 6, '62
J. Wm. Vaughan, died Camp
    Priceville, Miss., July 8, '62
John Walters wV
James N. Ware died Columbus,
    Miss., June 10, '62
Wm. C. Ware died Columbus,
    Miss., Aug. 8, '62
Jeremiah V. Warren died Camp
    Priceville, Miss., June 15, '62
Benj. F. Watson
Wm. A. Watson
William H. Wheelock
Wm. F. Wise died in hosp., July,
    '62.
John L. Yardley died Enterprise,
    Miss., June 16, '62

COMPANY F

Raised in Galveston, Texas, by Captain John Muller.

Personnel

Captain John Muller kC
1st Lieut. J. S. McMahon died
    Dec. 7, '62, Jackson, Miss., at
    rank of Captain.
2nd Lieut. Gustave Prellwitz
3rd Lieut. A. K. Leigh
James Foster wC
Joseph Bruecher wV
1st Sgt. Joseph J. Salberg kC
2nd Sgt. Wm. Rollfing died
    Columbus, Miss., Aug. 17,
    '62
3rd Sgt. D. Soete wC, died Nov.
    27, '62
4th Sgt. Adolph Stroube
5th Sgt. Hermann Marten
Frederick Dieterick wV
1st Corp. B.S. Lott

2nd Corp. Wm. Halley
3rd Corp. Joseph B. Brueher wV
4th Corp. J.H. Berlocker wS, wC,
    captured, died in prison.
Leopold Rauschenberg kV
Frederick Adler wS, captured,
    died City Gen. Hosp., St.
    Louis, Mo., May 19, '62

Privates

Wm. Altenbrun wS
John Baumgartner
August Beckmann wS, captured,
    Camp Dennison, Ohio
Wm. Beckmann wS, captured,
    Camp Chase, Ohio
H. Bindschadler wC, POW
G.W. Betts mC

F. Billigmann
———— Brocks wC
A. Burghard
James Clanton POW
J.A. Cole died Oct. 1, '64,
    Galveston, Tex., yellow fever.
John Deffenhoff
James Derby wounded Oct. 16,
    '62, died Nov. 17, '62
F.E. Dewey died Oct. 28, '64,
    Galveston, Tex., yellow fever.
Fred. Dieterick wV
John Dietz cS, Camp Douglas, Ill.
Louis Duersch
Henry Duman
F. Falkenhagen
John Fiarro
Jose Frankisko
Gerhard Funk cC
Fred Gropp mV
John Gross cC
Henry Harlan captured near
    Vicksburg, Miss., May 19,
    '63, died Camp Morton,
    Ind., July 21, '63
A. Haussmann
H. Heine mS
J. F. Hencke
R. J. Hill mC
Louis Hitzfield, found dead on
    road from Corinth to
    Baldwyn, Miss., June '62
H. D. Holland wV
E. Huebner
August Ingle
Peter Johnson
Chas. Kelogg died Oct. 3, '64,
    Galveston, Tex., yellow fever.
John Kitzinger
John Krinn mC
Christian Kroeger wS
Peter Koelsch
Joseph Legg

Fredrich Lentz kS
H. Loewing
John Maye
Louis Meyer cS, Camp Douglas,
    Ill.
Valentine Mayer
Gust. Wm. Melchers
John Nelson
Peter Nelson mS
Fred Nieder
Wm. Otto
Wm. Phlenderer cS, Camp
    Douglas, Ill.
Henry Phloen wC
John Ponsel wV
John Poore wV
U. S. Powell wV
R. H. Price kV
Louis Rusch mS
Charles Runald
Frank Sattler died Aug. 20, '62.
T. H. Sattler died Galveston,
    Tex., Oct. 4, '64, yellow
    fever.
Charles Schlemmer
Charles Schmidt captured at
    Battle of Iuka, died New
    Orleans, La., July 27, '63.
Edward Seifarth killed Nov. 29,
    '62, on road from Jackson to
    Vicksburg, Miss.
Peter Smith kC
John Teubner
J. D. Vubrush
W. Walker
Wm. Weber
F. Wessels died Okolona, Miss.,
    June 2, '62.
Peter West
H. Wilson wV
Anton Wilbur
Anton Wrede

COMPANY G

The Burleson Guards, from Burleson County, raised by Captain John W. Hood.

Personnel

Captain John W. Hood wS

1st Lieut. Christopher Columbus McGinnis wV, Mexican War Veteran

2nd Lieut. Elijah James Chance

2nd Lieut. J. C. Rowland

1st Sgt. John S. Atchison

2nd Sgt. Charles Coleman Chance wS

3rd Sgt. T. N. Persons kC

4th Sgt. G. W. Parker wV

5th Sgt. G. F. Johnson wS

1st Corp. J. W. Randolph wS, died Holly Springs, Miss., May 15, '62

2nd Corp. G. W. Randolph wS, wC

3rd Corp. John K. Addison wC

4th Corp. J. E. Thomas

Privates

Elbert Abercromby kV

A. W. Armstrong mC

Thomas Armstrong wV

G. M. Arnold

Alexander Autrey kV

Joseph C. Barham wS, captured, died Camp Douglas, Ill., May 18, '62

Thos. Barham cS, Cincinnati, Ohio

John F. Boren wS

William Burks kS

J.H. Burnet mS

H.C. Burrow died Okolona, Miss., June 17, '62

John Cairns

J.J. Calcote

Allen Carr

Titus Carr

D.W. Cates

R.C. Cates died Grenada, Miss., June 10, '62

D.A. Clanton wS, died on battlefield

James Clanton cS, died Camp Douglas, Ill., Aug. 29, '62

Madison Clanton wS

W.A. Clanton wS, died July 4, '62

B.F. Clark died July 4, '62

E.E. Cottingham

E.F. Cottingham wS

J.O. Cottingham

Benton Courtney died Jan. 5, '62, Houston, Tex.

W.W. Covington wS, died Okolona, Miss., May 16, '62

Jesse Daniels died Corinth, Miss., Apr. 24, '62

Thos. R. Daniels kC

J. Deichrich wV

John E. Dean wS, mC

Wesley Dear

Harris Denton

B. F. Drake died March 12, '62.

Edwin H. Emseyler wS, mC

Charles I. Evans

J. W. Farmer wS

W. L. Foster died Jan. 10, '62, Houston, Tex., typhoid fever.

Geo. L. Gee

Van R. Gee

E. H. Green

S. T. Green

J. J. Hardy wC

H. H. Hart wV

John Hart wV

L. H. Hart died Columbus, Miss., Sept. 24, '62

Cyrus Holt wS, POW, Camp Chase, Ohio

Elias Holt cC

F. R. Holt

R. A. Hope died Okolona, Miss., May 16, '62

A. J. Horton

A. E. Howell wS, died July 19, '62.

Wm. Hunt wS

J. W. Ivy wS, died Okolona,
    Miss., Apr. 20, '62

C. C. Jackson wS

J. A. Jackson kV

Frank Johnson

George Johnson wS

G. J. Johnson wS

I. W. Johnson wS

W. A. Johnson mS

J. L. Jones

J. R. Jones wS

J. W. Joy

P. D. King wS

Jasper N. Kirby wS, died
    Quitman, Miss., Nov. 27, '62

C. G. Knight

W. J. Latham died Gen. Hosp.,
    Okolona, Miss., Aug. 30, '62

James Lindsey

W. S. Loden kV

S. R. Marsh

A. J. Martin mS

L. H. Martin

Hope Mills kV

W. B. Montague

J. W. Morgan died in hospital,
    July 10, '62

S. M. Morgan

J. M. McClendon

John McDonald wS, died Holly
    Springs, Miss., June 1, '62

W. H. McGary died Okolona,
    Miss., June 9, '62

W. L. McGary wC

J. T. McMannis wV

A. M. Nichols died Quitman,

Miss., Dec. 10, '62

A. Parker

Benj. Parker

Milton Parker wV

E. L. Parkill

T. N. Persons wC

Albert Pluhker, died Jan. 9, '63.

J. M. Randolph

R. L. Robinson wS, captured
    Tullahoma, Tenn., Oct. 12,
    '63, Alton Military Prison,
    Ill.

J. H. Ryan

J. S. Ryan

M. R. Ryan

P. B. Scott

R. W. Scott

W. L. Scott died Aug. 11, '62.

W. T. Scott wC

G. W. Simpson wC

Montreville Simpson mC

George M. Smith wS, died
    Corinth, Miss., Apr. 27, '62

W. S. Soden kV

G. M. Springer died July 16, '62.

J. S. Standifer wS

W. B. T. Teal

J. D. Thomas died Grenada,
    Miss., May 16, '62

J. D. Thomson

T. C. Thomson

W. H. Walton wS

Thos. H. Watson died Columbus,
    Miss., Sept. 1, '62

W. B. Wilkinson

Calvin Wilcoxen

Wm. G. Wood wC

COMPANY H

The Lexington Grays, from Lee County, raised by Nobel L.
McGinnis.

Personnel

Captain Nobel L. McGinnis wV

1st Lieut. Thomas S. Douglass
    wV

2nd Lieut. Jerome B. McGinnis

2nd Lieut. Jr. George W. Harris

1st Sgt. William A. Knox

2nd Sgt. Francis Marion Parks
    wV

3rd Sgt. Oscar L. Broaddus wS,
    kV

4th Sgt. William D. Burns

5th Sgt. Ben F. Allen

W. W. Carrington wS, captured, Keokuk, Iowa

Corp. Wm. R. Meeks

J. Watt Thomas

James B. Clemens

Wilson Rogers

Wm. M. Shackelford wS

Drummer R.L. Griffin

Privates

W. Baylor Allen died March 12, '62, Houston, Tex.

Oswell C. Alsup died Dec. 26, '61, Houston, Tex.

Wm. R. Anthony cS, died Camp Douglas, Ill., May 8, '62

Geo. B. Barbee wounded by bomb, Corinth, Miss., May 28, '62

Geo. D. Bell wS

Jabus T. Benson wC, died Oxford, Miss., Oct. 15, '62

Q. Benson kC

George M. Betts

Eugene Henry Brenen wS, POW, Sandusky, Ohio.

Eugin Henry Brewer kS

David Bridges wounded Corinth, Miss., May 28, '62, died Camp Priceville, Miss., July 26, '62

Henry C. Broaddus

Leland W. Broaddus

Reuben G. Broaddus

Richard P. Brooks wC

James S. Brown

Jackson Brymer wS, died Hazelhurst, Miss., Apr. 30, '62

Jasper Brymer wS

John T. Brymer

Newton T. Brymer wS, kV

Thomas W. Bryson

Henry A. Burns died Okolona, Miss., June 4, '62

Alex H. Carpenter died Columbus, Miss., Sept. 6, '62

F. M. Cawdson wV

James L. Chiles died Vicksburg, Miss., Feb. 1, '63

Lewis A. Cleibius

Frank M. Condron

Thos. M. Condron wV

Daniel Craig

Thos. Crawford

Wm. H. Crump died Feb. 25, '62, Houston, Tex.

Francis Marion Curry died Jackson, Miss., Sept. 8, '63

Francis C. Drake kV

James Ellis

Cannon B. Farris wV

Joseph Fay mS

Henry Feisler cC

James H. Flannagan died Quitman, Miss., Jan. 15, '63

James Floyd

Thomas Floyd

E. L. Ford wS

John A. Ford wS

Windsor Fort died General Hosp., Miss., Apr. 19, '62

Granville Fry died Okolona, Miss., July 15, '62

Thomas Jefferson Gardiner kS

Michael Gibbins wS

Henry H. Gilley

John J. Gilley died Quitman, Miss., Nov. 17, '62

Wm. H. Gilley died University, Miss.

Wm. C. Givins wS

Thos. T. Goodwin

Eastham T. Harper wS, died Corinth, Miss., May 27, '62

John M. Hecoman kC

Robert S. Henry kV

J.E. Hibbits

James E. Hightower died Okolona, Miss., June '62

Henry Hill kS

John B. Hill died Okolona, Miss., June 16, '62

Robt. J. Hill wC, POW, died Iuka, Miss., Oct. 7, '62

Thos. G. Hill

John R. Holland mS

Mordecai Houston

Edward N. Hudson

James P. Hutchins

James D. Hutson died Okolona, Miss., May 9, '62

Turner Ivy wV

A. Jackson

Robert Jackson wS

Palmer Johnson

Turner Joy wV

Fredrick Lampe died Columbus, Miss., June 20, '62

John Lastor captured Pleasant Hill, La., Apr. 19, '64

Henry Lawrence wS, died West Point, Miss., May 29, '62

Henry Lee

Leroy Lee wS

Arthur K. Leigh wC

Moses B. Lipscomb

Lorenzo B. Little

Wm. T. Lucas

Charles Luitner wS

Fredrich Manning kS

John Mark mC

John W. Meek wC

W. H. Meeks kV

W. H. Mohondro cV July 4, '63, died New Orleans, La., July 24, '64

Dorsey Morse wV

Drury Morse cC

Henry Morse died Grenada, Miss., July '62

James B. McArthur

Robt. E. McArthur captured near Vicksburg, Miss., May 11, '63, Prison Camp, Elmira, New York.

J. Harvey McClanahan

Giles J. Nance

John M. Newman wS

Fredrich Neitman

Isom P. Olive wS

Peter J. Pankey died Okolona, Miss., June 2, '62

Wm. A. Pankey wS

C. B. Parish wV

John R. Parks wC

Samuel Peebles wS, captured, Camp Douglas, Ill.

Jacob C. Pettyjohn wS

John Pettyjohn died West Point, Miss., June 19, '62

Simon Philip

John L. Pleasants

James B. Rogers wS

Wm. K. Rogers died Columbus, Miss., June 18, '62

James T. Runkle wC, died Columbus, Miss., June 18, '62

William G. Scales wS

Fredrich Schmidt mS

Wm. M. Shackelford wS

John M. Shelton

Thos. Smith died Hazlehurst, Miss., Apr. 30, '62

James B. Stanley died in Miss.

John T. Stanley died in Okolona, Miss., June 30, '62

Wm. H. Stanley

Henry Stockhardt died Meridian, Miss., July 21, '62

Lonis L. Stuart

Theodore D. Sullivan wS, captured, Camp Douglas, Ill.

J. Alexander Thomas wV

H. Wm. Tisdale kV

Benj. F. Townsend

John Trump

H.S. Westbrook died Okolona, Miss., May 12, '62

John Wells

John Weymer kV

William Travis White died Okolona, Miss., Apr. 30, '62

Stephen Wilkinson

Howard B. Wilson died Okolona, Miss., Apr. 30, '62

Chas. Zoellnar cS, Camp Douglas, Ill., wV

COMPANY I

The Gonzales Invincibles, later known as the Wilson Rifles,

raised by George Washington Lafayette Fly from Gonzales and Wilson Counties.

Personnel

Captain G. W. L. Fly
1st Lieut. J. D. McFarland
2nd Lieut. R. Debord wV
Lieut. Geo. Weekley died Guntown, Miss., June 6, '62
Lieut. W. D. Goff
1st Sgt. Leonidas J. Duren wS
2nd Sgt. James E. Harper wounded Franklin, Tenn., Nov. 30, '64, captured at Nashville, Tenn., Fort Delaware Del.
3rd Sgt. D. L. Kokernott
4th Sgt. John M. Bell wV
5th Sgt. W. C. Billings wC
W. W. Kimbro wS, died Okolona, Miss., May 13, '62
1st Corp. John A. Porter wV, died Galveston, Tex., Oct. 23, '64, yellow fever.
2nd Corp. D. W. Smith died Grenada, Miss., June 9, '62.
3rd Corp. H. W. Kendall
4th Corp. T. A. Lambert
E. C. Barton kS
Drummer J. E. Lang

Privates

W. W. Alden
Albert Anderson wS, wC
M. B. Anderson
J. M. Avant
R. S. Baker wV
J. H. Ball
J. H. Battle
John M. Bell wV
J. H. Billings
J. R. Billings
W. C. Billings wC
John B. Bishop wC, wV
F. Boatwright died in hospital,Columbus, Miss., June 27, '62
T. Boyd
John S. Braid wV, POW
E.C. Burton kS

B.F. Butler captured Vicksburg, Miss., May 17, '63 Camp Morton, Ind.
W.H. Chapman kV
B.F. Clark
James Clemens captured Fort Pemberton, March 23, '63, Gratiot Street Prison, St. Louis, Mo.
James K.P. Clemens kS
H.L. Clements
Enoch D. Cooksey wS, captured, died City Gen. Hosp., St. Louis, Mo., Apr. 24, '62
Samuel Cooper
John H. Coulter kC
J.N. Craig captured July 17, '63, died Gratiot St. Prison Hosp., St. Louis, Mo., Oct. 14, '63
J. Cunningham captured Hines Co., Miss., Fort Delaware, Del.
Aaron Daniels
J. Davis wV
J. H. Debord
E. E. DeShane wV
Wm. Edwards died in Gen. Hosp., Aug. 13, '62
A.M. Eicholtz died Sept. 6, '64, Galveston, Tex., yellow fever.
R. M. Ferguson
J. H. Fesson
W. S. Gray died Mason, Miss., May 19, '62
G. H. Grey died Jackson, Miss., June 21, '62
James D. Harper wounded Franklin, Tenn., Nov. 30, '64, captured Nashville, Tenn., Fort Delaware, Del.
W.E. Harris died Jackson, Miss., June 1, '62
James H. Hesson wS, died Galveston, Tex., Oct. 21, '64,

yellow fever.
Fayette Hodges kV
G. W. Howard died March 7, '64,
   disease.
J. S. Jolly wC, died Quitman,
   Miss., Dec. 18, '62
L. H. Kendall
L. D. Kendall
Bosman Kent wV
Josiah Lambert wS, died May 12,
   '62, Hazlehurst, Miss.
Nathan Lambert wV
F. T. Letney kV
P. K. Linthicom died Jan. 22, '63.
Rufus Littlefield kV
W. S. Loden kV
Michael McManus wC
M. C. McMene
R. U. Peebles died Okolona,
   Miss., May 22, '62
Modesto Pena wS, wC, captured
   Corinth, Miss., died Iuka,
   Miss., Nov. 20, '62
C. S. Powe
R. H. Price kV

James Priestly wV
John Reed wC, died Oct 4, '62.
William Riddle cS, Camp
   Douglas, Ill.
G. W. Ritchie cS, died Camp
   Douglas, Ill. Aug. 1, '62
Lewis Robinson kC
H. B. Sands died Oct. 24, '64,
   Galveston, Tex., yellow fever.
W. L. Seale died Columbus, Miss.,
   July 20, '62
Clay Smith kV
Daniel Smith wV
D. W. Smith died Grenada, Miss.,
   June 9, '62
John Smith wS, died Camp
   Priceville, Miss., Aug. 10, '62
W. N. Smith cS, died Camp
   Douglas, Ill., May 31, '62
J. A. Strickland
T. N. Walker
Benjamin Weed wS, died Camp
   Sloan, Miss., Nov. 25, '62
E. S. Weisager

COMPANY K

The Texana Guards, raised in Jackson County by Captain
Clark Owen, a veteran of the Texas Revolution.

Personnel

Captain Clark Owen kS
1st Lieut. M. K. Simons
2nd Lieut. J. M. B. Haynie kC
2nd Jr. Lieut. W. F. Kirk kV
1st Sgt. Henry McDonnell
2nd Sgt. Leander Garrett wV
3rd Sgt. Wm. B. McDowell mS
4th Sgt. E. A. Matthews
5th Sgt. James W. Allen
1st Corp. F. W. Armstrong
2nd Corp. C. W. Andrews
3rd Corp. A. O'Berry died in
   hospital, June 10, '62
4th Corp. S. Laconey
Lance Corp. Geo. F. Simons mC

Privates

T. J. Ainsworth wC
James A. Andrews

Z. Bankhead
Geo. W. Baylor kS
M. H. Beatty died Galveston,
   Tex., May 22, '62
Winchester Beaumont
L. Z. J. Bectly
D. Bennet wV
John A. Bolling wC
John Bourke
Max Brandt
Jessie Brook
Wm. Brook
David Burnet wV
F. M. Burrell
E. P. Clary wV
Isiah Cole died in hospital, May
   16, '62
A. D. Coleman
W. H. Coleman

Harmon Cook wV
A. Cox wV
Saml. W. Dutart
T. J. Ewing
Jim H. G. Farthey kS
Wm. Felday captured near
Jackson, Miss., July '63, died
Camp Morton, Ind., Oct. 10,
'63
W. S. Ferrell
Geo. Flayer
Robt. Fleury cC
J. W. Fountain died in Miss.
J. G. French died Memphis,
Tenn.,Apr. 6, '62
J. H. G. Futhey died in camp near
Corinth, Miss., Apr. 6, '62
Adolphus German cC
Abraham Gisler cC, wV
W.D. Goff cC, veteran of the
Mexican War
A. Gorman kS
Michael Green wC
T.P. Harlan
Geo. W. Harper died in hospital,
Apr. 29, '62
F.W. Henry wS, POW, died City
Gen. Hosp., St. Louis, Mo.,
Apr. 21, '62
John S. Hicks cS, Camp Douglas,
Ill.
Amos Jordan wV
W.M.H. Kirk kS
John L. Logan wV
Eugene B. McDowell mS
Wm. B. McDowell died in
hospital, Winona, Miss.,
June 5, '62
Thos. Menefee died in hospital,
Grenada, Miss., June 7, '62
Mack C. Merchant wS
Henry Meyer kS
Henry P. Mills died Okolona,

Miss., June 19, '62
Wm. H. Moore died in hospital,
May 6, '62
W. Morehead wV
E. F. Murphy died in hospital,
May 3, '62
Eli O'Berry kV
Israel O'Berry died Galveston,
Tex., Oct. 4, '64, yellow
fever.
James O'Berry died in Hospital,
Nov. '62
Joseph O'Berry died July 6, '62.
P. H. O'Dell died Quitman,
Miss., Aug. 28, '63
Zachariah Oppenheimer kV
R. R. Payne
J. Louis Probst wS, died Nov. '62.
S. D. Robb
John A. Rogers died Grenada,
Miss., June 15, '62
John A. Sanford wV
Isaac Seely died Okolona, Miss.,
June 15, '62
I. J. Sheppard
Wm. Sheppard
W. H. Simons
T. J. Sims kV
Ralph Smith wS, captured, Alton
Military Prison, Ill.
Wm. Staton
John A. Stulting
L. G. Thurmond kV
Jonathan Vess died in hospital,
May 6, '62
L. F. Wells
Louis Werg kV
Chas. Whaley kC
C. M. Whittington died in
hospital Apr. 15, '62
David Wilkins
A. W. Wiseman
N. M. Wiseman kV
Dr. James Woolfork

SONGS AND POETRY
OF THE SECOND TEXAS INFANTRY

This first song appears in *Reminiscences of Civil War,* and Ralph Smith assures his readers that someone from the regiment is the author.

Shiloh

(Set to the tune of Joe Bowers)

Anonymous

Draw near my gallant comrades and
    a story to you I'll sing,
A sad and mournful song of war,
    tears to your eyes will bring.
One April morn on Shiloh's plains the
    rising sun displayed,
One hundred thousand soldiers in
    battle line arrayed.
Soon drum and fife proclaimed the
    hour that we must march away,
Mid canon's roar and musket's crack
    to mingle in the fray.

Chorus

Cross Shiloh's field the bullets sped,
On Shiloh's hills full many bled —
On Shiloh's plains lay thousands dead
While Shiloh's rills ran red with blood.
Time after time we charged the foe
    who made a stubborn stand,
And ere the sun had reached the
    West we fought them hand to hand.
At last their solid ranks we broke
    and scattered them afar,
And then the vail of night fell down
    and closed the scene of war.
The memory of that bloody day the
    heart with anguish fills,
For dead and dieing everywhere lay
    thick on Shiloh's hills.

When morning's light once more appeared
    drums beat to arms again,
Unmindful of the dieing and heedless
    of the slain;
And soon the canon's deadly mouth
    renewed its angry roar,
Ten thousand fell and thousand sped
    to battle nevermore.
Each place in ranks may be refilled
    but not in heavy hearts
That watch and pray for their return
    throughout our country's parts.

From *Southern Patriotic Songs* we find a song written by M.B. Smith, Company C, to be set to the tune of "Dixie."

The Land of Texas

Texas is the land for me;
On a winter morning the wind blows free;
    Away, boys, away down South in Texas!
In Texas land, where I was born in,
Early one fine summer morning;
    Away, boys, away down South in Texas!

Chorus

In the happy land of Texas, hurrah, hurrah!
In Texas land we'll take our stand,
And fight and die for Texas land,
Hurrah, hurrah! hurrah for the boys of Texas!

Texas land is the land for Cotton,
Piney hills or sandy bottom;
    Away, boys, away down South in Texas!
Here the finest corn we raise,
With oats, wheat, barley, peas and maize;
    Away, boys, away down South in Texas!

Here we have all sorts of game,
The numerous kinds I will not name;
    Away, boys, away down South in Texas!
The beasts of the field and birds of the air
Are found in Texas everywhere

Away, boys, away down South in Texas!

Here the Southern sun doth shine,
Which makes all nature look sublime;
 Away, boys, away down South in Texas!
O, Texas land is the land forever,
Up the hill or down the river;
 Away, boys, away down South in Texas!

Here the men grow stout and steady,
Ever brave and always ready;
 Away, boys, away down South in Texas!
Here we have the finest ladies,
Girls as sweet and pretty as daises,
 Away, boys, away down South in Texas!

Texas is my home by birth, —
And shall be until the day of death —
 Away, boys, away down South in Texas!
When I fall, then will I cry,
"Farewell, Texas! let me die —
 Away, boys, away down South in Texas!"

The *Tri-Weekly Telegraph* of Houston published this anonymous poem on December 22, 1862, lamenting the death of Colonel William P. Rogers.

Can We Ever Forget Col. Rogers?

Forget him who met the savage foe,
 Where battle droops not his clotted wing;
Where weapons clash, and cannons roar.
 Where loud war whoops so keenly ring?

Forget him, who hung his banner out,
 And spread it to the Southern breeze?
How firm his purpose in every rout;
 How deep his words, how plain his ease.

Forget his successful repluse of the horde,
 As they advanced upon our own free soil,
With hurling shot and glittering sword
 He drove them back and save the spoil.

Forget our hero, who gallantly fell
    At post and place with sword in hand?
Ah no, his deeds of valor will tell
    To the unborn sons of freedom's land.

Forget Col. Rogers? No, Texians, no;
    Not while the mind can rove at will;
For he it was that charged the foe
    That did for us his own blood spill.

Forget him? no, our bleeding country cries
    For vengeance and quick amends.
Like Romans of old, we'll valiantly arise,
    To slay his oppressors what ere attends.

Forget our patriot at Corinth, I ask,
    Where his daring courage surprised the foe?
No Maury, no Moore, be this your task
    To laud his service where ere you go.

From *Tri-Weekly Telegraph* of December 22, 1863, there appears a strangely biographical poem written by Sam Houston, Jr.

The Soldier's Prayer

Sam Houston, Jr.

Almighty God! and wilt thou list,
To this a supplicant soldier's prayer?
And wilt thou guide a wandering boy,
Far from a mother's constant care?

And may I ask Almighty God!
That thou would'st shield me from all harm
And when the battle rages thick,
Then wilt thou nerve this young right arm.

I ask not for earth's golden store,
To me 'twould be but sordid dust —
I have a country to defend,
A sacred high and holy trust.

And if, oh God! it be my lot
to lie amid the noble slain,
While this life's blood is ebbing fast,
And this poor body racked with pain.

And when my moments here are few,
Before my soul from earth is riven,
A soldier's grave is all I ask —
And then, oh God, a home in Heaven.

ENDNOTES

CHAPTER 1   Organization of the Second Texas Infantry

1. Special Orders No. 19, X.B. DeBray to Ashbel Smith, Ashbel Smith Papers, Eugene C. Barker Texas History Center, University of Texas.

2. *Reminiscences of Civil War* by Ralph J. Smith, Sometimes Private, San Marcos, Texas, 1911. This reference will hereafter be referred to as Ralph Smith.

3. Personnel of the Civil War, Volume 1, William F. Amann, ed., A.S. Barnes, New York, 1961.

4. *The Tri-Weekly Telegraph,* Houston, Texas, July 16, 1862.

5. *Texas in the War 1861–1865,* Col. Harold Simpson, Hill County Press.

6. *The Handbook of Texas.*

7. *Old River Country — A History of West Chambers County,* Flavia Fleischman, published privately. This information was supplied by Kendon L. Clark of the Chambers County Historical Commission, a great-grandson of Barton Clark, member of the Bayland Guards.

8. "Ashbel Smith trained Civil War unit here," Wanda Orton, *the Baytown Sun,* January 8, 1981. Also supplied by K.L. Clark.

9. *A Comprehensive History of Texas 1685 to 1897,* Dudley G. Wooten, editor, William G. Scarff, Dallas, 1898. This reference will hereafter be referred to by the name of its Second Texas Regimental biographer, Charles I Evans.

10. Louis Trezevant Wigfall and Williamson Simpson Oldham were both staunch advocates of the political theory of States rights and bitter political and personal enemies of Gen. Sam Houston and his Know-Nothing party. Wigfall was a noted duelist, having killed one man and wounded another in trial by combat. Wigfall was elected to the United States Senate in 1859 and to the Confederate Senate in 1862. Oldham was a newspaper editor and became a member of the provisional Confederate Congress, which wrote the Constitution for the Confederate States of America. For this anecdote on General Houston, the author is indebted to Jon P. Harrison of McAllen, Texas, a member of the Second Texas Infantry Reenactment Society of Austin.

11. From the book, *A Thumbnail History of the City of Houston, Texas,* by Dr. S.O. Young, Houston, Texas, 1912, comes the following:

"The Confederate Grays was a fine infantry company from Houston that saw much active service, first at Shiloh under Johnson and afterwards in the campaign in Mississippi and at Vicksburg. After the capture of Vicksburg they were exchanged and transferred to this side of the river."

From the military record described by Dr. Young, the infantry company must belong to the Second Texas Infantry, and since four of its companies came from Harris County and three could be named from other sources, the fourth company must be as named above. However, this name sounds the same as the name of Company B, the Confederate Guards, so that a dim memory might have confused the two.

12. *Historical Recollections of Robertson County,* Richard Denny Parker, Anson Jones Press, Salado, Texas, 1955.

13. *A History of Robertson County, Texas,* J.W. Baker, sponsored by the Robertson County Historical Survey Committee.

14. *Galveston — History of the Island and City,* Charles W. Hayes, Jenkins Garrett Press, Austin, 1974.

15. For the local designations of Companies G and H, the author is indebted to Mrs. Catherine G. Alford of Caldwell, Texas, President of the Burleson County Historical Society.

16. *Astride the Old San Antonio Road, A Pictorial History of Burleson County,* Burleson County Historical Society, Taylor Publishing Co., 1980.

17. *History of Lee County Texas,* Lee County Historical Survey Committee, Mrs. James C. Killen, Editor; Mrs. R.L. Vance, Assistant Editor, Nortex Press, Quanah, Texas, 1974.

The author is also indebted to Mrs. Jan Conn of Ledbetter, Texas, Chairperson of the Lee County Historical Commission, and Mrs. Robert Vance of Lexington, Texas, for locating the descendants of Captain Douglass.

18. The author wishes to thank Mrs. H.H. Vollentine of Gonzales, Texas, Chairperson of the Gonzales County Historical Commission, for her help in locating the company name through the county court records.

19. The author is indebted to Dr. W. Lamar Fly, former President of Hill College in Hillsboro, Texas, for this letter and several other letters and documents on his grandfather, George Washington Lafayette Fly, as well as the picture of Major Fly appearing in this book. Federal District Judge Robert M. Hill of Dallas, Texas, also kindly supplied information on the life of Major Fly.

20. This anecdote is from an undated, untitled newspaper clipping furnished by Dr. W.L. Fly.

21. *George W. Brackenridge, Maverick Philanthropist,* Marilyn McAdams Sibley, Univ. of Texas Press, 1973.

22. *The Handbook of Texas.*

23. Ralph Smith. [See Note 2.]

24. "The Maurice Kavanaugh Simons Diary," Dr. J.E. Connor, Department of History (ret.), Texas A&I University. This unpublished manuscript was kindly furnished by Thomas A. Simons III, Houston, Texas.

25. "George Washington Trahern, Texan, Cowboy, Soldier; from Mier to Buena Vista," Vol. XLII, *Southwestern Historical Quarterly,* page 67.

26. "The Maurice Kavanaugh Simons Diary." [See Note 24.]

27. Special Orders No. 19, X.B. DeBray to Ashbel Smith, Ashbel Smith Papers, Eugene C. Barker Texas History Center, University of Texas.

28. *Generals in Gray — Lives of Confederate Commanders,* Ezra J. Warner, Louisiana State University Press, 1959.

29. *Hood's Texas Brigade: Lee's Grenadier Guard,* Colonel Harold B. Simpson, Texian Press, Waco, Texas, 1970. Louis T. Wigfall's temperament and excessive consumption of spirits renders him unfit to command. Colonel Simpson, writing about General Wigfall's leadership of the Texas Brigade while on picket duty on the Potomac, states that, "The nearness of the Federal troops played havoc with the nerves of Brigade Commander Wigfall. Highstrung and nervous by temperament, the General seemed to panic at the slightest movement or noise from the north of the Occuquan or from

across the Potomac. Even the rustling of wind through the surrounding forests and underbrush appeared to be an excuse for the panicky leader to order his brigade drummer to beat the long roll . . . Wigfall was known to sip a little social liquid (he had a particular fondness for hard cider) from time to time and unfortunately appeared intoxicated on several occasions both on and off duty in the presence of his troops."

30. The biography of William P. Rogers is a composite from three sources, *A Comprehensive History of Texas 1685 to 1897*, Dudley Wooten, Vol. II, Wm. G. Scarff, 1898; *The Handbook of Texas, and the Lost Account of the Battle of Corinth and the Court Martial of Gen. Van Dorn* by unknown author, edited by Monroe F. Cockrell, McCowat-Mercer Press, Jackson, Tennessee, 1955.

Interestingly enough, all three sources list different birth dates, so the last source was chosen, which was written by Rogers's daughter.

Colonel Rogers's kinship to the wife of General Sam Houston was acknowledged by Mrs. H.N. Bringhurst, daughter of Sam Houston, in the article, "Col. W.P. Rogers, Tributes to His Memory," appearing in *Galveston Daily News*, March 8, 1896.

31. "The Maurice Kavanaugh Simons Diary." [See Note 24.]

32. "The Diary and Letters of William P. Rogers, 1846–1862," Eleanor Damon Pace, *The Southwestern Historical Quarterly*, Vol. XXXII, page 259.

33. Second Texas Infantry C.S.A. Authenticity Documentation, Austin Reenactment Society, Inc., undated.

34. Simons Diary. [See Note 24.]

35. Ralph Smith. [See Note 2.]

36. *Battles of the Civil War Complete, Kurz and Allison Prints*, Fairfax Press, New York.

37. Report of General, Stephen A. Hurlbut, U.S. Army, Commanding Fourth Division, Army of the Tennessee, *War of the Rebellion: A Compilation of the Official Records of the Union and Confederate Armies*, Series 1, Volume X, Chapter XXII, page 204.

38. Ralph Smith and Charles I. Evans both report similar versions of this speech, which the author has closely followed. [See Notes 2 and 9.]

CHAPTER 2   The Battle of Shiloh

1. Shiloh National Military Park, Tennessee, Albert Dillahunty, National Park Service Historical Handbook Series No. 10, Washington 25, D.C., 1955.

2. *Texas in the Confederacy*, Col. Harry McCorry Henderson, The Naylor Company, San Antonio, Texas, 1955.

3. "Some Confederate War Incidents," Gen. J.C. Moore, *Confederate Veteran*, Volume XII, March, 1904.

4. [See 3], above.]

5. *Tri-Weekly Telegraph*, Houston, Texas, May 9, 1862. Due to slow communication, first detailed accounts of Shiloh arrived about this time to the Houston area. A soldier of the regiment using the nom de plume, "Sioux," writes this account.

6. *Tri-Weekly Telegraph*, Houston, Texas, April 25, 1862. This article is a

letter from Major H.G. Runnels to Dr. Cushing, editor of the paper, describing the battle of Shiloh.

7. "The Late Col. W.P. Rogers," *Tri-Weekly Telegraph,* Houston, Texas, Nov. 7, 1862.

8. "Shiloh Reviewed," Maj. Gen. Don Carlos Buell, *Battles and Leaders of the Civil War,* Vol. 1, Thomas Yoseloff, Inc., New York, 1956.

The map on page 502, along with the excellent official report of the battle given by Colonel Moore, enables the reader to pinpoint the movements made by Second Texas throughout the day on Sunday.

9. "Letters from the 2d Texas Regiment," *Tri-Weekly Telegraph,* Houston, Texas, July 16, 1862.

This account of the battle of Shiloh was written by another regimental soldier with the nom de plume, "Confederate."

10. *Tri-Weekly Telegraph,* Houston, Texas, July 10, 1862. An account of the Battle of Shiloh written by Capt. William Christian, Company A.

11. "Letters from the 2nd Texas Regiment." [See Note 9.]

12. *Tri-Weekly Telegraph.* [See Note 10.]

13. "Shiloh Shadows," Sam Houston, Jr., *The Southwestern Historical Quarterly,* Vol. 34, 1930.

Mr. Houston claimed in this article that the Second Texas captured General Prentiss's camp. However, the camp of General Prentiss was too far to the west to be in the path of the Second Texas.

14. Private correspondence from Mr. Madden Hill to Dr. W.L. Fly, Sept. 10, 1964.

The author is indebted to Dr. W.L. Fly, Cuero, Texas, for a copy of this letter.

15. "Shiloh Shadows," Sam Houston, Jr. [See Note 13.]

16. *Tri-Weekly Telegraph,* Houston, Texas, April 25, 1862.

17. *Tri-Weekly Telegraph.* [See Note 6.]

18. Charles I. Evans. [See Chapter 1, Note 9.]

19. *The War of the Rebellion,* pgs. 560–563, Series 1, Volume X, part I, Government Printing Office, 1884.

These volumes will afterwards be referred to as O.R.

20. *The War of the Rebellion.* [See Note 19.]

21. In the article, "Once Right in the Eyes of God — The Amazing Career of Ashbel Smith," by Elizabeth Silverthorne, appearing in *Civil War Times Illustrated,* Dec. 1980, Smith's reaction to being struck by the bullet is recounted. "As the Captain (Smith) and his men were fighting toward the Union camp, a bullet struck his arm, wounding him severely. One of Smith's soldiers, who was nearby when the bullet seared his leader's arm, reported that Smith exclaimed, 'God damn it!' But a moment later he recovered himself and prayed, 'Lord forgive me!' "

22. It is clear that the Second Texas captured at least a portion of General Prentiss's cadre, but what portion remains unclear. Many Confederate units at Shiloh will later claim credit for the capture of General Prentiss, and the controversy will rage on for years in print until the last veteran "crosses the river." It is small wonder then that our sources are confused about what happened. Ralph Smith said, "I witnessed the General (Prentiss) surrender his sword to Colonel Moore and saw the men lay down their arms and

march to the rear under guard." If this were so, Colonel Moore would defi-
nitely have mentioned this great honor in his official report, which he did
not. Captain William Christian of Company A, in a letter to the *Tri-Weekly
Telegraph* of Houston, July 4, 1862, said, ". . . and the 14th (Mississippi), Lt.
Col. Mason Commanding, and ourselves, forced Gen. Prentiss to surrender.
Our regiment in front, they got on the enemy's flank, and they soon hoisted
the white flag; Capt. Hood, of Company H, of our regiment, taking the
colors from the hands of the division Ensign." If Captain Hood had seen the
division colors, then Colonel Moore would have known what unit the Second Texas captured, and it would have been included in the official report.
The accepted version for the text was the one supplied by C.I. Evans, a private
in Captain Hood's company. About all that sly old Colonel Moore would say
about the incident appeared forty years later in the journal, *Confederate Veteran*,
(Vol. X, 1902), ". . . and we soon came in contact with that Prentiss much captured brigade, since rendered famous by so many writers in the *Veteran* claim-
ing the credit for different commands. The Second Texas has never entered the
claimant contest, but living members return some recollection of having been
'there or nearby' on that occasion, as was shown by the captured colors and
prisoners they turned over to the proper authorities."

23. "Shiloh Issues Again," *Confederate Veteran*, Volume X, 1902.

24. *The War of the Rebellion*. [See Note 19.]

25. Ralph Smith. *Reminiscences of Civil War*. [See Chapter 1, note 2.]

26. The fate of Lieutenant Gallaher is uncertain, until May 8, 1862,
when a soldier from the regiment picks up a scrap of newspaper from the
battlefield at Farmington, Mississippi. From this paper it is learned that the
following members of the regiment are being held as prisoners of war in St.
Louis, Missouri: Lieutenant Gallaher, B. Buddy, W.R. Anthony, Joe
Wright, James A. Rhea, H. Bartlett.

27. The body of water was known to the Confederates as "Bloody
Pond." Both Sam Houston, Jr. and Captain Fly reported this water as being
too contaminated with blood to be potable.

28. "Shiloh Shadows," Sam Houston, Jr. [See Note 13.]

29. *The War of the Rebellion*. [See Note 19.]

30. *Tri-Weekly Telegraph*, Houston, Texas, July 4, 1862. This article is a report from Captain William Christian of Company A on the Battle of Shiloh.

31. This obituary for Clark L. Owen was published by *Tri-Weekly Telegraph*, Houston, Texas, May 6, 1862.

"Capt. Clark L. Owen was mortally wounded on Monday by a ball
from a Belgian musket, that entered his stomach, and went out near the
backbone. He was taken to the hospital on the field, and is still there unless
dead. The hospital is in the hands of the enemy he is too badly wounded to
bring away."

This is an extract from a private letter written by a member of Terry's
regiment, and from it and other sources, we have reason to believe that
Clark L. Owen is no more.

The news will sadden many a heart, especially in Western Texas,
where his name, in the dark hours of the Texian revolution, was a tower of
strength to the people; for often did he lead the advance to repel the invad-

ing Mexican, and never did he resign command until the enemy was beyond the border.

The people of this section looked up to him and followed him with confidence, obeying him in the field and loving him at home. Many, very many old Texians will recount his virtues and deeds, and weep that he is dead. No truer patriot, nor more gallant soldier, has shed his blood for his country.

As commander of the south western Army of Texas during the revolution as a member of the Old Congress and Legislature of Texas, as Captain of a company, early enlisted at Galveston in Col. Moore's regiment, he has proven himself equal to his duties, commanding the confidence and respect of all who know him in these positions.

From his qualifications, antecedents and experience, he had a right to look to high command in this crisis; but true to the instincts of the patriot and soldier, he thought not of himself but of his country and his duty; he raised a company in his county and enlisted in the war in the regiment named.

He was a modest man and a good one; he was a positive man in his opinions and actions, as the people of Jackson County, where he lived so long, well know. That people will mourn his loss with no common sorrow; they will feel that one of their main pillars has fallen, for the name of Owen is a household word there. The body is dead but the name lives in his character and actions; his name is a cherished one in Texas as well as in his native State of Kentucky, one that his bereaved wife and children may not only love, but admire and revere.

Would that the writer, who from his youth has known him, could speak more fully of his deeds and virtues. He has fallen! and when the news of his death reaches western Texas, it will be felt as a void not to be supplied, that no more gallant, true or better man is left behind, and the hearts of the people will apply to his fall the lines of Sir Walter Scott:

> "Now as the stately column's broke,
> The beacon light is quenched in smoke,
> The trumpet's silver sound is still,
> The warder silent on the hill."

32. *Tri-Weekly Telegraph*, Houston, Texas, July 4, 1862. The list of casualties for the battle of Shiloh is sent by Sioux to Dr. Cushing, the editor.

33. Ralph Smith reports good treatment from the Federals as one of the prisoners "Whom the United States had kindly sent North to spend the summer and recuperate and gather strength for the fatigue of coming campaigns." He was treated and released from a hospital in St. Louis, Missouri, and spent the remainder of his confinement in a prison at Alton, Illinois. He will be exchanged in the summer of 1862, and have a joyous reunion with General Moore. [See Chapter 1, Note 2.]

34. Letter from Colonel William P. Rogers to his wife, May 1, 1862, William P. Rogers Papers, Eugene C. Barker, Texas History Center, University of Texas, Austin, Texas.

35. O.R. Vol. X, Series I, pages 566–571.

36. Letter from Colonel William P. Rogers. [See Note 34.]

37. Charles I. Evans. [See Chapter 1, Note 9.]

38. Capt. Ashbel Smith to Sam Houston, April 16, 1862, reproduced by

permission of the San Jacinto Museum History, Deer Park, Texas. Elizabeth Silverthorne, Temple, Texas, brought this letter to my attention.

39. "Bullet Marks Psalm in Bible Given Sam Houston, Jr. by Mother; Good Book's Stirring Adventures in Civil War Battles Related," Temple Houston Morrow, *The Dallas Morning News*, March 5, 1939.

Sam Houston, Jr. is well treated by Federal surgeons and recovers well enough to be moved from hospital facilities in early summer. He is interned in Camp Douglas, Chicago, Illinois, for a short while, and then exchanged for a Federal prisoner. By late summer, young Sam is taken to Vicksburg, Mississippi, and released. However, his wound continues to disable him and he is finally discharged from the army by fall, 1862.

40. Letter from Colonel William P. Rogers. [See Note 34.]

CHAPTER 3   Camp Life in Mississippi

1. *Tri-Weekly Telegraph*, Houston, Texas, May 30, 1862.

2. *Tri-Weekly Telegraph*, Houston, Texas, July 4, 1862.

3. *Tri-Weekly Telegraph*, Houston, Texas, May 30, 1862.

4. Letter from William P. Rogers to Helen Rogers, Aug. 21, 1862, William P. Rogers Papers, Eugene C. Barker Texas History Center, University of Texas, Austin.

5. *Kate: The Journal of a Confederate Nurse by Kate Cumming*, edited by Richard Barksdale Harwell, Louisiana State University Press, Baton Rouge, 1959.

Miss Cumming is at Corinth only two days before she meets Pvt. Eli Wasson of Company C, Second Texas Infantry, who has been wounded in the Battle of Shiloh. As a young, inexperienced nurse she makes the forgiveable error of becoming personally concerned in his welfare. With his death something seems to die inside of her as she learns to separate her emotional feelings for a patient from her professional duties. Never again in her diary is a patient described in such personal and human terms.

On April 13, 1862, she writes concerning her patients,

". . . About eight were in the room, among them Mr. Regan of Alabama and Mr. Eli Wasson of Texas, both of whom had lost a leg. I paid these special attention as they were worse than others. They were very grateful and thanked me all the time. Mr. Wasson said that he knew that he would get well now. They are both unmarried, and talk much of their mothers and sisters, as all men do now.

April 15 — Mr. Wasson is cheerful, and is doing well; tells me much about his home in Texas and the nice fruit there; says that I must go home with him, as his family would be so glad to see me.

April 17 — Mr. Wasson felt better and knew that he would soon go home. I asked the surgeon who was attending him about his condition and was much shocked to learn that neither he nor Mr. Regan would live to see another day. . . . I tried to control my feelings before Mr. Wasson, as he was so hopeful of getting well. He looked at me once and asked me what was the matter; was he going to die? I asked him if he was afraid. He replied no; but he was so young that he would like to live a little longer, and would like to see his father and mother once more. I did what I could to prepare him for the great change which was soon to come over him, but I could not muster courage to tell him that he was going to die.

About dark a strange doctor was visiting the patients. When he came to Mr. Wasson, I was sitting by his bedside. He asked me if this was a relative. I informed him that he was not, but I had been attending to him for some days, and he now seemed like one. Mr. Wasson looked at him and said, 'Doctor, I wish you to tell me if I am going to die.' The doctor felt his pulse and replied, 'Young man, you will never see another day in this world.' A pallor passed over his countenance, and for a little while he could not speak. When he did, he looked at me and said, 'Sister, I want to meet you in heaven,' and then requested me to get a clergyman to visit him. There happened to be one in the hospital. I sent for him, and he prayed and talked with him for some time. Mr. Wasson then asked me if I could not let his brothers know his condition; he had two or three in Corinth. A friend who was with him did all in his power to inform them, so that they could see him before he died, but it was of no avail. They were sick, and we could not ascertain in what hospital they were confined. He was much disappointed in not seeing them. He then asked me to write to his mother, who lives in Grimes, County, Texas. He desired me to inform her that he had made his aeace with God, and hoped to meet her in that land where all is peace and happiness.

April 18 — I remained with Mr. Wasson all night. A child could not have been more composed. He told me how good the Lord was in giving him such peace and strength at the last hour. About 4 o'clock AM he insisted that I should leave him, as I required rest. He begged so hard that I left him for a little while. When I returned he had breathed his last."

6. *The Lone Star Defenders,* S.B. Barron, The Neale Publishing Company, 1908.

7. *Tri-Weekly Telegraph,* Houston, Texas, May 30, 1862.

8. Charles I. Evans. [See Chapter 1, Note 9.]

9. O.R. Volume X, pt. 1, Series I, page 804.

10. *Tri-Weekly Telegraph,* Houston, Texas, June 12, 1862.

11. Letter from Colonel William P. Rogers to wife, June 25, 1862, William P. Rogers Papers, Eugene C. Barker Texas History Center, University of Texas, Austin.

12. O.R. Volume X, pt. 1, Series I, page 861.

13. Charles I. Evans. [See Chapter 1, Note 9.]

14. Letter from Colonel William P. Rogers to wife, undated, camp near Itawamba Co. Miss., Eugene C. Barker Texas History Center, University of Texas, Austin.

15. Letter from Colonel William P. Rogers. [See Note 14.]

16. Letter from Colonel William P. Rogers to wife, June 19, 1862, Eugene C. Barker Texas History Center, University of Texas, Austin.

17. Letter from Dr. William McCraven to Colonel William P. Rogers, July 29, 1862, Eugene C. Barker Texas History Center, University of Texas, Austin.

18. *Tri-Weekly Telegraph,* Houston, Texas, July 16, 1862.

19. *Tri-Weekly Telegraph,* Houston, Texas, July 4, 1862.

20. "Before, During, and After the Battle of Iuka," Captain G.W.L.

Fly, Company I, unpublished manuscript. This document was kindly furnished by Dr. W.L. Fly, Cuero, Texas.

21. Ralph Smith. [See Chapter 1, Note 2.]

22. Ralph Smith. [See Chapter 1, Note 2.]

23. Two versions of this story are reported, one by Ralph Smith and the other by S.B. Barron, in *The Lone Star Defenders*, see Note 6.

Smith remembers the incident occurring at Wise's Bluff enroute to Shiloh, while Barron's version is reported to have occurred at Baldwyn, Mississippi, among the men of the 3rd Texas during the summer of 1862. Since the 3rd Texas reported this story, it is quite likely to have taken place when the two regiments were camped together, and since Ralph Smith knows the name of the auger-wielding culprit, the 2nd Texas receives the credit. It is quite possible that "Sargeant Bill's" auger benefited both regiments.

24. Letter from Colonel William P. Rogers to Dr. Wm. McCraven, Aug. 14, 1862, William P. Rogers Papers, Eugene C. Barker Texas History Center, University of Texas, Austin.

25. Letter from Colonel William P. Rogers to wife, Aug. 14, 1862, William P. Rogers Papers, Eugene C. Barker Texas History Center, University of Texas, Austin.

26. Letter from Colonel William P. Rogers to wife, Aug. 21, 1862, William P. Rogers Papers, Eugene C. Barker Texas History Center, University of Texas, Austin.

The feeling of hostility that Colonel Rogers perceives to exist between himself and President Jefferson Davis is an old one that could pre-date the Mexican War. In "The Diary and Letters of William P. Rogers, 1846–1862," Eleanor Damon Pace, *The Southwestern Historical Quarterly*, Vol. XXXII, April 1929, Rogers wrote on Aug. 24, 1846, "Col. Davis and Lieut-Col. A.K. McClung I do not think are my friends."

This article further states that Colonel Rogers's promotion to Brigadier General is approved, and he receives the appointment only a few hours before his death.

27. *Tri-Weekly Telegraph*, Houston, Texas, Sept. 3, 1862.

28. Charles I. Evans. [See Chapter 1, Note 9.]

29. Letter from William P. Rogers to wife, Aug. 24, 1862. William P. Rogers Papers, Eugene C. Barker Texas History Center, University of Texas, Austin.

30. "Before, During, and After the Battle of Iuka," Capt. G.W.L. Fly, Company I, unpublished manuscript.

CHAPTER 4   The Battle of Corinth

1. *Decision in Mississippi*, Edwin C. Bearss, Commission on the War Between the States, Jackson, Mississippi, 1962.

2. O.R., Volume XVII, pt. 1, Series I, page 376.

3. Letter from K. to E.H. Cushing, Oct. 14, 1862, published in *Tri-Weekly Telegraph*, Houston, Texas.

A biographer of Sterling Price, Albert Castel, [see 7] states that while Price strongly disagreed with the plan at its onset, once a final decision was made on the attack he agreed to carry out all of his allotted assignments in good faith.

4. Few detailed accounts exist of the activities of the armies during the first day's battle at Corinth on October 3. The account given relies heavily on the official reports and maps in O.R., Volume XVII, Series I.

Especially useful are the accounts given by Generals John C. Moore C.S.A., Mansfield Lovell C.S.A., Thomas J. McKean U.S.A., John McArthur U.S.A., and Colonels John C. Oliver U.S.A., John Shane U.S.A., and Elliot Rice U.S.A.

To a lesser degree, the book, *The Lost Account of the Battle of Corinth and the Court Martial of Gen. Van Dorn,* edited by Monroe F. Cockrell, McCowart Mercer Press, Jackson, Tennessee, 1955, was used.

Gen. John C. Moore's official account varied with that of Charles I. Evans on several points which were ruled in favor of the former. [See Chapter 1, Note 9.]

5. The capture of 300 prisoners by the counterattack is reported by Charles I. Evans, but no mention is made of such a number of either Moore, McArthur, or Colonel Babcock of the 7th Illinois. In fact, only 319 Federal troops are reported missing or captured in the entire Battle of Corinth. However, many captured Federal troops are released by the Confederates during the hurried retreat from Corinth, and perhaps these numbers do not show on the final Federal tally sheet. [See Chapter 1, Note 9.]

6. [See Note 4, this chapter.]

7. *General Sterling Price and the Civil War in the West,* Albert Castel, Louisiana State University Press, Baton Rouge, 1968.

8. "With Col. Rogers When He Fell," J.A. McKinstry, *Confederate Veteran,* Volume 4, 1896.

McKinstry, a seventeen year old private in the Forty-second Alabama Regiment, was wounded in six places during the attack on Battery Robinett. He managed to elude capture and went on to fight with General Moore in Tennessee and General Joseph Johnson in Georgia.

9. *Tri-Weekly Telegraph,* Houston, Texas, Nov. 5, 1862. This article is written by a Northern correspondent at Corinth during the battle. The note is found on Rogers's body, as well as the bullet pierced armor vest, a portion of which is now on exhibit in the museum of the Wisconsin Historical Society, Madison, Wisconsin. [See illustrations] This vest probably was carried north by a member of the 17th Wisconsin as a souvenir of the battle.

10. *The Lost Account of the Battle of Corinth.* [See Note 4.]

11. *The Galveston Daily News,* Galveston, Texas, March 8, 1896.

12. This mysterious illness has been suspect by many writers throughout the decades. General Hebert did not file a report on the battle and, as far as can be determined, never attempted to explain this illness in print. Some historians [see note 7] felt that Hebert had opposed the attack on Corinth from its inception and simply refused to participate. It is also possible that Hebert realized the futility in attacking such a strong defensive position and failed to give the order.

13. "With Colonel Rogers when He Fell." J.A. McKinstry. [See Note 8.]

14. *The Lost Account of the Battle of Corinth.* [See Note 4.]

15. "Rosecrans Whips Van Dorn at Corinth," from *The Blue and The Gray*, Henry Steele Commager, The Bobbs-Merrill Company,. Indianapolis, 1950.

16. Letter from Thomas Hagan to his father, Oct. 22, 1862, found in 7.

17. Letter from Matt Conklin, Oct. 11, 1862, published in *Tri-Weekly Telegraph*, Houston, Texas.

Halbert Rogers followed the regiment to Mississippi with his father, Colonel W.P. Rogers. He is a youth and his father at first strongly opposed his joining the regiment. In a letter of May 1, 1862, Colonel Rogers writes to his wife, "Halbert shall not join the army as long as I can help it. Our soldiers are badly treated and unless the war soon ceases I fear very much for the future . . ." However, the elder Rogers, probably due to the pleadings of his son, relents somewhat and by June 19 writes, "Halbert is now attached to Van Dorn's staff. I have never had occasion to regret the advice I have given him and if you could see how our privates are treated you would agree with me." The transition to soldier is completed by September 24 as the Colonel, writing about the Battle of Iuka says, "Halbert was also in our last fight and handled his gun properly." The younger Rogers survives his wounds and after the war lives in Corsicana, Texas.

18. "With Colonel Rogers When He Fell." [See Note 8.]

19. *Tri-Weekly Telegraph*, Houston, Texas, Nov. 5, 1862. The father of Joel Bryan, Dr. Louis A. Bryan, of Houston, also travels to Mississippi, not as a soldier, but on an errand of mercy. With funds contributed by the citizens of Houston, he forms the Texas Hospital at Quitman, Mississippi, to treat sick and wounded Texas soldiers of the confederacy. Many Confederate veterans will owe their lives to the medical care and treatment received from Dr. Bryan.

20. "With Colonel Rogers When He Fell." [See Note 8] and, *The Lost Account of the Battle of Corinth*. [See Note 4.]

21. Charles I. Evans. [See Chapter 1, Note 9]

Private Weed, a lad of 18, lives only three weeks longer, dying in the Texas Hospital at Quitman from exposure contracted during the Battle of Corinth.

22. *History of Texas, together with a biographical history of Milam, Williamson, Bastrop, Travis, Lee, and Burleson Counties,* the Lewis Publishing Co., Chicago, Ill., 1893.

Of John Lloyd it was said, ". . . he brought out with his regiment the flag, which was pierced by bullets several times while in his hands."

23. *Tri-Weekly Telegraph*. [See Note 9.]

24. *Tri-Weekly Telegraph*. [See Note 9.]

25. "The Assault on Corinth — Rosecrans Holds Firm," in *The Photographic History of the Civil War*, Volume 2, Francis Trevelyan Miller, Editor, Castle Books, New York.

The body of Colonel Rogers is buried with military honors by order of General Rosecrans in a single grave close to where he fell at Battery Robinett. The other brave Confederate attackers are buried in a mass grave. Both graves lie undecorated and unnoticed in the passage of time. An 1884 photograph shows Colonel Rogers's grave in the turn row of a field covered with weeds and surrounded by a sagging picket fence. However, an article

in the *Galveston Daily News,* 1892, written by J.R. Wiles, entitled, "A Ne-
glected Texan's Grave," sparks the interest of Texans and by March 8,
1896, we read in the same paper, "There is in Texas what is known as the
Rogers monument association created for the purpose of erecting and main-
taining a monument to Colonel W.P. Rogers. . . . Membership in the association may be secured upon the payment of $5 and it may be paid in in-
stallments. John N. Simpson, president of the National Exchange Bank of
Dallas, Tex. is the treasurer. The association is fully subscribed." "Monument to Colonel Rogers," appearing in the *Confederate Veteran* ,March, 1913,
describes the monument and its unveiling.

"The fine shaft is of white marble and bears these inscriptions:
East side facing the grave:

William P. Rogers,
A Native of Alabama
December 17, A.D. 1817
Captain of Mississippi Rifles,
1845–1847.
First Man to Mount Walls of Monterrey.
United States Consul to Mexico, 1849.
Signed Ordinance of Secession of Texas, Feb. 1, 1861.
Colonel 2d Texas Infantry.
Brevet Brigade Commander.

North side:

Fell Leading Moore's Brigade, Fort Robinette,
October 4, 1862.

'He was one of the bravest men that ever led a charge. Bury him with military honors.' (Maj. Gen. W.S. Rosecrans, Commanding army of the Cum-
berland, U.S.A.)

South side:

'The gallantry which attracted the enemy at Corinth was in keeping with
the character he acquired in the former service.' (Jefferson Davis)

His last words were: 'Men, save yourselves or sell your lives as dear as
possible.'

West side:

'Erected by the Texas Division, United Daughters of the Confederacy, the
surviving members of the family, and admiring friends.

August 15, A.D. 1912.'

At the same time that the monument was dedicated a beautiful marker
to the unknown dead of Colonel Rogers's charge was unveiled through the
generous work of Mrs. G.W. Bynum, assisted by the Rogers brothers, of
Grand Junction. . . . Then the monument was unveiled by Mabel and Bollin
Outlar, great-grandchildren of Colonel Rogers, and there was a salute to the
monument by John Austin Saunders, great-grandson of Colonel Rogers,
with the sword of his famous ancestor. . . . After the decoration of the graves
by the veterans, assisted by a group of lovely little girls, the band with muf-
fled drum played, 'Massa's in the cold, Cold Ground.' " [Monument is in
Corinth, Mississippi.]

26. O.R., Volume XVII, part 1, Series I, page 381.

27. *The Lost Account of the Battle of Corinth.* [See Note 4.]

28. "The Forgotten Heritage: The Battle of Hatchie Bridge, Tennessee," Robert W. McDaniel, *The West Tennessee Historical Society Papers.*

Sources are at variance on whether or not Second Texas crossed Davis Bridge with the rest of Moore's Brigade. Charles I. Evans states that the heavy Federal cannonade destroyed Davis Bridge before Second Texas could cross it, but this version is not likely, since the Federal attack will cross the bridge later in the day. Col. Harold Simpson, in his manuscript, "The Civil War Record of George W.L. Fly," states that the Second Texas crossed the bridge, and a portion was surrounded and captured, including Captain Fly. However, Captain Fly claims [See Note 19, Chapter 1] in this letter to have been captured at Corinth in the Federal counterattack to recapture Battery Robinett. Gen. John C. Moore, in his official report, states, "As we were filing off to the right the enemy's batteries opened on us from the hill at Metamora. The Second Texas, being in the rear, was cut off by this fire and did not form in line with the other regiments."

29. *The Lost Account of the Battle of Corinth.* [See Note 4.]

CHAPTER 5   The Campaign of Vicksburg

1. *Tri-Weekly Telegraph,* Houston, Texas, Nov. 5, 1862.

2. *Tri-Weekly Telegraph,* Houston, Texas, Nov. 12, 1862.

3. Charles I. Evans. [See Chapter 1, Note 9.]

4. Charles I. Evans. [See Chapter 1, Note 9.]

5. Charles I. Evans. [See Chapter 1, Note 9.]

6. This letter was kindly furnished by Colonel Edward C. Moore, Jr. (retired) of Dallas, Texas, the grandson of General John C. Moore. Colonel E.C. Moore's father remembered the General as, ". . . a person who if he thought he was right, would buck anyone regardless of what might happen." This letter offers ample evidence of the truth of that statement.

7. Charles I. Evans. [See Chapter 1, Note 9.]

8. O.R., Vol. 17, pt. 1, page 685.

9. Lieutenant Colonel Timmons death occurs in Vicksburg, not on the battlefield at Chickasaw Bluffs. We can infer from the transcription of the diary of M.K. Simons. [See Note 24.] The regiment is obliged to Mrs. Holt for her care of Timmons and soon has an opportunity to repay her kindness. From Simons's diary, the entry for June 15, written during the height of the Vicksburg siege, we read,

"I received a note this morning from a Lady asking me for Gods sake to sell her a peck of meal & some peas that she had laid in six months supply but that her house & all she had had been burnt; I sent her the asked for articles, as a gift, for I know that every true man would be willing to divide his last ration under such circumstances; it was at this Ladies house that Col. Timmons died, Mrs. Holt . . ."

10. *Tri-Weekly Telegraph,* Houston, Texas, Feb. 20, 1863.

11. This story is taken from the article, "Feminine Fortitude in War Times," written by George W.L. Fly and appearing in *Confederate Veteran,* Vol. 11, No. 6, June, 1903. This article was supplied by Dr. Lamar Fly, Cuero, Texas.

12. Service Record of Colonel Ashbel Smith, Rebel Archives, National Archives, Washington, D.C.

13. Ralph Smith. [See Chapter 1, Note 2.]

14. Ralph Smith. [See Chapter 1, Note 2.]

15. Ralph Smith. [See Chapter 1, Note 2.]

16. Report of Lieutenant J.H. Wilson, O.R., Vol. XIX, Series I, pt. 1, page 387.

17. Report of Major General W.W. Loring, O.R., Vol. XIX, Series I, pt. 1, page 415.

18. Ralph Smith. [See Chapter 1, Note 2]

19. Charles I. Evans. [See Chapter 1, Note 9]

20. Lieutenant Daniel C. Smith to Lt. B.H. LeCompte, Adjutant, Camp Pemberton, March 31, 1863, Ashbel Smith Papers, Eugene C. Barker Texas History Center, University of Texas at Austin.

Lieutenant Daniel C. Smith survives the war to return to Houston and live out his life. He becomes active in politics, serving as mayor of Houston. The Federal Government forgives Smith for his Rebel activities, and he also serves as postmaster of Houston for many years.

21. Ashbel Smith from Captain Timmons, April 30, 1862, to the *Tri-Weekly Telegraph,* Houston, Texas.

22. Charles I. Evans [See Chapter 1, Note 9.]

23. Charles I. Evans [See Chapter 1, Note 9.]

24. This remarkable diary kept by Major Maurice Kavanaugh Simons is an eyewitness account of the siege of Vicksburg, giving daily entries from April 14, 1863, to October 5, 1863. The original diary, now in the possession of Capen Robert Simons of Kingsville, Texas, was carefully transcribed by persons unknown to this author and a copy placed in the Texas State Library.

The transcription, a hefty 105 page manuscript, is the account of a very acute observer. While Major Simons's spelling leaves a little something to be desired, his rhetoric and keen sense of human nature are solid gold.

Parts of this diary have appeared in "The Vicksburg Diary of M.K. Simons, 1863," edited by Walter H. Mays, *Texas Military History,* Spring, 1965. This diary will here after be referred to as M.K. Simons.

25. Charles I.L Evans. [See Chapter 1, Note 9.]

The ball-and-buck cartridge contains a standard smooth bore musket ball and two to four buck shot, making a particularly vicious weapon when fired at short range.

26. O.R., Ch. XXXVI, page 382.

27. Charles I. Evans. [See Chapter 1, Note 9.]

28. Charles I. Evans. [See Chapter 1, Note 9.]

29. Simons Dairy. [See Note 24.]

30. Report of Colonel Ashbel Smith on the Siege of Vicksburg, O.R., Ch. XXXVI, Series 1.

31. Union Brigadier General Michael Lawler is an enormous man weighing close to 300 lbs. with a girth so large that no sword belt can fit his waist. He carries his sword suspended by a strap from his shoulder, and fights in his shirtsleeves in the sultry Mississippi weather. An Illinois farmer and a devout Catholic, he inspires confidence in his men.

32. Report of Colonel Ashbel Smith. [See Note 30.]

33. Charles I. Evans. [See Chapter 1, Note 9.]

34. Report of Colonel Ashbel Smith. [See Note 30.]

35. Charles I. Evans. [See Chapter 1, Note 9.]

36. Simons Diary. [See Note 24.]

37. *Astride the Old San Antonio Road, A History of Burleson County Texas,* Burleson County Historical Society, 1979, Taylor Pub. Co., Dallas, Texas.

38. Furnished by Albert Scheller, Park Technician, Vicksburg National Military Park.

39. M.K. Simons. [See Note 24.]

40. M.K. Simons. [See Note 24.]

41. *Burleson County.* [See Note 37.]

42. This incident is from an article written by Sterling Fisher, "The Amenities of War," published in *Blue and Gray.*

43. Sterling Fisher. [See Note 42.]

44. In the Jennie Howell Collection at the Texas State Library in Austin, Texas, one page of a tribute to Col. W.P. Rogers by the men of the regiment can be found to which is attached the following marginal statement, "Picked up at Milldale (Mississippi) July 9th 1863 please keep this for me till I return it appears to be the original preamble and resolutions of the within named committee & I wish to keep it as a relic of our campaign in Mississippi. Signed Kermit S. Bostwick."

45. Ashbel Smith Papers, Eugene C. Barker Texas History Center, University of Texas, Austin, Texas.

CHAPTER 6   A Regimental Postscript

1. *Reminiscences of the Boys in Gray, 1861–1865,* Miss Mamie Yeary, Wilkinson Printing Company, Dallas, Texas, 1912, page 513.

2. "Feminine Fortitude in War Times," George W.L. Fly, *Confederate Veteran,* Vol. 11, No. 6, June 1903.

3. *The Lone Star State — Houston and Galveston,* page 492, Texas State Library, Austin, Texas.

4. "Battle of Lookout Mountain," General John C. Moore, *Confederate Veteran,* Vol. VI, September 1898.

5. Same as 1, page 216.

6. Ralph Smith. [See Chapter 1, Note 2.]

7. Ralph Smith. [See Chapter 1, Note 2.]

8. "Old War Records," Ben C. Stuart, *Galveston News,* October 13, 1907.

9. Letter to the Editor, *Galveston News,* October 18, 1907.

10. *40 Years A Peace Officer,* Lewis S. Delony, privately printed.

CHAPTER 7   Reminiscences

1. M.K. Simons's Vicksburg Diary. [See Chapter 5, Note 24.]

2. "Battle of Lookout Mountain," General John C. Moore, *Confederate Veteran,* Vol. VI, Sept. 1898.

3. O.R., Vol. XLIII, page 852.

4. *General William J. Hardee — Old Reliable,* Nathaniel Cheairs Hughes, Jr., Louisiana State University Press, 1965.

5. "Battle of Lookout Mountain." [See Note 2.]

6. This letter was kindly furnished by Colonel E.C. Moore, (ret), Dallas, Texas.

7. Hughes. [See Note 4.]

8. "Battle of Lookout Mountain." [See Note 2.]

9. "Battle of Lookout Mountain." [See Note 2.]

10. There is strong evidence to indicate that General Moore had penned this message early enough in the day so that strong counter measures could have been taken. No action is taken on the message, which leads to the "surprise attack" on the Confederates occupying Lookout Mountain. After the disastrous defeat of the Confederates on November 24–25, an informal investigation is held, and Moore's message is mysteriously "missing." From O.R. Volume XLIII, page 683, we find the following:

"Headquarters Cheatham's Division
"January 9, 1864

"Major General Stevenson:

"General: I have just received your note of this date, inquiring about a communication received by me from General Moore on the 24th November last, and forwarded to you 'to the effect that the enemy were massing a force on the Chattanooga road, apparently with an intention of moving on us from that direction.'

"I inclose to you a copy of the only note I have from General Moore. It was received in the morning and is not the one to which you refer.

"The information you refer to came by me, not only from General Moore, but from officers of pickets, who escaped by the Kelley's Ferry road across the foot of the mountain. I recollect the information but cannot give you the contents of the note. It was in consequence of this information (finding that we were so seriously threatened) that I first went up to confer with you.

"Yours truly, John K. Jackson."

11. O.R., Vol. XLIII, page 677.

12. O.R., Vol. XLIII, page 704.

13. In his official report on the battle [See Note 12], Moore again comments on the issue of inferior equipment to his men. "We had now been engaged nearly three hours. We had but 30 rounds of ammunition at first, that being the capacity of the cartridge boxes issued to the brigade, and this supply was now nearly exhausted — entirely so with some of the men." A standard issue of ammunition for that period of the war for combat was 60 cartridges.

14. [See Note 12.]

15. O.R., Vol. XLIII, page 741.

16. O.R., Vol. XLIII, page 852.

17. O.R., Vol. XLIII, page 849.

18. O.R., Vol. XLIII, page 851.

19. O.R., Vol. XLIII, page 849.

20. This letter was kindly furnished by Colonel E.C. Moore (Ret), Dallas, Texas.

21. This letter furnished by Colonel E.C. Moore.

22. *Guide to the Archives of the Government of the Confederate States of America,* Henry Putney Beers, GSA, Washington, 1968.

23. [See Note 22, above.]

24. Hughes. [See Note 4.]

25. Charles I. Evans. [See Chapter 1, Note 9.]

26. A copy of this recollection was kindly furnished by Mr. Cox Robert Crider of Mexia, Texas. The original manuscript resides in the Gibbs Memorial Library, Mexia, Texas.

27. Letter from G.W.L. Fly to Rev. Walter J. Johnson, December 5, 1899. This letter was kindly furnished by Dr. Lamar Fly, Cuero, Texas.

28. Dr. Lamar Fly, a grandson of Major Fly, relates that during the heyday of the Stonewall Institute, Major Fly wrote General Robert E. Lee offering him the position as president at Stonewall Institute. General Lee replied by return mail that while he was flattered by the offer, previous commitments forced him to decline the position.

29. Letter from G.W.L. Fly to Ashbel Smith, July 8, 1880, Ashbel Smith Papers, Eugene C. Barker Texas History Center, University of Texas at Austin.

30. A biography on the life of Ashbel Smith by Elizabeth Silverthorne is soon to be released by the Texas A&M Press.

31. *Old River Country — A History of West Chambers County,* by Flavia Fleischman, published privately.

32. Service Record of Colonel Ashbel Smith, National Archives Washington, D.C.

33. "Col. Ashbel Smith, of Texas," James A. Stevens, Burnet, Texas, *Confederate Veteran,* Vol. XXVIII, Jan. 1920.

34. "Col. Ashbel Smith, of Texas," James H. M'Neilly, Nashville, Tennessee, *Confederate Veteran,* Vol. XXVIII, Dec. 1919.

35. M'Neilly. [See Note 34.]

36. Ashbel Smith to my young friend, April 8, 1863, Ashbel Smith Papers, Barker Texas History Center, University of Texas, Austin, Texas.

37. Stevens. [See Note 33.]

38. Stevens. [See Note 33.]

39. Service Record of Colonel Smith. [See Note 32.]

40. H.H. Merritt to Colonel Ashbel Smith, April 17, 1877, Ashbel Smith Papers, Barker Texas History Center, University of Texas, Austin, Texas.

41. "Once Right in the Eyes of God," Elizabeth Silverthorne, *Civil War Times Illustrated,* Dec. 1980.

42. Ashbel Smith to My dear Friend, July 31, 1862, Ashbel Smith Papers, Texas State Library, Austin, Texas.

INDEX